BRITAIN'S NEW TOWNS

'It is not enough in our handiwork to avoid the mistakes and omissions of the past. Our responsibility, as we see it, is rather to conduct an essay on civilisation. By seizing an opportunity to design, evolve and carry into execution for the benefit of coming generations the means for a happy and gracious way of life.'

Lord Reith, Chairman,
The New Towns Committee, 1946

Between 1946 and 1976, beginning with Stevenage, Harlow and Basildon and culminating in Milton Keynes, thirty New Towns were created across the UK. Today more than two million people live in the New Towns, and as they undergo phases of regeneration and renewal, this book revisits their story. How did these towns come to be built, how have they aged, and what lessons do they provide for regeneration or the creation of new urban developments today? The New Towns have been described as a social experiment; so what has this experiment proved?

As a national project, the New Towns sat alongside the creation of the National Health Service as an ambitious programme of the post-war government, aimed at promoting social and economic progress in the wake of the Great Depression and the Second World War. Both Labour and Conservative governments created New Towns to meet housing demand and encourage economic growth. Their origin in the campaigning vision of the Edwardian Garden Cities Movement meant pioneering new approaches for the design and management of the towns. These new principles meant a radical break with the traditional form of British towns and cities, which together with the rise in road transport came to epitomise twentieth-century urbanism.

The evolution of Britain's New Towns, their successes and failures, provides a vital lesson for the similarly courageous goal of creating sustainable communities today.

Anthony Alexander is a writer and consultant working in urbanism and sustainability. He has contributed to masterplanning, sustainable transport strategies and environmental policy at regional and national levels, including the UK government's Carbon Challenge programme and Eco-Towns Initiative. His previously published work includes contributions to *Learning from Place* and *Sustainable Urban Design,* second edition.

BRITAIN'S NEW TOWNS

GARDEN CITIES TO SUSTAINABLE COMMUNITIES

Anthony Alexander

Routledge
Taylor & Francis Group

LONDON AND NEW YORK

First published 2009
by Routledge
2 Park Square, Milton Park, Abingdon, Oxon OX14 4RN

Simultaneously published in the USA and Canada
by Routledge
270 Madison Avenue, New York, NY 10016, USA

Routledge is an imprint of the Taylor & Francis Group, an informa business

Typeset in Avenir by Keystroke, 28 High Street, Tettenhall, Wolverhampton
Printed and bound in Great Britain by the MPG Books Group, UK

British Library Cataloguing in Publication Data
A catalogue record for this book is available from the British Library

Library of Congress Cataloging-in-Publication Data
Alexander, Anthony.
    Britain's new towns: from garden cities to sustainable communities/
    Anthony Alexander.
        p. cm.
    Includes bibliographical references and index.
    1. New towns–Great Britain–History–20th century. I. Title.
    HT169.57.G7A43 2009
    307.76'80941–dc22   2008049954

ISBN13: 978–0–415–47512–9 (hbk)
ISBN13: 978–0–415–47513–6 (pbk)
ISBN13: 978–0–203–87565–0 (ebk)

ISBN10: 0–415–47512–0 (hbk)
ISBN10: 0–415–47513–9 (pbk)
ISBN10: 0–203–87565–6 (ebk)

Contents

Foreword

Building new towns is not a new idea, and we ignore the lessons of the past at our peril. An evaluation of the principles, practices and performance of previous attempts to create new or expanded settlements can help us ensure that present and future new towns avoid the problems of the past and build upon the positive aspects of previous experience. But providing these lessons from previous eras of policy and practice is no easy task, and it is a task made all the more difficult by the fragmented nature of many existing assessments.

This book attempts to redress the balance and is important for three reasons. First, it provides a new 'cut' of familiar material by offering a policy commentary alongside an assessment of popular perceptions; the grand visions and designs of planners are set against the expectations and experiences of the actual new town pioneers. Second, it makes a deliberate and determined effort to identify lessons that can be used to inform current and future thinking. Third, it does not concentrate on plans and interventions to the exclusion of an assessment of implementation and outcomes.

Learning from past experience of developing and managing new settlements has never been more important. As we face the challenge of creating new and expanded settlements that provide additional housing in the form of sustainable communities, it is essential that we emphasise the positive experiences evident from earlier generations of new towns, and, most importantly, don't waste time and resources 'reinventing the wheel' of proven practice. Although it is essential to plan, develop and manage each settlement as an individual place, there are many generic lessons that can help to guide our aspirations and actions.

Chief among those lessons is the need to develop and manage settlements through integrated programmes of action. Fragmented, silo thinking and working has bedevilled many new towns (and other places) in recent years, and the recognition of the merits of the sustainable communities model and the 'single conversation' mode of integrated place development and management offers a much-needed response.

Drawing on both familiar evidence and new insights, Anthony Alexander provides a novel and refreshing assessment of the new towns programme and offers the reader many valuable lessons. The title tells part of the story of the new towns, whilst a longer version could be: from garden city, through new towns, to sustainable communities.

This book is a useful addition to our collective knowledge and understanding of the trials and triumphs of new towns. Whilst it does not flinch from identifying problems and failures, it also offers lessons that can help inform what we do now and in the future. It represents an important contribution to our toolkit of skills and knowledge.

Professor Peter Roberts
Chair of the Homes and Communities Academy

Notes on writing style

The New Towns Programme is capitalised as a formal project title. New Towns is generally capitalised as an abbreviation of this for towns built as part of the New Towns Programme initiated by the 1946 New Towns Act. Other towns built in the same time, but not part of the New Towns Programme, such as Cramlington near Newcastle, are referred to as a new town but not a New Town. Similarly, Expanded Towns is capitalised to refer to the towns of the Expanded Towns Programme created by the 1952 Housing Act. New Town Development Corporation is capitalised as a formal name, and often the name of an organisation, such as Stevenage Development Corporation. However, references to development corporations in general, are not capitalised.

Government is capitalised when referred to as a name, such as the Macmillan Government, but government in general is not capitalised. Similarly, local government, local councils and local authorities are not capitalised. However, within quotations, the original capitalisation is preserved.

The title of this book is 'Britain's New Towns', however, a brief mention is made to the extension of the New Towns Programme into Northern Ireland. Informally, Britain is often thought of as the same as the UK (United Kingdom), however the formal name of the country is the United Kingdom of Great Britain and Northern Ireland. This consists of four nations, England, Scotland, Wales and Northern Ireland. England, Scotland and Wales are part of the landmass of Britain, though historically the islands of Britain and Ireland have been named The British Isles. The island of Ireland consists of two countries, Northern Ireland (part of the UK) and the Republic of Ireland. Technically therefore, the Northern Ireland New Towns are not British, though they are included in part as little has been written about them elsewhere.

The total number of New Towns under consideration is also subject to some further definition. The New Towns Programme is commonly thought of as having resulted in thirty-two towns in the UK (see Table on page 49). Five in Scotland, two in Wales, four in Northern Ireland (of which only one, Craigavon, was a new settlement, the rest saw development corporations managing urban expansions), and twenty in England, of which the majority were the expansions of existing settlements, including three that were run by development corporations working in partnership with an existing local authority (Warrington, Peterborough and Northampton). These towns have stronger historic identities than some of the immediate post-war towns. In the case of Welwyn Garden City, a single development corporation was created to take over the assets of the existing Garden City Corporation, but also oversee the creation of Hatfield, which is a separate town. Peterlee and Newton Aycliffe were also run by a single development corporation. During the 1980s, the development corporations of Runcorn and Warrington were merged. Finally, three New Town's designated in the 1970s were terminated, including Llantrisant in Wales, Stonehouse in Scotland, and the Central Lancashire New Town in England. Only the last of these is included in the list of real New Towns as land was purchased and a small amount of development begun, before the plans were curtailed. Alternative names for this town, such as Preston City are not commonly known, though some references appear to this site as the acronym CLNT.

Acknowledgements

Sincere thanks to all those who have helped with research and images: David Devine (Museum of Harlow), Jo Ward and Claire Sutton (Stevenage Museum), Jenny McLellan (Milton Keynes City Discovery Centre), Kate Henderson and Nick Matthews (Town and Country Planning Association), Victoria Brindle (West Lancashire District Council), Madelyn McAlpine (Corby Borough Council), Joan Grady and Wiebke McGhee (North Lanarkshire District Council), Claire Critchell and Will Schofield (Transforming Telford), Peter Phippen (PRP Architects), Hertfordshire Archives and Local Studies, Jon Wright (Twentieth Century Society), Professor Peter Roberts (Homes and Communities Academy).

Other original photographs are by C.J. Clarke (Basildon), Matt Robson (Milton Keynes), Quinton Smith (Crawley), Anthony Alexander (Harlow, Milton Keynes, Welwyn Garden City, Stevenage), and courtesy of Alan Baxter & Associates (Bracknell, Crawley, Basildon, Milton Keynes); Heike Corina Zieher (figuregrounds), Brian Horton (growth maps), Paul Gillespie (British Isles map and timeline).

To Kirsten Gogan, Matt Norris, Stephen Coley, Susan Lawson, David Taylor and Robert Thorne for their invaluable comments on the manuscript, and to Caroline Mallinder, Alex Hollingsworth and Catherine Lynn at Taylor and Francis. We have made every effort to contact copyright holders, but if any errors have been made, we would be happy to correct them at a later printing.

This book was funded with assistance from the Alan Baxter Foundation.

Mark Hall North 1951

The Mark Hall North neighbourhood of Harlow takes shape, 1951.

Introduction

The New Towns in a
new light

The Centre: Milton Keynes, 2008.

The twentieth century was a time of huge social and technological change. The industrialisation that began in the nineteenth century accelerated in the twentieth. The industrialisation of warfare created atrocious mass carnage and persecution in two world wars, the execution of which drove new technological advances. The motorcar, radio, radar, the passenger jet, electronics and computers all saw huge advances during this time. They changed the way we live, and gave the British economy new opportunities in the post-war world. The urban development of the twentieth century reflects these changes.

The dawn of the century found the new industrial towns and cities of the nineteenth century densely overcrowded. Death and sickness rates were high in urban areas and traffic congestion increased as motorcars replaced horse-drawn vehicles. As suburbs spread outwards along transport links, they further added to the sheer numbers of people working in the centre. The response to these urban problems in the aftermath of the Second World War was a deliberate policy of 'decentralisation', encouraging people to move out of Britain's cities. The bombed-out city centres were to be rebuilt and entirely new towns were to be created, both using new designs specially adapted for this new modern age.

The post-war New Towns Programme was the largest public house building programme of its kind. The places created now house more than two million people in settlements with populations ranging from ten thousand to as high as a quarter of a million each. The towns were to be built by dedicated development corporations, receiving loans from the government to get construction underway, to be repaid at current rates of interest. This town-scale mortgage loan, originally set for repayment over 60 years, was then supplemented by ad hoc subsidies and other sources of income. The last of the loans were repaid in 1999, with the final sum estimated at £4.75 billion (CLG, 2006: 31).

It was a massive undertaking. The creation of entire towns required new infrastructure including roads, water, sewers, electricity and gas networks, as well as large volume construction for housing, commercial and civic buildings. People who needed houses were housed, and companies seeking to expand were able to build new premises outside of the restraining conditions of the dense inner cities that were often in cramped and deteriorating conditions. Since then, surplus land assets in the New Towns have generated a further £600 million profit for the government (House of Commons, 2002a). In the long term, it can be argued that the New Towns have proven to be value for money as the investment made has been recouped.

However, the towns that were created – more than thirty in total – have long been an unfashionable topic for urban theorists and journalists. They have often been derided for having unspectacular architecture or dismissed as a failed social experiment, with headlines such as 'Fallen Utopia' (BBC, 2007) or 'Brave New World' (*Guardian*, 2007). Their reputations have been tarnished by pockets of extreme deprivation and a vicious spiral of decline, and in some cases, chronic problems of maintenance, widespread abandonment and ultimately demolition. The New Towns have long ceased to be regarded with the attention they deserve. The aspirations they originally set out to meet resulted in some cases in a total reversal of fortunes.

Yet, between the late 1940s and the late 1970s, the New Towns not only attracted the most talented and creative professionals of the day, but also inspired similar urban development around the world. Many senior figures in British architecture and urbanism worked on the New Towns and much of the published literature, dating from the 1960s and 1970s, celebrated their achievements. Comparing current construction programmes with those that existed when the New Towns were proposed and built, a number of questions arise. How did such a large programme of construction come to be? How was it organised? How did things start to go wrong? What are the lessons for similar programmes today?

A number of reports from think tanks, campaigners and internal government research projects have sought transferable lessons for today. These reports have often been aimed at an audience of policy-makers, and focused on the immediate development plans, such as the Growth Areas. Academic research papers or books have assessed the long-term effectiveness of the stated aims of the policy, or examined specific issues such as transport. Various books describing the growth of individual towns or the memories of early residents have been published over the years. The success of the stated aims of the policy has been scrutinised. The story of each town over the years has also been subject to their unique circumstances. Yet, many attempts at researching the New Towns have been hampered by a historic failure to record basic information. A government research unit set up to follow the progress of the towns at the start of the programme in the late 1940s was scrapped after only 18 months. Later, in 1992, the government ceased to classify the New Towns as a specific area of public policy, regarding them as no different from other towns, disguising their socio-economic performance from public statistics (House of Commons, 2002a).

This book attempts to provide a fresh review of the New Towns by taking a broad look at their historical origins and subsequent development. Where did the New Towns Programme originate, and what ideas were used? What was the experience like of building the towns and later living in them? What are their prospects today, and what does their experience tell us about future urban development? Each town was truly a product of its time: designed according to the latest ideas of urbanism, adapted to modern realities, and aiming to solve problems that had become intractable in Britain's older towns and cities. They broke with the past, rejecting traditional street and building layouts in favour of experimental new design ideas. They responded to the view that the old, historic urban form was failing in the face of technological change.

The need for this response was clear and unambiguous. Britain's existing towns and cities had indeed become polluted, unhealthy and dysfunctional – unfit for the modern world. Created in the era defined by the arrival of cars and television, the story of the New Towns demonstrates the changing character of urbanism in the twentieth century. The 'brave new world' that Aldous Huxley had written about in 1932 was that of the ever-growing North American culture of consumer capitalism. Changes in the way that people live – or rather, the ways they were expected to live – are carved into the urban fabric of the New Towns. From the walk-to-work neighbourhoods of the first generation, to 'full motorisation' later, the New Towns show how movement profiles have changed. The expectations and opportunities for entertainment, the role of shopping in British society and the approach to green space, are all subject to a radical rethink. The reform of the old status quo, informed by debates in the 1930s, 1940s and 1950s, can be compared to similar debates today about how to make better places, and address the challenges of sustainable development. The early twenty-first-century guidelines for urban design practice, deter-

mining the layout of buildings, streets and public spaces are in marked contrast to the approaches taken then (DETR and CABE, 2000). Will new waves of reform in the principles of urbanism and architecture go a similar way?

The New Towns pioneered the use of car-free routes and centres.

New Towns in the future

Major new urban developments today, from large-scale town expansions to the Government Eco-Towns Initiative, also seek to attract new thinking. This is necessary because of fundamental concerns that contemporary urban Britain has again become deeply dysfunctional, this time in terms of environmental sustainability. Yet the words 'new town' have become so much associated with the post-war New Towns Programme, and these towns have attracted such bad press in recent times, that these words have become anathema in discussions on building more new towns today. Instead they are euphemistically rephrased as new settlements or completely re-branded and reconceived as Eco-Towns. Whatever their label, strong environmental performance must be paramount in all new developments, as well as existing settlements, in order to address the enormity of climate change and other negative ecological reactions to industrialisation.

Progressive house building in Willowfield, Harlow, early 1960s. Copyright: Museum of Harlow.

Changes in lifestyle throughout the twentieth century reveal the way that society can be rapidly transformed, in ways that are extremely difficult to predict. How can designers and planners make plans that will still be robust in twenty years' time, when society clearly will experience considerable change in twenty years? This change is certain, but the exact nature of change will be inherently unpredictable. The lesson for today must be to anticipate change as inevitable and design in inherently flexible and adaptable ways. The story of the New Towns reveals the actions of the first generation of people to work in the new British planning system. This new legal environment sought to guarantee that urban development was planned in the public interest. Yet this new planning system, based on predicting future needs for the first time, had to respond to accelerating change in the twentieth century.

The period of time it took to develop the New Towns is also a salient lesson for built environment professionals today. Although the programme started in 1946, legal challenges delayed initial work and an economic crisis in 1948 stalled progress almost completely. Construction of the first towns only really got underway in 1952 – six years after the programme had been started. In 1955 the situation slumped again, rising to a peak of productivity in 1957, then declining to its lowest point in 1964. Between then and 1970, with a new generation of towns commissioned, prospects were looking up, before collapsing again after 1972 (Osborn and Whittick, 1977). With the global economic crisis of 2008, the most severe since the Wall Street Crash of 1929, plans for sustainable communities may take a similarly long time to come to fruition. Major publicly funded construction works during the Great Depression helped stimulate economic activity, as they may well do so again. The lesson is that there may be little benefit in being too contemporary in design aspirations, given the length of time from drawing board to the capping-off of construction.

As the New Towns have passed the fortieth, fiftieth or sixtieth anniversaries of their designation, they have entered phases of renewal. The nature and quality of the places that resulted highlights the challenge of such ambitious urban growth. Some of these challenges are unique to the New Towns whilst others affect all similar urban development in the UK dating from this post-war era. These include the design qualities of industrial estates and housing estates built on the edge of countless towns, the road infrastructure that often isolates their town centres and the modern precincts or shopping developments in the inner cities or the urban fringe. Bristol, Coventry, Gloucester, Plymouth, Leeds, Birmingham, Swindon, Huntingdon, Thetford or Canterbury, all display the problems of such post-war urban development. All these places will be forced to address this legacy in their future development.

Nowadays, the fact that our streets tend to fill up with traffic would be regarded as a fault of the traffic rather than the street. Transport planners of the post-war era assumed that the circulation of vehicles through the arterial roads of the country was vital for the economic health of the nation. The impact of ring roads, one-way systems, roundabouts and underpasses has led to towns suffering from a breakdown in the circulation of human movement, affecting the economic life of town centres. The urban structure of historic towns is inherently more sustainable as they have a finer grain of buildings, creating a built environment that is easy to change incrementally, and a scale of development that is designed to be walkable and hence has low car-dependency.

Local leaders in British cities such as Birmingham have been overcoming political obstacles and remodelling their cities to a more human-scale and less car-centred form. The stranglehold of the post-war ring-road infrastructure has been removed by a series of strategic interventions around the city centre. The large-scale post-war housing estate at Castle Vale has been completely demolished and replaced by a more traditional pattern of streets and buildings (Mournement, 2005).

The New Towns face different challenges in terms of their scale and urban character, and different economic circumstances. Yet there are clear parallels. The story of the New Towns also cannot be separated from that of other towns in Britain. The ubiquitous urban features of the latter half of the twentieth century – multi-lane highways, multi-storey car parks, shopping malls, high-rise housing – all made their first appearance in Britain via the New Towns Programme, which in the immediate aftermath of the Second World War provided a major platform for innovation.

The ambition was impressive, and the need was great. The New Towns Programme was a vital response to Britain's damaged condition in the immediate aftermath of the Second World War. Factories that were once the vanguard of industrial progress, overloaded to mass-produce weaponry, were collapsing through lack of maintenance. A staggering 500,000 homes had been destroyed and a further 500,000 damaged by enemy action, of which the majority were in London (Hennesey, 1992: 104).

Set alongside emergency pre-fabricated housing and new construction in the inner cities, the concept of the New Town provided an ambitious, large-scale solution, yet it did not appear from nowhere. The origin came from attempts in the late Victorian and Edwardian era to address industrial pollution and poor housing conditions created in the nineteenth century. As such, many basic design ideas applied in the New Towns were devised far earlier than the post-war era. The New Towns Programme presented a vision of the future, but many of its key concepts were born a generation earlier. Understanding the long campaign that prompted the creation of the New Towns Programme is vital to understanding how these towns came to be realised. Following their evolution over time highlights the range of factors that influenced their relative successes and failures by the end of the twentieth century.

Problems lie in the disparity between intention and achievement. The New Towns were intended to produce healthier places to live, carefully planned to meet the needs of their future residents. This meant demonstrating the latest approaches in architecture and urban design, with extensive car-free areas and traffic-free routes. The same sentiments are echoed today in the call for sustainable communities. Stern warnings are provided by the wind-swept, economically depressed pedestrian shopping precincts and car-free housing estates of the New Towns, inspired by experimental layouts in Scandinavia and the USA. In the new quest to build zero-carbon communities it is vital that lessons from the New Towns are not lost.

The New Towns were intended to showcase the work of a new generation of architects, as well as the pioneering new profession of town planner. They aimed to create low levels of outward commuting by ensuring that local jobs were available to local residents. Marketing strategies were developed to attract businesses, which also helped to create a strong sense of identity for the towns. The employment of arrivals officers to help new residents settle in quickly emerged as a valuable way to monitor the success of the new communities. In later stages, brand new approaches to community consultation were pioneered. New places that offered a better quality of life than before were created, and new opportunities and new lifestyles did result. As the first report of the New Towns Committee declared,

> It is not enough in our handiwork to avoid the mistakes and omissions of the past. Our responsibility, as we see it, is rather to conduct an essay on civilisation, by seizing an opportunity to design, evolve and carry into execution for the benefit of coming generations the means for a happy and gracious way of life.
>
> (cited in Gallagher, 2001)

The parallels with the urban regeneration of recent years are clear. The Sustainable Communities Plan, published by the Labour Government in 2003, sought to address poor-quality architecture and urban development through a new agenda for design quality and a planning system refocused on the public good. Sustainable communities were defined as,

places where people want to live and work, now and in the future. They meet the diverse needs of existing and future residents, are sensitive to their environment, and contribute to a high quality of life. They are safe and inclusive, well planned, built and run, and offer equality of opportunity and good services for all.

(ODPM, 2003)

The question of how best to design our towns and cities grew with the rising profile of the urban designer in the late 1990s. The government established the Commission for Architecture and the Built Environment (CABE) to arbitrate on questions of quality. The experience of the New Towns Programme serves as a test case as to what worked and what did not in design terms, and how issues of delivery and management affect long-term success.

The disconnection between the hope and the reality in both the above statements of intent is a salient warning for the future. Given the decades-long timescale for a town to be designed and built, occupied and grow, and, eventually, undergo incremental change as parts are replaced, the original creators are seldom around to see whether their design ideas remain valid over the long term. But neither can success or failure be anchored in a single point in time. The success of places can rise and fall, perhaps many times over. Economic slumps are followed by reinvigoration. A place that has value, even if just in the assembly of buildings and roads, can always be revisited. Places must continually reinvent themselves as circumstances in the wider world change, and the role they once played changes. As such, the New Towns Programme represents a huge achievement. Compared to the rate of house building at the turn of the millennium, the New Town Development Corporations produced a colossal output.

They may not seem so new any more, but they can still be thought of as young, especially when compared to many of Britain's towns, some of which have existed for more than two thousand years. They are, at present, moving from youth into adulthood, maturing as places. Part of their absence as a topic for study has come from the fall in their reputation. Commentators have failed to look in detail at the origin of the problems in the New Towns. These problems are, first, those resulting from their design features, shared with almost all other developments of their era, and, second, specific problems that have emerged as a result of the unique way that they were run. Their economic planning and subsequent demographic evolution is also a major factor.

Post-war Britain, after more than a decade of economic depression, entered the eponymous swinging sixties with huge increases in average wages and resulting improvements in quality of life. Britain briefly regained its position as an industrial manufacturing economy, this time for cars, plastics and electronics. The New Towns reflect this. Today, they bear the marks of Britain's post-industrialisation, and assume car-based labour mobility. The reality is ambiguous. The New Towns, for their faults, remain centres of light industry, including high-tech sectors, and host major services such as distribution. They are car dependent to a greater extent than historic towns, but perhaps no less so than very many other parts of the country. Looking to the future, as they themselves enter major phases of renewal, the New Towns today offer an interesting lens through which to view the prospect of building sustainable communities in a changing world.

In the early years of the twenty-first century, Britain's long-term urban growth strategy, outlined in the Sustainable Communities Plan, presented the largest urban development drive since the New Towns Programme. Within the neglected inner cities the 'urban renaissance' has seen the regeneration of former industrial heartlands into new attractive places for people to live and work. Creative industries now flourish in former warehouses in London, Newcastle and Manchester. Meanwhile, outside the core cities, three major strategic 'growth areas' in the South East included Milton Keynes and the South Midlands (MKSM), the London–Cambridge–Stanstead–Peterborough Corridor (LCSP) and the Thames Gateway. A later update added 'growth points' across the whole of England, where housing growth should be targeted.

The Thames Gateway concept first originated as a plan for a string of 'New Towns' along the Kent and Essex coasts to regenerate London's post-industrial hinterland (Ward, 1993). Ebbsfleet, on the south bank, is the culmination of that vision. It is an emerging twenty-first century new town, connected to both London and Paris by high-speed rail, with a target population of 40,000, and showcasing new environmentally sustainable designs. Meanwhile, on the north bank of the

Thames Estuary, the post-war New Town of Basildon is the key site for growth, benefiting from the creation of the vast new deep-water container port at nearby Shellhaven. The Milton Keynes South Midlands (MKSM) sub-region is based around the greatest of the New Towns, increasing its size from 220,000 to 350,000, with the adjacent towns of Corby and Northampton, also products of the New Towns Programme, set for increased growth. The Cambridge–Peterborough Corridor includes the post-war New Towns of Harlow and Peterborough. At the time of writing, the new town of Northstowe was awaiting final approval from the local planning authority. An exemplar of environmental sustainability, this satellite town north of Cambridge, linked via a high-speed guided bus system, was planned for 15,000 to 20,000 people. This complemented the creation in the early 1990s of Cambourne, a new town with a target population of 10,000, a few miles east of Cambridge.

Then there is the Eco-Towns Initiative. This has sought to drive the development of new environmental infrastructure such as zero-carbon energy systems by creating economies of scale for developers. Many of the sites being considered contained large areas of so-called 'brownfield' land – sites that have previously been developed and are categorised as non-agricultural land, such as military bases, airfields, quarries or coalmines. Against the need to put sites such as disused army bases to new uses is the need to target urban development where it will assist regional planning objectives. Adding a critical mass of population along a new public transport route can help complement the growth of existing town centres through the principle of linked settlements (TCPA, 2007: 38). Balancing the availability of sites, existing regeneration problems and broader strategic planning issues of the best location for new settlements has been central to the inevitably complex evolution of the Eco-towns Initiative.

The long-term plans for urban development in the UK are proceeding with a number of existing and potential new towns, such as Northstowe in Cambridgeshire, Poundbury in Dorset and Sherford in Devon. Major growth of many post-war New Towns is also well underway. The urgent need to meet housing demand without increasing Britain's dangerous greenhouse gas emissions means all this growth is intended to drive the creation of low-carbon communities. Although the Sustainable Communities Plan, the Eco-Towns Initiative and the government's new housing standard, The Code for Sustainable

Homes, seek to create new places that meet this requirement, it must also be recognised that the post-war New Towns are themselves already pioneering environmental sustainability. Peterborough is building on its engineering base, attracting an emerging cluster of environmental businesses, and re-branding itself as Britain's premier eco-city. Milton Keynes is fuelling its city centre redevelopment with a major installation of low-carbon energy infrastructure. Telford's Lightmoor Millennium Village is a large-scale development built to high sustainability standards. Washington and Peterlee are host to wind-powered industrial sites and academic energy research centres.

It is of course a cliché that to fail to learn history means being doomed to repeat it, but the aspirations of the mid-twentieth-century New Towns Programme are so similar to those of early twenty-first century that the message is clear. What can the next generation of planners, architects and urban designers to deliver Britain's new sustainable communities learn from this particular period of the recent past? How will the desperately needed homes and places be delivered successfully, and in ways that are sustainable? What should be done differently to ensure that future urban development does not repeat the mistakes of the past?

There are many apparent contradictions at the heart of the New Towns project that have persisted without resolution. The timescales involved in building a town are so long that coherence can often fail. Indeed, the stated reasons for the creation of New Towns changed over time. Incoming governments inherited an existing programme someway through completion and with a substantial amount of momentum and could easily justify the continuation of the programme as a relatively uncontroversial, minor arm of public activity. There were relatively few significant debates in the House of Commons on the New Towns Programme. Significant points raised in these debates, and the subsequent decisions made, sometimes seemed of little concern. Attention was understandably focused on the short term and the desire to get matters started in order to address the problems in hand. Yet, these sometimes seemingly small decisions set in action chain events whose significance were to take years, if not decades, to become apparent. A lack of initial certainty over how the activities of the New Town Development Corporation would ultimately be concluded had an impact that resonated over decades.

Another crucial factor in understanding the New Towns Programme is the sheer complexity of the issues. In the case of society-at-large, and the case of the New Towns in particular, a huge range of influencing factors is at work. This can make the long-term outcome of decisions inherently unpredictable. The turbulent mix of ideas about how to design the New Towns coupled with the near total failure to capture evidence or to evaluate them in practice has made the ultimate success of the programme difficult to assess.

Each individual town took a different form, shaped by its geography and by the people that worked on it. Each therefore has a distinct story and this book cannot give all of them the attention they deserve. Some are discussed in more detail than others to help illustrate particular points in the following chapters, whilst others, regrettably, have been neglected. Each town has a contribution to make in terms of increasing understanding of the New Towns' story and can provide lessons for urban development today. They do not deserve to be ignored by urban theorists; they define an era of urban change that is central to the form of the modern world.

To look at the New Towns in a new light is to see their true colours. What do they tell us about the nature of British urban life in the twentieth century? How do they function as places and how did they come to be built? The New Towns offer lessons for today, some for good, some for bad, but we must learn from these lessons. Current urban development is not doing something that has never been done before. Rather than neglect the past, the link between this period from the 1950s to the 1970s and the present needs to be understood in more detail. As a unique phase in urban development, they provide illumination on how to make all places work better.

The huge loss of life in the first half of the twentieth century meant losing the working knowledge of generations of builders, craftsmen, designers and administrators. This tragedy is seldom remarked upon. The new approaches that were created in the wake of the Second World War have since become, in many instances, deeply problematic. The hunger for newness and change came from the sense that the world needed to be reborn in the aftermath of war. Many of the ideas that took hold, such as car-free areas, neighbourhood heating systems or industrialised off-site manufacture of building materials, are promoted today just as they were in the 1950s and 1960s. The zeal to create new forms of urbanism and new forms of architecture to answer the challenge of sustainability and climate change must learn from this experiment in design and delivery. The New Towns Programme offers a living case study, and a clear sign that place making requires a long view over many decades and ultimately centuries into the future.

The New Towns epitomised the desire to forge a new way and embraced the opportunity to benefit from new technologies and techniques. It was also the product of a unique historical circumstance, with levels of public support for housing growth unimaginable in contrast to recent times. While the optimism and enthusiasm of the post-war period is not matched today, nonetheless a new generation of designers is emerging who are dedicated to tackling the challenge of securing a sustainable future. They are optimistic that the problems of unsustainability can be solved through better buildings and urbanism. The story of Britain's post-war New Towns Programme therefore sets an important historic precedent in achieving such transformational goals.

Construction begins in Mark Hall North, Harlow, 1951.

Part 1

Planning the New Towns

A bit of a bombshell

Extensive bomb damage from the blitz created a severe housing crisis in Britain.

The story of Britain in the twentieth century is dominated by the two world wars. Although surviving to victory in both wars without the homeland being invaded by enemy troops, Britain was diminished from being the centre of a global empire to a mere nation state. The role it once held as the world's superpower in the nineteenth century would instead be contested between the United States of America and the Union of Soviet Socialist Republics, and their competing ideologies for world order in the age of the atom bomb.

Although Britain had held off the threat of invasion, the technological development of the aeroplane meant that the Second World War had a new frontline, the Home Front. 'Total War' meant that both sides attacked civilians in their homes, with London and other British towns and cities attacked initially by aircraft and later by long-range missiles. Over the six years from 1939 to 1945, Britain's towns and cities were subjected to air attacks whose explosives and firebombs obliterated half a million homes, and left a further half a million severely damaged. De-mobilised soldiers were returning to homes that no longer existed. The country faced critical shortages of housing, employment and supply of goods.

Throughout the 1940s, just as it had been in the decades previously, the cinema was the number one form of mass media entertainment. The silver screen was a lifeline to another world; every week millions of people were transported from their immediate reality. Despite the spirit of optimism, the aftermath of the Second World War was grim and fearful, with wartime austerity and rationing destined to continue for another eight years after victory.

Cinema's role for escapism and entertainment persists today, but before the rise of television in Britain in the 1950s, cinema was also a major source of news and information. Besides the main feature presentation, programmes included newsreels, Saturday morning serials for children, cartoons and government information films. In London, news cinemas showed newsreels round the clock.

In 1948, three years after the end of the war, after a bitter winter and major floods the following spring, cinema-goers enjoyed historical epics such as *Anna Karenina* and thrillers such as *Appointment with Murder*. Cinema programmes also included newsreel highlights from the 1948 London Olympic Games – the first since Berlin in 1936 – and films from the government's Central Office of Information.

A number of these films were entertaining Disney-like animations featuring a character called Charley, a chirpy everyman whose experiences helped inform audiences about new government programmes. In 1948, films covered new schools being built or the arrival of the new National Health Service. One called 'Charley in New Town', promoted a major new government programme for post-war housing in brand new communities to be built in open countryside away from existing towns and cities. The film makes no mention of the war but it perfectly summarises – in cartoon form – the ideas behind in the New Towns Programme. The film (now available on the National Archives website) is worth summarising in detail (see page 2 of the colour plate section).

It came about because of the immediate political context and policies enacted in the aftermath of the war. As a significant aspect of the promotional campaign for the New Towns Programme, it provides an immensely valuable summary of the fundamental arguments and ideas: first, of the overall arguments for why New Towns were needed; and, second, of the planning and design principles that would be used.

The film opens on an aerial view of a New Town. White, rectangular buildings lie in a square grid, separated by open green space. Charley is seen cycling through empty streets, along a dedicated cycle-path, wearing what look like army fatigues. The oversized eyes of his cartoon face are accompanied by a cheekily bouncing quiff of hair. As he pedals along to the film's chirpy soundtrack, he passes a woman pushing a pram, then an elderly gentleman cyclist, and greets them both with a cry of 'Hallo!' and 'Morning!' before turning to face the viewers in the cinema.

'My, what a way to start the day,' he says, as he cycles along. 'A bit different from what it used to be, I can tell you.'

The screen dissolves in a swirl of smoke as we flashback to Charley sitting on a packed double-decker bus.

'I can remember it like it was yesterday. It wasn't half so comfortable. It took a bloke a good hour to get to work.'

The crowded bus chugs along an endless row of 1930s semi-detached housing. The journey, long and polluted is described by Charley, illustrated with the unique expressiveness of cartoon animation. The music, now orchestral and scary as the route becomes increasingly dark and smoke-filled, builds to a crescendo of anxious violins, until the scene passes a lone tree, covered in smoke, to rest on three downcast children, kicking a ball in an alley.

'And not even a bloomin' place for the kids to play. Poor little blighters,' he says. A lonely, tragic violin solo accompanies the ball, bouncing out into the street to the sound of a car's brakes screeching.

Arriving at work, his quiff marking him out in the ant-like crowd, he declares, 'One day I was proper fed up with it all. It seemed to me we'd made a real mess of things in our town. Still, if you can make a muck up of things, you can put 'em right.'

At a meeting of citizens and town planners, the vision for a new community is laid out on screen. The Planner, as Edwardian gentleman in a tailcoat, with waistcoat and bow tie, a bald head and moustache, brings the meeting to order, providing a quick history of urban development to date.

'Let's start by seeing how our town looked 150 years ago,' says The Planner. 'Small. Compact. Thriving. Small population. Then, the industrial revolution happened. Industry moved into the town – it needed workers.'

The town and its green surroundings fill-up with vast factory buildings and warehouses. Lines of ant-like people start to fill the streets. Buildings soon crowd every available space in the town. Long lines of back-to-back terraced housing, and vast gas cylinders appear. A railway train enters the frame, and toots its way out of the city, new buildings springing up in its wake. The view now is of a city on a river whose rough edges are expanding outwards in waves. Like a bacterial culture, the monstrous city expands until it fills up the entire view.

The solution then described represents a number of ideas long campaigned for by social reformers and architect-planners. A Green Belt is defined around the edge, an idea put into law in 1938 to prevent the indefinite outward spread of towns and cities, and beyond it a new town is started. Here the town is planned from the start to separate housing and industry into dedicated estates. This idea known as zoning answered the problem of factories and housing being mixed up together, with pollution from the factory chimneys affecting health, by separating them into housing estates and industrial estates.

The problems of commuting were solved by planning these towns to be a specific size and with the number of jobs available perfectly balanced with the number of houses. No one would need to commute elsewhere. Not only was this to reduce traffic congestion but also the short cycle ride to work was to be made even safer and easier by having a network of special cycle paths. Young mothers could also push their prams to the centre of town and back along car-free pedestrian routes.

'Our town was going to be a good place to work in, and a grand place to live in,' says Charley, 'with plenty of open spaces, parks, and playing fields which people could enjoy. Flower gardens. And of course, there'd have to be an attractive town centre too, with plenty of room for people to meet, shops, a posh theatre, cinemas, a concert hall, and a civic centre.'

The animated blueprint of the town shows bright, modernist buildings springing up from plan to reality. Homes of all shapes and sizes, houses with gardens for families, bungalows for pensioners and flats for young singles. The final view is of buildings separated by wide green spaces; the tiny dots of people moving between them spread out, in marked contrast to the dense urban scene of the old industrial city.

'I'm telling you. It works out fine,' says Charley, cycling off to his job in the bright, new factory, and with a suggestive wave of his cartoon finger, he grins, 'Just you try it!'

Planned decentralisation

This vision of life in new towns was doubtless appealing to Londoners living in neighbourhoods scarred with bombsites. The lack of green space that was the inevitable consequence of the pressure for land in the old cities made the parks and gardens of the New Town seem idyllic. A new life in a New Town compared with the one lived in war-torn London seemed an obvious choice. Professionals saw the logic too. Employers liked the chance to expand and architects and planners were eager to be involved in forging a new and better society from the ruins of the old. By the end of the 1960s the population of the New Towns numbered more than 700,000.

The overarching government policy, of which the New Towns Programme was a major aspect, was one of planned decentralisation. This meant building houses away from the cities in order to tempt inner-city residents to relocate. They would have better living conditions, better housing and jobs in

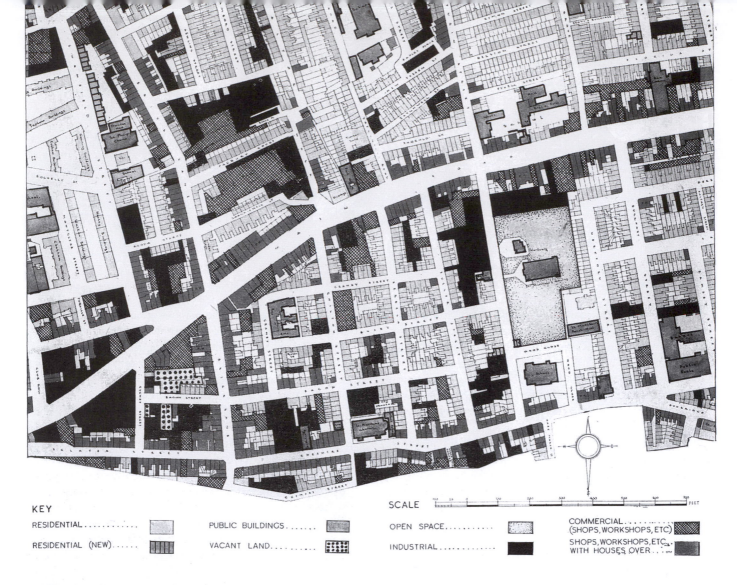

KEY

RESIDENTIAL · · · · · · · · · · ·

RESIDENTIAL (NEW) · · · · · ·

PUBLIC BUILDINGS · · · · · · ·

VACANT LAND · · · · · · · · · ·

SCALE

OPEN SPACE · · · · · · · · · ·

INDUSTRIAL · · · · · · · · · · · ·

COMMERCIAL · · · · · · · · · · · ·
(SHOPS, WORKSHOPS, ETC)

SHOPS, WORKSHOPS, ETC.,
WITH HOUSES OVER · · · · · ·

TYPICAL AREA IN THE EAST END, SHOWING THE EXISTING INTERMIXTURE OF INDUSTRY, HOUSING ETC.

The reconstruction plan for London highlighted the extent to which factories were located immediately adjacent to housing. Crown Copyright.

Instead, radical new forms of urbanism and architecture were proposed, so that people could live in dedicated housing estates, designed to maximise light and air. Crown Copyright.

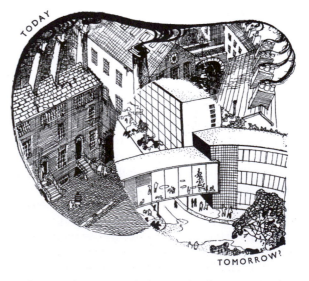

Modernist architecture and urbanism thus became central to Britain's post-war reconstruction. Crown Copyright.

modern factories. Meanwhile, with fewer people to re-house in the inner cities, they could be rebuilt to lower densities. Bomb sites in the cities created new open spaces that made people realise how tightly crowded the city had been. The new housing to be built in these demolished spaces of the city promised more space, better light and air and less congested roads and walkways. The building of this dream was to take another twenty years, and the policy of planned decentralisation from Britain's cities was only to formally end in 1976.

Post-war reconstruction was understandably one of the largest projects ever undertaken in British history. It is astonishing to consider this process from the perspective of the 1960s and 1970s, when extensive areas of dereliction still existed and the discovery of unexploded Second World War bombs was still common. The places created – the hallmarks of Britain of the late twentieth century – were largely a result of the ideas put in place by the country's leading town planner, Professor Sir Patrick Abercrombie. In 1942, he produced a plan for the post-war reconstruction of Plymouth, and with the London County Council chief architect, F.J. Forshaw, he issued plans for the reconstruction of London in the County of London Plan, in 1943. These were published in a defiant spirit to boost morale and promised a new vision for Britain.

Unlike many European cities, such as Rouen, Rheims, Bruges, Liège or Köln that restored their bomb-ravaged areas to their previous scale and along their historic street patterns, Britain embraced a new vision for its cities that went with the grain of the existing programmes of slum clearance. Abercrombie's plans promoted a new approach to urbanism based on the ease of movement of the motorcar, the separation of pedestrian movement from road traffic, and the separation of housing, commercial and industrial into dedicated estates. The architectural paradigm of modernism, established in France, Germany, Russia and America during the 1930s, was central. An army poster in 1942 by Abram Games, one of the government's leading graphic designers, showed an illustration of a terraced street of small, working-class housing, shattered by bombing, with a tall, clean, white, spacious buildings bursting from the ruins with the bold caption, 'Your Britain: Fight for it now' (please see page 1 of colour plate section).

Abercrombie's vision for London extended beyond the boundaries of the old London County Council (what are now London's inner boroughs) out to the region as a whole. To express this plan, the government's new Ministry of Town and Country Planning, created in 1943, commissioned Abercrombie to produce the Greater London Plan in 1944. Whereas the London Plan addressed a vision for the capital rebuilt with zoned industrial estates, high-capacity road networks, new green spaces and modernist housing estates, the regional plan – the first of its kind – aimed to reduce the population of the city by encouraging them to move elsewhere. In 1939, the population of Greater London had been more than eight million. Abercrombie's plan was for one million people to be offered the chance to be re-housed outside the capital. Some 515,000 people were to go to New Towns located in an orbit around London just beyond the Green Belt.

Although their election manifesto made no mention of New Towns, the image of a better future after the war was an essential plank of the Labour Party's election campaign held just eight weeks after the end of the war in 1945. The landslide win gave the Labour Party their first ever overall majority in government. Asked why the voters had turned against Churchill in the 1945 election, Labour Prime Minister Clement Atlee said, 'They did not turn against Churchill, they turned against the Conservatives. They remembered what had happened in the 1930s' (Hennessy, 1992). The conditions for Britain's working class were essentially unchanged since the nineteenth century. In the wake of the stock market crash of 1929 they were transformed dramatically for the worse. Selwyn Parker's account of the Great Depression describes the conditions in Scotland's largest city, Glasgow, as the worst in Europe. "In 1930, nearly 85,000 people were squeezed into . . . soot-blackened tenements in which half a dozen families might share a single outside privy . . . Most of the dwellings were within sight and sound of the belching smoke stacks, and the crashing and clanking of heavy industry." (Parker, 2008: 72).The promise of emancipation had considerable magnetism and the post-war mandate was thus not only to repair the damage and rebuild the economy but to establish a welfare state to abolish poverty and exploitation. The vision of the New Towns slotted in readily alongside free health care for all, free pensions, free legal aid and so forth.

The first part of Abercrombie's plan was soon made law by the New Towns Act of 1946. Over the next four years this led to the designation of eight satellite towns for London: Stevenage, Hemel Hempstead, Hatfield and Welwyn Garden City in Hertfordshire; Crawley in Sussex; Harlow and Basildon in Essex; and Bracknell in Berkshire. In addition, six sites were designated elsewhere: East Kilbride near Glasgow; Glenrothes in Fife; Cwmbran in South Wales; Corby in the East Midlands; and Aycliffe and Peterlee in County Durham. All were to be built by specially appointed development corporations with legal powers to compulsorily purchase land at agriculture value, grant planning permission and then capture the resulting increase in value to invest in subsequent stages of development.

The second aspect of the Abercrombie plan came into effect as the first major housing policy of the Conservative Government of 1951 to 1964. The Town Development Act of 1952 created the Expanded Towns Programme where development was run by local authorities rather than development corporations. The largest of these towns to receive over-spill population from London were Basingstoke and Swindon, each receiving around 13,000 new homes. Others including Andover received around 6,000, while Banbury, Aylesbury, Thetford and Wellingborough were to receive around 3,000 each. Other cities also attempted similar programmes, such as Birmingham, which created housing estates for 3,000 families in towns such as Daventry and Droitwich (Town and Country Planning Journal, 1967b: 99).

Facilitated by government grants in the 1950s, the Expanded Towns were built using the same thinking as the New Towns, but the scale of delivery did not come close. By 1961, the government changed tack and initiated a second phase of the New Towns Programme, returning to New Town Development Corporations to design, build and run the towns. Skelmersdale and Runcorn in Lancashire, Dawley in Shropshire (later renamed as Telford), Washington in Northumberland and Livingston in Central Scotland, were all designated by the Conservative Government in the early 1960s.

Cumbernauld in Central Scotland was also a lone New Town designated by the secretary of state for Scotland in the mid-1950s to further support the objectives of East Kilbride in depopulating inner-city Glasgow. Under the new Labour Government of 1964 to 1970, the final stage of the New Town Programme saw Scotland's final New Town, Irvine, Milton Keynes in Buckinghamshire, the aborted Central Lancashire New Town, and major expansions for Newtown in Mid-Wales, Warrington in Cheshire, Peterborough and Northampton.

By the time the policy of planned decentralisation reached its official end in 1976, around two-thirds of a million Londoners had relocated to New Towns and around one-third of a million relocated to Expanded Towns. This was roughly the reverse of the ratio originally proposed by Abercrombie. Besides London, planned decentralisation had been investigated for other cities. Leeds and Sheffield decided they had room to accommodate additional population within their city boundaries. Nottingham and Leicester had considered building out-of-county housing of some sort but did not determine how or where. Bradford and Hull did not believe they had a problem that demanded decentralisation. In the end only Glasgow was to follow London's lead in the 1940s, with Birmingham, Manchester and Liverpool following in the later phase.

Alongside these plans were those for the reconstruction of the bomb-damaged cities. Coventry, Bristol and Plymouth were all to have centres rebuilt according to new principles to address problems in their design that had emerged over time: traffic congestion along streets designed for horse and carriage, pollution from vehicles and factories, and poor quality, working-class housing that was generally overcrowded and squalid. In Plymouth, a city that lost 40 per cent of its buildings through bombing, Abercrombie produced a microcosm of what was to become the national plan, by decentralising the population into a series of satellite suburbs around the city edge. These followed similar design principles outlined for the New Towns – well-defined neighbourhoods of several thousand homes around a local centre containing shops and other basic facilities (Plymouth, 2005).

Two visions for urban reinvention

The argument for new housing either in purpose-built towns or as extensions to existing towns was coupled with a drive for new forms of architecture and urban planning. These came from an acute awareness that the nature of city living had become deeply problematic. The causes, laid out in plain language in Abercrombie's plan for London, but also in many other publications of the era, was that cities had developed industry

Top: Air raids during the Second World War saw extensive areas of London and other British towns and cities damaged or destroyed. Crown copyright.

Bottom: The reconstruction in Britain was directly linked to the political message promoted by the modernists. This propaganda poster from 1942 shows architect Maxwell Fry's Kensal House, Ladbroke Grove, London (a 68 apartment, workers' housing block completed in 1937), rising from a shattered nineteenth-century working-class terrace. Copyright: Estate of Abram Games.

Charley in New Town, 1948. Produced by Halas & Batchelor on behalf of the Central Office for Information, for the Ministry for Town and Country Planning. Crown copyright, courtesy of the British Film Institute. To watch the film online please go to http://www.nationalarchives.gov.uk/ films/1945to1951/filmpage_cint.htm. Last accessed 19 March 2009. Moving to a New Town was promoted on the grounds of the high quality of the environment compared to the old cities. The green belt, finite size of new town, zoned separation of industry and housing, modernist town centres and the neighbourhood unit are all part of the appeal.

Welcome to Harlow, Development Corporation publication produced in 1961. Copyright: Museum of Harlow.

Stevenage's celebrated pedestrian precinct prompted a generation of similar schemes across the UK.

Furnace Green in Crawley, a neighbourhood halfway between urban and rural. Source: Quinton Smith.

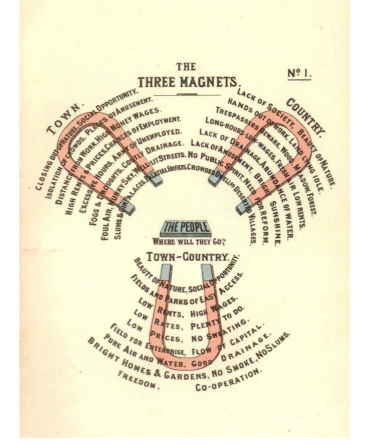

Ebenezer Howard's concept of the Garden City sought to address the problems of both the city and the countryside, as illustrated in his famous 'three magnets' diagram (top left). Once they grew to a specific size development was to stop and a new Garden City was to be established, linked to its parents and siblings via canals and tramways. Together this would form 'the social city' (bottom), a cluster of self-sufficient, ecologically benign settlements. Images courtesy of Hertfordshire Archives and Local Studies, ref: DE.Ho.F4.1 and 13.

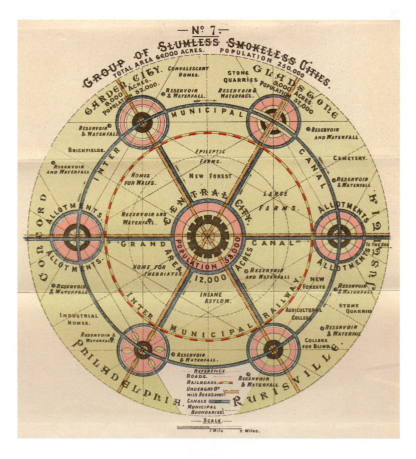

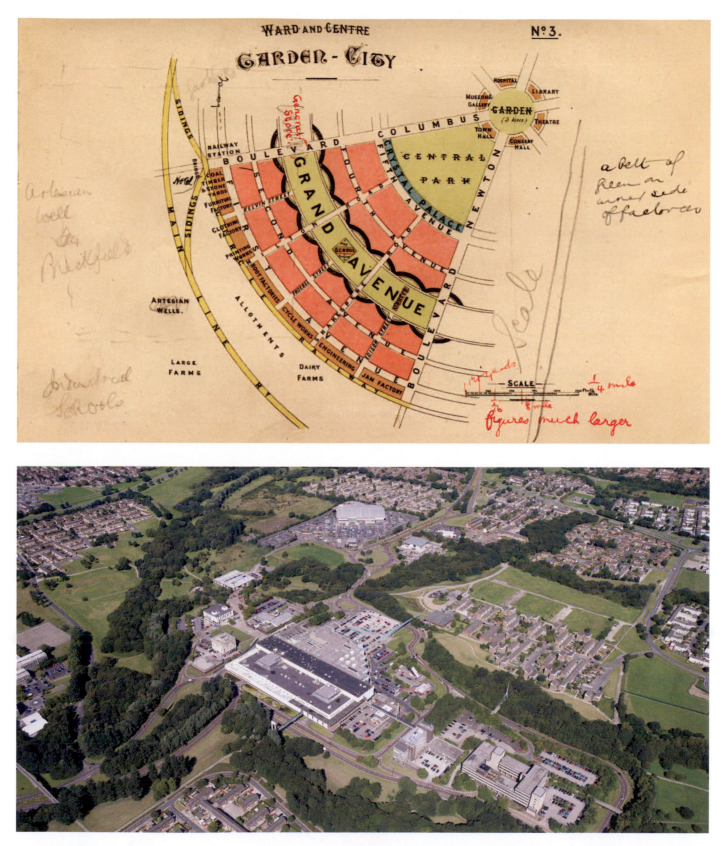

Howard's urban plan for the Garden City separated residential and industrial zones into concentric rings around a civic centre, central park and 'crystal palace' shopping arcade (top). Image courtesy of Hertfordshire Archives and Local Studies, ref: DE.Ho.F4.2. This design concept is clearly echoed in the New Towns. As can be seen in this aerial photograph of the centre of Skelmersdale (bottom), the central park and landscape wedges intended to unite town and country, the 'crystal palace' shopping mall, low-density housing arrangements in 'neighbourhood units', and industry located in dedicated estates on the outer edges, are the direct legacy of Howard's ideas. The later influence of Osborn ensured that the New Towns would be built to segregate traffic and pedestrian movement so that the roads would go 'to but not through' the town centre and similarly the surrounding housing estates would have no through roads but sit in their own self-contained road systems. Image courtesy of West Lancashire District Council.

Skelmersdale's low-density, garden city attributes are seen in figureground (top). A recent plan for the regeneration of the town (bottom) proposes adding new housing to the expansive green space to increase the total population, introduce a more traditional high street, new education, leisure and commercial sites. Image courtesy of West Lancashire District Council.

By the 1990s, some (though by no means all) New Town residential estates were showing signs of neglect and their car-free, landscaped areas offered little amenity value.

The most successful of all the New Towns is Milton Keynes – by virtue of the size of its population, wide mix of employment, including the Open University, and its strategic location on the M1 between London and Birmingham.

Milton Keynes' shopping centre remains a major destination for the surrounding region. The town is attractive for people wanting to relocate from nearby Aylesbury or North West London, and recent expansion plans aim for considerable growth for the centre and surrounding housing areas.

and housing in an ad hoc manner that damaged human health through pollution and that traffic congestion had become a chronic problem that damaged the economic life of the city.

With the damaged cities to be redesigned rather than merely repaired, the decentralisation of the population provided the opportunity for these problems to be tackled. The mass demolition of so-called slums took place alongside the pulling down of bombed-out buildings. Huge areas of the inner cities were replaced with modern housing estates, arranged in new, non-conventional ways. Simultaneously, the New Towns were to embrace the ideals of the same new, modern designs on large, coherent scales. Ultimately many towns and cities were to adopt these principles, with modernist tower blocks, zoning of industrial estates and housing estates, and new highways infrastructure of ring roads and underpasses.

Today, many of these urban characteristics are commonly thought of as belonging to the 1960s (when their construction was completed) but they actually originated in the wartime plans of the 1940s. The design principles, meanwhile, originated in the decades before that. A rich debate on city design began at the start of the twentieth century with the Garden Cities Movement. This highlighted the social damage resulting from poor conditions in the heart of the industrial cities and called for people to leave to build new communities in the economically depressed rural areas of the country. These were to be planned from first principles as the colonial cities of Australia or America had been. Started by social campaigner and grandfather of the British planning system, Ebenezer Howard, this movement produced two planned towns, Letchworth Garden City and Welwyn Garden City, in the countryside north of London, inspiring planners and designers around the world. In the UK, the assiduous campaigning of Frederick Osborn, Howard's right-hand man, led directly to the creation of the New Towns Programme.

By the 1920s, city design was increasingly subject to the growing influence of traffic engineers such as Algar Tripp, the Metropolitan Police head of traffic management, and Robert Moses, the New York highways engineer who was arguably the most influential city builder since Haussmann. Where the Garden Cities Movement sought to build places that balanced urban living with an appreciation of the rural way of life, twenty years after their origin, the new up and coming ideas were those

of the Modern Movement, spearheaded by the Swiss architect Le Corbusier.

Born the son of a clock-maker, Le Corbusier (whose real name was Charles-Edouard Jeanneret) designed a number of inspiring buildings utilising the properties of new materials such as concrete. His vision of the future where motorisation was central to society was published in the 1923 book *Vers Une Architecture*, published in English four years later as *Towards a New Architecture*. His Ville Contemporaine was a proposed city of three million people, composed of a line of large megablocks separated by freeways and linear parks.

The new realities of the private motorcar, widespread in America from the 1920s, had rapidly led to major congestion problems in historic towns. Corbusier and his sympathisers dismissed these towns as having been designed in the era of the horse and cart. Instead, urban expressways, ring roads and underpasses were essential to the lifeblood of modern technological society. In America, Robert Moses did not just argue the case but directly transformed New York by carving major highway infrastructure across the city through a vast road-building programme throughout the Depression. As well as highway infrastructure, American approaches to urban planning had been developing, driven by legal reform campaigners such as Alfred Bettman. They argued for the community benefits of separating employment and housing into distinct zones of industrial estates and housing estates. These ideas rapidly became widespread as many different architects and designers came to similar conclusions about the nature of contemporary urban living. The American modern architect Frank Lloyd Wright developed the idea of Broadacre City, a prototype for a region constructed from separate suburbs and urban centres linked by freeways.

In Abercrombie's plan for the reconstruction of London, these ideas came together on the ground to address the unhealthy conditions of Victorian smokestack factories surrounded by housing for their workers. For businesses too, the mass of historic buildings and streets meant expanding the size of their operations was extremely difficult, and maintaining their ageing buildings was expensive. As a result, the plans for the new country that would be built from the ruins, intrinsic to the morale boosting communications, were all of a deliberately different form than before. The continental approach to rebuilding bomb-damaged areas in the post-war era using their original street layout and building forms was not the priority in Britain.

The two camps of the Garden Cities Movement and the Modern Movement had both been arguing their case throughout the years leading up to the Second World War. At times each had been antagonistic to the other. The Garden Cities Movement had been in existence for much longer than the Modernists, and had entered the political mainstream. By the 1940s, sufficient common ground between these two groups campaigning for change meant that the New Towns became a hybrid of their two perspectives. The Modern Movement was optimistic about new technology and campaigned for buildings and cities that embraced industrial design, mass production and high-speed transport.

The Garden Cities Movement by contrast had its roots in a nineteenth-century reaction against industrialisation. It shared common ground with the Arts and Crafts Movement, who from the late Victorian period had sought to protect the trade of traditional artisans from the ravages of cheaper industrial mass-production. Some were traditionalists while others were radicals – pastoralist romantics who sought to preserve or recreate a rural idyll of man in communion with nature and God. Yet, these spiritual undertones did not betray a pragmatic resourcefulness. The social campaigning element of Ebenezer Howard's work meant what mattered was achieving a change on the ground, not just winning a philosophical argument. In this he was clearly in tune with the famous epitaph of Karl Marx – philosophers have interpreted the world, the point however is to change it.

Such was the success of Letchworth Garden City that the style of housing and the residential street layouts used in the Garden Cities soon influenced the design of Britain's vast inter-war suburbs in the 1920s and 1930s. Hampstead Garden Suburb became the first of countless similar developments that steadily receded from Howard's original vision. As will be discussed later, the reinvigoration of Howard's campaigning organisation, the Garden Cities Association in the 1930s, renamed the Town and Country Planning Association, played an increasingly influential role in prompting and then shaping the New Towns Programme after the Second World War.

With the Modernists in ascendance in the 1930s, thirty years after the Garden Cities Movement began, they were able to pour scorn on the architecture of suburbia while showcasing dramatic new creations clearly belonging in the present and pointing to the future rather than staying weighed down in the past. This was not entirely fair, as the Garden City had been a radical and forward-looking concept that sought an alternative to suburban sprawl. Howard himself had little interest in archtecture but was concerned with how towns operated as entities in their own right. The mock-Tudor facades and Garden Suburb layouts that spread across Britain and overseas in the 1920s and 1930s paid a disservice to Howard's core vision just as huge amounts of British modern architecture of the 1950s and 1960s was to be a poor copy of the work of Le Corbusier and other modernist pioneers such as Walter Gropius and Mies van der Rohe.

Ultimately, the fundamental principles of the Garden City Movement culminated in the post-war New Towns Programme. This link is so strong that Britain's New Towns cannot be properly understood without explaining a little of the story of the Garden Cities Movement. The essential principles of town design included a careful balance of jobs and housing to avoid local unemployment and prevent inward or outward commuting. Towns were to be of a specific size that meant they would be self-contained, capable of hosting all the functions needed for a town without being dependent on a larger city for their survival. Howard's Garden City was also conceived as self-sufficient in terms of food supply and energy production – a significant precursor of the idea of environmental self-sufficiency that emerged in the 1970s. He also wanted to achieve a balance between an urban way of life and a rural setting, leading to an approach to town planning designed to give the impression of being in the countryside whilst still being inside a town.

The Garden Cities Movement was arguably at the height of its powers in the 1940s, whilst the height of the influence of the Modern Movement in Britain came in the early 1960s when British construction was in full swing. As such, the Garden Cities Movement gave the New Towns Programme its political impetus, basic investment model and fundamental design concepts, such as zoned-separation of housing and industry, self-containment within a green belt, and extensive use of green spaces within the towns' boundaries. The detailed design of buildings, however, was undertaken increasingly by members of the Modern Movement. The later phase of the New Towns Programme that began in the 1960s, and the completion or expansion of the early New Towns in the late 1960s and

Wine makers Gilbeys expanded into gin and whiskey production, with new offices and distillery in Harlow, shown here in 1964. Copyright: Museum of Harlow.

continuing into the 1970s, showed the increasing influence of the Modern Movement.

Ultimately, the way the New Towns were a hybrid of these two distinct movements meant the design principles were pulled in two different directions. One set of core values – that of the

Garden Cities Movement – related to a vision of urbanism fundamentally concerned with the relationship between society and nature. The other, of the Modern Movement, was one fundamentally concerned with the relationship between society and technology. This contrast is central to the underlying character

PLANNING THE NEW TOWNS

of the New Towns. It has shaped their evolution and it is an essential part of what makes them distinct from any other type of town or instances of similar styles of architecture or urban design within larger cities. The character of the New Towns really is a combination of both the fast and urban, and the quiet and rural. This is vital for understanding the sort of places they are.

Building the better future

Another key element of this story was the birth of the British planning system. Besides the policy that there should be new towns and new principles for how they should be designed, a new legal system controlling all development was introduced in order to prevent dysfunctional places from ever being created again. The planning system meant that landowners could no longer build whatever they wanted, wherever they wanted. Instead, they were to be subject to development plans controlled by local government officials, who would grant permissions in an open forum to which local residents could contribute. This was a central reform undertaken by the post-war government. Immediately prior to the war, the accompanying legislation of the Green Belt Act 1938 was based on the principle that existing towns and cities should be prevented from expanding without limit. London had expanded rapidly in the previous two decades, alarming many. The Green Belt was a zone around each town and city in which development was to be strictly controlled or avoided altogether. Rather than a static band where development was banned outright, the Green Belt was a zone to ensure that towns and cities did not blend into each other, creating a homogenous sprawl of urban development.

Building in Britain is thus subject to a hierarchy of restrictions. Building on the Green Belt is extremely difficult and despite a return of the fear of urban sprawl, its designated size increased substantially after 1997 (ODPM, 2003). Building on Areas of Outstanding Natural Beauty, Sites of Special Scientific Importance or high-quality agricultural land is effectively forbidden. Building of any sort is subject to planning permission from the local or regional planning authority, which can only be overturned by the government in exceptional circumstances (and thus remains a hotly contested area for new airport run-

ways or nuclear power stations). Reform of the planning system, to reduce the delays in granting permission for domestic house extensions or increase focus on sustainable development, means the issue is never quite off the boil.

The impetus for the New Towns Programme thus arose from a number of factors coming together. Abercombie had long been a supporter of the Garden Cities Movement. In 1926, he helped create the Campaign for the Protection of Rural England, aimed at preventing urban sprawl, curtailing the outward expansion of towns and cities. This campaign had common cause with the Garden Cities idea for entirely new self-contained towns. Then, in his role as Professor of Planning at Liverpool University in the 1930s, Abercrombie became influenced by the work of the Modernists. Together with leading figures in the Garden Cities Movement he formalised the idea of depopulating the inner cities and enshrined it in public policy. The first pillar of the planning system, the Green Belt Act 1938, meant that government could begin to control development. The outbreak of war meant that nothing would be built without direct government control. By the end of the war, the planning system was implemented as a de facto continuation of the command and control systems of the wartime economy. The arguments from the 1930s now had the mechanism of state involvement, and would now be applied to achieve the peacetime aims of physical and economic reconstruction.

High-quality housing in well-designed communities drew wide support from both the man in the street and senior figures in the political establishment as a matter of social justice, and throughout the early twentieth century this campaign grew. With the Labour Party achieving a landslide victory in the general election a mere eight weeks after the end of the Second World War in 1945, the government mandate was to build a new society on the ruins of the old. The New Towns were visible proof of this and represented a major expansion in state provision for housing. In any case, private sector provision was virtually impossible until around 1954 when construction materials were no longer subject to rationing and government control on building licences was eased. State-built housing was itself a further idea long campaigned for by social reformers, just as universal education and access to healthcare had been. The council house or council flat was another pillar of the welfare state, and the challenge of building enough houses fast enough was one of the pre-eminent concerns during the immediate post-war years. Many were housed in some 150,000 emergency 'pre-fabricated' houses, mass produced in factories that weeks earlier had been making military aircraft. Some (up to 50,000) squatted in derelict properties (Hennesey, 1992). Eliminating slums from the face of Britain's cities had been a long-standing concern, but the New Towns would not provide immediate relief.

Rebuilding in London commenced on a site-by-site basis and the essential infrastructure of roads and water was already present – even if damaged. To build a New Town required considerable masterplanning, complex negotiation and large-scale organisation. Some of the first sites had been identified before the war, so plans were already in existence, such as the first town to be designated, Stevenage in Hertfordshire, which had been earmarked by its local authority for expansion in the 1930s from a town of 7,000 people to one of more than 30,000. The Ministry of Town and Country Planning was able to absorb it within the New Towns Programme, 'as a matter of urgency' (Osborn and Whittick, 1977: 177) and announce it as soon as the New Towns Programme was announced. However, the fact that the plans were well known meant that residents of 'Old Stevenage' had created a well-established and well-funded protest group numbering in the thousands. The impression was not the happy utopia portrayed in the government's jolly promotional cartoon, *Charley in New Town*, but shock and outrage. As one existing inhabitant, Jack Franklin recalled,

> It came as a bit of a bombshell to everybody. We were a contented little town . . . nobody would want to deny places for people to live but we thought it a bit unfair to plan to plonk about 80 or 90,000 people on this wretched little village, and, people got very hot under the collar . . . I'd just bought a cottage beyond the cricket field, a nice little Georgian cottage . . . recently got married and . . . we had it about three weeks before we got a letter through the post box saying, 'Sell this or else!'
>
> (Stevenage, 2007b)

On 6 May 1946, plans were presented at a packed public meeting in the town where the government minister responsible, Lewis Silkin, and leader of the Garden Cities Movement, Frederick Osborn, were booed and heckled 'dictators'. In what would now seem a titanic public relations disaster, Silkin declared the residents' views as irrelevant since the town was going to be built. The mood turned angry and the minister fled to find his car had been sabotaged (Kynaston, 2007: 163).

Later Franklin's friend Clarence Elliott coined the name 'Silkingrad', in reference to Soviet authoritarianism. In January 1947, having skilfully manufactured fake railway signs baring this name, they rebranded Stevenage Station (with the tacit support of the local policeman) and got a photograph in the press that soon spread the message of their campaign as far as America and New Zealand (Stevenage, 2007b). The PR campaign against the New Town also benefited from celebrity support, such as from writer E.M. Forster, who had set the novel *Howard's End* in Old Stevenage. He declared the New Town would be like, 'a meteorite upon the ancient and delicate scenery of Hertfordshire'. Some small irony given that the novel, written in 1921, described central London increasingly choked by pollution. The problems of the city were widely agreed, but the proposed solution to create new places outside of the city where people could live a healthier life inevitably met resistance. As Frederick Osborn put it,

> naturally there was resentment and tough opposition on the part of the owners of the land that had to be compulsorily acquired in assembling the sites, and by private residents who had settled in pleasant countrified surroundings and did not want their Arcadia invaded by what they envisaged as a horde of urban slum-dwellers. On the other hand, the retail traders, and the majority of employable workers already in the designated area generally welcomed the prospect of a new town.
>
> (Osborn and Whittick, 1977: 59)

His appeal that the needs of the urban many should outweigh the desires of the rural few marked a conflict between urban and rural, and the political camps of Labour and Conservative, that had long repercussions. A public inquiry ensued – as it did in many of the subsequent New Town designations – but to no avail. The Court of Appeal and the House of Lords eventually ruled in favour of the policy as being in the national interest and hence, in 1949, a whole three years after designation, the first

new houses at Stevenage began construction. The engineering of infrastructure – roads, water supply and other services – preceded development and the first neighbourhood, Bedwell, was not completed until 1956, seven years later. Only by the end of 1962, thirteen years after construction of the New Town had begun, had the town centre and four of the initial six neighbourhoods neared completion.

Mr and Mrs Sulzbach and son, at 4 Broadview, Stevenage. The first tenants to move into the Bedwell neighbourhood, photographed in 1958. Copyright: Stevenage Museum.

The early New Towns

New Towns were attractive to families with children, resulting in the nickname of Pram Towns. Gibberd's Morley Grove scheme, Harlow. Copyright: Museum of Harlow.

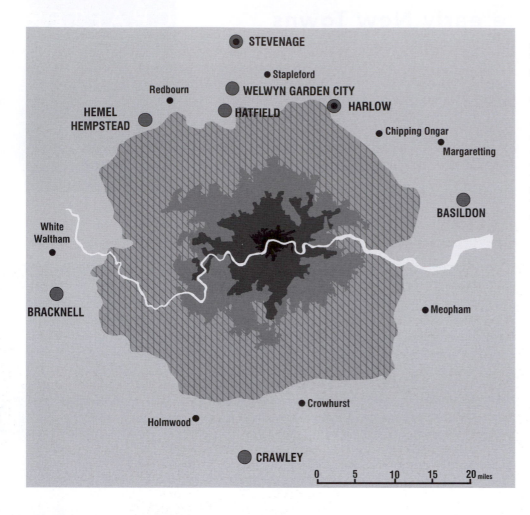

STEVENAGE

• Stapleford

Redbourn   WELWYN GARDEN CITY

HEMEL   HATFIELD   HARLOW
HEMPSTEAD

• Chipping Ongar

• Margaretting

White
Waltham

BASILDON

BRACKNELL

• Meopham

• Crowhurst

Holmwood •

CRAWLEY

0   5   10   15   20 miles

London expanded in waves of suburban growth, beginning with the West End in the Georgian era, railway suburbs in the Victorian era, and the Interwar suburbs in the early twentieth century. The introduction of the Green Belt (shown in hatched lines) proposed in Abercrombie's Greater London Plan curtailed further outward expansion. Meanwhile, future growth was to be accommodated in New Towns beyond the Green Belt. The dots indicate the sites suggested by Abercrombie, and the circles show the sites eventually developed under the New Towns Programme.

The origin of the New Towns Programme came in the New Towns Act of 1946. By 1950, eight sites had been identified in a ring around London to meet the policy of decentralisation, plus a further one in the Clyde Valley to decentralise population from Glasgow, which also had appalling slum conditions. In addition, a further five sites for New Towns had been designated: two in the North East, one in the East Midlands, one in Fife, Scotland, and one in South Wales. These additional sites sought to provide improved living conditions or housing for workers in new sites for mining or industry.

Abercrombie's Greater London Plan of 1944 had put forward ten sites to accommodate inner-city Londoners. The sites identified and the target populations were White Waltham (60,000), Chipping Ongar (60,000), Harlow (60,000), Margaretting (30,000), Stevenage (60,000), Redbourne (60,000), Stapleford (25,000), Meopham (40,000), Crowhurst (60,000) and Holmwood (60,000). The rest were to relocate to existing towns either in the region or more remotely (Abercrombie, 1944). The plans were subject to official scrutiny by civil servants throughout the war. Of the sites originally proposed, five were selected to go forward: Stevenage, Hemel Hempstead and Hatfield in Hertfordshire; Crawley in Sussex; and Harlow in Essex. A further three were added soon after: Bracknell in Surrey; Welwyn Garden City in Hertfordshire, to combine with neighbouring Hatfield under a single Development Corporation; and Basildon in Essex.

In the East Midlands, Corby was a steel-working town that

had been built by private enterprise in the 1920s. In County Durham, Peterlee was a new community for families living in poor-quality housing built by private mining companies, while Newton Aycliffe was the site of a major military munitions works. Glenrothes in East Fife was also to serve a growing coal-mining area, while Cwmbran in South Wales was to provide a new town for employees commuting long distances to a variety of employers in the area.

Each of these towns took well over a decade to build, with the actual rate of housing completions fluctuating in response to the wider economic conditions of the 1950s and 1960s. House building peaked at around 1,000 homes per year per town in 1957 (around 15,000 homes per year in total), but by early 1960s, completions slumped to below 7,500 homes per year (Osborn and Whittick, 1977).

The New Towns Programme was a major undertaking, but was not the only house building being embarked on. Major housing estates were also being built through the Expanded Towns Programme, introduced through the 1952 Town Development Act, and throughout the inner cities. The principal difference for the New Towns was that the scale of development achieved was entirely as a result of the new type of management regime created – the New Town Development Corporation. This had the power to force the purchase of land at its agricultural value and reinvest the profits from leasing the land, once the town had been built.

Frederick Gibberd, architect planner of Harlow New Town. Gibberd's other major works included Liverpool's Catholic Cathedral, Didcot Power Station, The London Central Mosque and Heathrow Airport.

The Harlow Development Corporation in 1949. From left to right, front to back, General R.P. Packenham Walsh (Deputy Chairman), Sir Ernest Gowers (Chairman), Eric Adams (General Manager), Countess P. Russell, B. Alsop, Mrs E. A. Newton, A. Reed, D.H. Whinney, R.O.C. Hurst, T.H. Joyce. Copyright: Museum of Harlow.

Front cover of the Harlow masterplan.

The New Town plans developed by the post-war Labour Government were actually built during the Conservative Government of the 1950s. Rather than creating new development corporations, the Conservative Government switched attention to encouraging local authorities to expand existing towns and produce high-rise housing in the inner cities. By the early 1960s, the Conservatives admitted the effectiveness of

Gibberd's eight-storey block, The Lawn in 1951, was Britain's first towerblock.

the New Towns Development Corporation model and commissioned a second generation of towns. The Labour Party, returning to government in 1964 for the first time since 1951, then designated a third generation. As such these three areas of housing growth all continued to be built well into the 1970s, under various governments.

The model of the development corporation was such that once commissioned they had relatively high levels of independence from government. Curiously, in order to determine the suitability of locations selected, an advisory committee on each New Town site had to be established and a tentative plan sketched out. In many cases, the people involved at this stage, including the planners, architects and local politicians, would go on to plan the actual towns and run their development corporations.

In each case the context was slightly different, and this was reflected in the way that the development corporations were established and who their members were. Each is covered in the official histories published by its development corporation. In the words of the 2006 government analysis of the New Towns,

these 'are unapologetically hagiographic in tone, similar in style to self-published company histories' (CLG, 2006: 13). The development corporations were in fact essentially like private companies with central government as their sole shareholder.

In the immediate aftermath of the war, they ran operations that were a unique fusion of public and private, with the powers of a public agency, but with the freedom of a commercial company to determine its own structure and choose who to employ. Each development corporation had a board made up of part-time members and a full-time general manager who did not sit on the board. The general manager then essentially ran the town-building project and hired the planners, engineers, architects, economic development experts and community development officers. The powers of the board varied from town to town with some acting like local authority committees and others just setting financial constraints and reviewing progress (Gibberd et al., 1980: 18). The success of each was thus a result of the nature of the relationship between the chairman of the board and the general manager.

The first generation

Although Stevenage is commonly thought of as the first New Town by virtue of being the first to be designated, the legal challenges by the existing 7,000 residents delayed the work of its development corporation. The town expansion had also already been outlined in the 1930s, so there was less imperative to create a fresh investigation for suitability. The second and third towns to be designated, Crawley in Sussex and Hemel Hempstead in Hertfordshire, were also subject to legal challenges.

As with Stevenage, Crawley New Town saw the high court ultimately ruling in favour of the government, with construction then beginning in 1950. The third New Town, Hemel Hempstead, had a substantially larger initial population, more than 20,000 people, who mounted a similar legal challenge against the designation order. The size of the existing population provides a good indication of the size of the existing urban fabric. With the population of Hemel Hempstead so great, rather than a new town with an existing village or industrial site forming part of the whole, this was effectively a trebling in size of an already major town, coupled with major renovations to the historic centre. The scale and complexity of this remodelling meant that the (now Conservative) secretary of state did not approve the plans until as late as June 1952.

In the fourth New Town to be designated, Harlow in Essex, the size of the existing community was small. Despite its proximity to London the site was a rural backwater and the land was owned by a small number of aristocratic families. Here, the Labour Party, rather than the ministry, conducted a successful public relations campaign to convince the local agricultural labourers of the opportunities they would have in the New Town instead of remaining in their present circumstances. Godfrey Arkwright, the first of the major landowners, also with some regret, acknowledged the arguments for the town. As such, the lack of prolonged legal proceedings meant that Harlow was the first New Town to get underway.

The Harlow Development Corporation began work in offices in London, moving to take over a country house north of Harlow in April 1948. Prefab sheds were built to house the architects, engineers and planners. The provisional plan the ministry had commissioned from Frederick Gibberd, one of leading lights of the Modern Movement in Britain, was put into action, and

Gibberd appointed as lead 'architect-planner' (Gibberd, et al., 1980: 29–30)

Gibberd was a member of the MARS Group, the Modern Architecture Research Group that had been founded in the UK by Le Corbusier's friend Wells Coates. MARS was the UK branch of the International Congress for Modern Architecture (CIAM). A major exhibition organised by MARS, and opened by Le Corbusier, in 1938, had established Modernism as the way forward for Britain. Gibberd, like Abercrombie, sought to combine Modernism with the objectives of the Garden Cities Movement. For Harlow, he produced a masterplan that aimed to achieve Ebenezer Howard's goal of a self-contained town, combining the qualities of the urban and the rural – the Essex landscape allowed him to pioneer the new discipline of landscape architecture.

Table 3.1 The 'Mark One', or first generation, New Towns, with the dates over which the sites were deliberated before official designation. Approval of each subsequent plan by the Secretary of State was then needed, with the pre-war Stevenage plan approved immediately, then Gibberd's plan for Harlow approved in January 1948. Some plans took over five years after designation before they were approved and construction could start.

New Town	First mentioned to Cabinet Committee	Designation order
Stevenage	25.11.1945	11.11.1946
Crawley	29.03.1946	09.01.1947
Hemel Hempstead	29.03.1946	04.02.1947
Harlow	29.03.1946	25.03.1947
Newton Aycliffe	13.05.1946	19.04.1947
East Kilbride	13.05.1946	06.05.1947
Glenrothes	02.11.1946	30.06.1948
Welwyn Garden City	01.02.1947	20.05.1948
Hatfield	01.02.1947	20.05.1948
Peterlee	19.07.1947	10.03.1948
Basildon	17.04.1948	04.01.1949
Bracknell	20.07.1948	17.06.1949
Cwmbran	20.09.1948	04.11.1949
Corby	See note below	

Note: The Stewarts & Lloyds steelworks built 2,200 houses on 113ha land in Corby between 1935 and 1939. The local authority, Kettering Rural District Council, had no involvement. The Corby Urban District Council was formed in 1939. Masterplanners for Corby New Town were appointed in August 1950.

Meanwhile, the buildings were to include a number of showcases of modern architecture, including Britain's first high-rise apartment block.

The creation of this block, the Lawn, was a point of considerable controversy. The housing commissioned to date throughout the New Towns had been uniform two-up, two-down terraces, and Gibberd wanted to create a landmark, visible from the surrounding roads. The ministry were adamantly opposed to the idea of building tower blocks in the countryside as this went against one of the fundamental arguments for why New Towns were necessary. If tower blocks were to be used, then why couldn't the housing crisis be met by accommodating people in skyscrapers in the cities (as indeed became the case later)? Instead, the Harlow Development Corporation saw this as a test case for whether they really did have independence from government. In December 1949, the government backed down, Gibberd got his way and Harlow got its landmark (Gibberd et al., 1980: 22). Harlow remains one of the best-preserved of the early New Towns, and the only one to have a coherent vision throughout. Gibberd stayed living in Harlow, working for the town for another thirty years.

The next New Town to be designated after Harlow was Hatfield. Here a poorly planned scattering of new factories built from 1934 onwards with employees largely commuting from St Albans, Welwyn Garden City and north London was to be turned into a town. The new De Havilland factory was to begin manufacturing jet engines for the new generation of aeroplanes. In neighbouring Welwyn Garden City, the population in 1948 was around 18,500. Since this was short of its creator Ebenezer Howard's target population of 50,000, it was identified as a further satellite town. With Hatfield so close, a single development corporation was established to tackle both towns within one organisation. The private Garden City Company founded by investors in the 1920s to build Welwyn was effectively eliminated in favour of a publicly backed New Town Development Corporation.

Basildon in Essex followed, also representing a chance to fix an area that had been seen as problematic. As part of a 'back to the land' movement and general property speculation marketed at Londoners in the 1920s, a series of self-build houses had sprung up in an ad hoc fashion among unmade roads with poor drainage and water provision. Retired soldiers, Cockney weekenders, radicals and the impecunious had created a sprawl of bungalow developments, which at best were akin to the Eastern European dacha, the wooden cottage in the country that town people would lovingly build during vacations, but at worst were effectively shacks, reminiscent of the rural poverty of the late nineteenth century. Basildon's start was complicated by the need to purchase land from thousands of existing landowners rather than a small number of aristocrats, as had been the case in places such as Harlow. The complexity of Basildon's infrastructure works and the less favourable economic climate at the time of building added to the difficulties in developing the New Town. The incoming population largely came from the East London districts of West and East Ham.

The last of the London satellites was Bracknell in Berkshire, a small village of a few thousand aimed for expansion initially of 25,000 people, increased to 60,000 people in 1961. The location was chosen in preference to Abercrombie's proposed site at White Waltham partly because of the higher quality of agricultural land that would have been lost there, and the impact on a nearby airfield. The new population was largely from the West London districts of Acton and Southall.

Hatfield and Basildon had shown that difficult unplanned areas could be fixed by becoming sites for a New Town. Away from London, Cwmbran in South Wales used the same logic to provide new housing and social facilities for workers commuting long distances to a variety of employers spread around the valleys near Newport. Corby in the East Midlands saw the expansion of a pre-war steel works, Stewarts & Lloyds, which had played a major role in the invasion of France, manufacturing the top secret oil pipeline PLUTO (PipeLine Under The Ocean). Scottish steel workers from Ravenscraig in the Clyde Valley had migrated down to man the plant as early as the mid-1920s, but now a major expansion of operations fitted well with the offer of a new life in England for Scottish steel workers.

In Scotland itself, East Kilbride in the Clyde Valley was the first New Town intended to accommodate population from the slums of inner-city Glasgow, while Glenrothes New Town was connected to the increased exploitation of coal-fields in the East Fife area between Edinburgh and Dundee. Coal was the essential driver of the British economy. It was the food for all industrial activity, for running the railways and for heating buildings. The more that could be mined the more the economy could grow.

For the Scottish New Towns, the minister responsible was the secretary of state for Scotland, who wielded far-reaching powers to co-ordinate the needs of the towns. Responsibility for planning, economic development and the scheduling of school and hospital building all resided with one person. The English New Towns fell under the Ministry of Town and Country Planning, later the Ministry of Housing and Local Government, and, ultimately, the Department of the Environment. The Welsh New Towns were also controlled from Whitehall. Scotland therefore avoided problems of co-ordinating delivery from different central government departments such as health, education and trade.

The expansion of coal production in East Fife, from 2 million tons per year to 6.5 million tons per year, required a doubling of the existing workforce to a new total of 13,000 men. The minister for Scotland, aware of the dangers of having a town dependent on a single sector, was able to successfully co-ordinate a strategy that created growth of alternative employment, which eventually overtook coal mining as the economic basis for the town. The total population of Glenrothes New Town was thus determined as 30,000.

The coal mining areas around County Durham in northern England produced the only New Town to be requested by local residents. Later renamed Peterlee, after mine union leader Peter Lee, the Easington New Town was an answer to the grim conditions of pit towns built in the area by private enterprise with no concern for wider social consequences. The residents were wholly reliant on their single employer and lived in conditions that showed no improvement on working-class life in the previous century. As an account by James Lansdale Hodson, published as *The Way Things Are* (1947), recalled of an area close to the future New Town site,

The streets are unpaved, with small knolls of hard earth and cinders and runnels caused by rain. Patches of grass grew boldly. The streets were almost an unbroken line of miserable brick hovels, each street about 400 yards in length, most horrible and dreary. Our coming brought a few unkempt women and ill-clad children to the doors. Two hefty young men eyed us sullenly. It was nearer to hell, I thought, than anything I had seen since Belsen.

(cited in Kynaston 2007: 159)

The nationalisation of industries such as coal and steel, effectively begun by Churchill's war economy, was formalised under the Labour Government. House building, too, previously also the domain of private speculative builders, was also effectively nationalised, with construction materials subject to extreme shortages, planning controlled by government, and a grave housing crisis. Responsibility for improvement in the Durham pit towns thus became a prime responsibility of the state, as demonstrated by the designation order for Peterlee New Town, which declared,

an outstanding opportunity for breaking with the unhappy tradition that miners and their families should be obliged to live in ugly, overcrowded villages clustered around pitheads, out of contact with people in other walks of life, and even for the most part with workers in other industries.

(Draft Easington New Town (Designation) Order, 1947, cited in Osborn & Whittick, 1977: 272)

Whether offering an alternative to smoky inner-city London or Glasgow, or the bleak pit towns from where the coal creating that smoke originated, the appeal and rationale of the New Town was incredibly strong. It offered the badly needed chance for the working classes to share in the benefits of modern society. As Elizabeth Darling puts it,

The middle classes had benefited to a considerable extent from progress and had achieved a state of intellectual and social modernity . . . For working-class people the experience of modernity was largely a negative one. Urbanisation and industrialisation had brought them not freedom but alienation, impoverishment, poor health and appalling living conditions, circumstances which, in effect, prevented them from even the prospect of entering a state of modernity.

(Darling, 2006: 85)

New designs for housing in brand new, rationally designed towns therefore became the moral imperative of the time. The use of modern architecture as an icon in the morale-raising poster campaigns during the war, showing clean, bright white, light and airy apartment blocks, schools and hospitals rising

The vast Apollo Pavilion sculpture by Victor Pasmore, Oakerside Drive, Peterlee New Town, was conceived as 'A villa for the space age'. Source: The Twentieth Century Society.

from bombed out Victorian streets resonated deeply with the British voters, contributing to the Labour landslide in 1945.

Central to the story of Peterlee is the role of the architect Berthold Lubetkin, who came to London, from Georgia via Paris, in 1930 with the ambition of bringing modern architecture to Britain. As a founder member of the architecture firm Tecton, Lubetkin built some of the most pioneering examples of modern architecture in Britain: the Highpoint flats in north London, the penguin pool at London Zoo and the Finsbury Health Centre, which featured on Abram Games' wartime propaganda posters as evidence for the better future Britain was fighting for. He also helped form the Modern Architecture Research Society (MARS). In Peterlee, Lubetkin intended to create a central civic plaza at the heart of the town defined by three tower blocks in a triangle.

Tragically for Lubetkin, the ground conditions of this former coal mining area meant that high-rise tower blocks were impossible, and by 1950 he had resigned from the project. His replacement, Professor Sir George Grenfell-Baines, then aimed to make up for lost time and the haste with which the town was planned and built had long-term implications. To restore confidence, the chair of the development corporation employed local academic, architect and artist Victor Pasmore to take charge of design for the town. The Sunny Blunts estate sought novel approaches to housing design, but Pasmore's most famous legacy for Peterlee was the 'Apollo Pavillion' – a vast, abstract sculpture made of concrete slabs described as a villa of the space age. Pasmore described it as

> an architecture and sculpture of purely abstract form through which to walk, in which to linger and on which to play; a free and anonymous monument, which because of its independence, can lift the activity and psychology of an urban housing community on to a universal plane.
> (cited in Ward, 1993: 16)

This 80 foot wide by 30 foot tall structure lay over a small lake in an area of green space in a housing estate near the southern edge of the town. Over the years it has been a focus for praise by architectural critiques and condemnation by local residents, who see it as out of keeping with the area.

The remaining example of the first generation of the New Towns – also in County Durham – shows the paternalistic idealism of that first majority Labour Government and the establishment of Britain's post-war welfare state. Newton Aycliffe was a New Town built around the abandoned remains of one of the country's most significant munitions factories. At the war's end, the site had employed a vast 17,000 people – mostly women, known as the Aycliffe Angels – and was made available for new industries. By 1947, the workforce on the site had dwindled to a mere 3,000 people working for fifty different firms. Clearly this presented a huge regeneration opportunity and the New Town was designated to provide homes for 20,000 people adjacent to the vast and now largely empty complex of buildings (*Northern Echo*, 2004).

One of the firms to move into the site was Bakelite, a name eponymous with the first generation of commercial plastics. This new technology would prove essential for Britain's economic boom in the 1960s, and British industry's move away from nineteenth-century sectors such as coal, steel and textiles. Yet, Bakelite would also soon be rendered obsolete by that technological advance.

The location of the Aycliffe site was allegedly because it was low-lying and frequently covered in mist and fog to counter possible detection and bombing by the enemy. As such it had a different logic to those of the other first generation towns. Its designation solved a problem of what to do with a large industrial site, and the designation may have seemed entirely justified by any argument at the time. However, the town was clearly to be smaller than the size Howard regarded as the minimum for a self-supporting community. Second, the industrial estate with housing estates adjacent containing basic community facilities offered little of the vision of a quality settlement demonstrated by architectural luminaries such as Gibberd. No consistency of dedicated planners and staff here. In fact, the planners were confounded in their attempts to design the place properly as the ultimate target population kept being modified by the Whitehall planners, causing calculations to be continually redrafted.

Attracting people away from poor-quality pit villages – labelled Category D 'scheduled to die' – into the New Town to new jobs in Aycliffe or Peterlee was seen as a good thing (Clare, 2008). But comparison with the residents' previous homes, such an important driver in creating the New Towns Programme, did not necessarily provide a long-lasting solution. The idea that living in the country air was certainly better than the smoke of the nearby cities may have been true, but this alone was not enough to produce a high quality of life. The officials developing the New Towns Programme well understood the nature of the problems, but at Aycliffe, Peterlee and many others, the real question was to what extent they understood the nature of the solution.

Newton Aycliffe is perhaps one of the least known of the British New Towns, yet it provides perhaps the most important lesson for today. It answered a number of problems such as providing much needed new housing for nearby people. It had a huge existing site of small factory and office units ready to receive new employers. Yet, the landscape and location presented problems for the architects concerned with quality place-making. The architects of Newton Aycliffe puzzled over the challenges of creating a sense of place, saying,

> we found it difficult to find any purpose for which tall buildings would be needed, and yet some variation in height of buildings is needed if the town is to have character and not look like a large housing estate.
>
> (Aycliffe Development Corporation, 1951, cited in Aldridge. 1979: 57)

Today part of the Sedgefield constituency, Newton Aycliffe soon became the centrepiece of Labour's vision for emancipation of the working class. None other than Lord Beveridge, author of the Beveridge Report in 1942 that defined the Welfare State as one where unemployment and poverty would be eliminated for good, was to chair its development corporation in order to put his vision into practice. As described by John D. Clare, historian of the town,

> He envisaged a classless town, where manager and mechanic would live next door to each other in council houses. Newton Aycliffe was to be a paradise for housewives, with houses grouped around greens so children could play safely away from roads. There would be nurseries (to look after children while their mothers went shopping), a sports stadium, a park and a 'district heating system', so dirty coal fires would not be necessary. The pubs were going to be state-run, and would sell nationalised beer. The town centre was to include a luxury hotel,

a college and community centre, a people's theatre, a dance hall and a cinema. There were even plans to use the Port Clarence railway to give townspeople a link to the seaside. The estimated cost of the town was £10 million; a local politician, Colonel Vickery, called it 'a scandalous and unnecessary waste of public money'.

Lord Beveridge opened the first house on Tuesday, 9th November 1948. Its tenant was D.G. Perry, an ex-army captain. While the newspapers hailed 'a dream town' and 'a bold experiment', Beveridge warned the first occupants that he could only offer them a life with 'no gardens, few roads, no shops and surrounded by a sea of mud . . . You have got to have the pioneering spirit,' Beveridge told the people, 'until you see the town of your hopes and dreams materialise'. . . . He even came to live in one of the houses, though he did not find 'life among the people' quite as easy as he had expected.

(Clare, 2008)

The key political moment for the New Towns Programme was when a hero from the war was introduced to his hard fought for home in this now little known town. The hopes and dreams in a sea of mud were to be the experiences of all the early New Town settlers. Like colonials setting out to found a city of dreams in the New World, the fundamental principle of the early New Towns was fundamentally utopian. It sought a better way of life.

In a previous generation, in the latter half of the nineteenth century, the creator of the Garden Cities Movement, Ebenezer Howard, had as a young man gone to Nebraska to be a pioneer. There he experienced the reality of creating a new settlement driven by the dream of a better future. The Garden City was inspired by how great colonial cities such as Washington and Adelaide had been brought into being. As Beveridge had made plain, the life of the early residents of the British New Towns bore many comparisons with the life of the settler. It was at times tough, and strange, but for the most part life for the New Town pioneers was filled with a spirit of optimism for the future, and of relief to be living somewhere better than before.

The later New Towns

CHAPTER 4

Netherfield in Milton Keynes. Copyright: English Partnerships. Image courtesy of Milton Keynes City Discovery Centre.

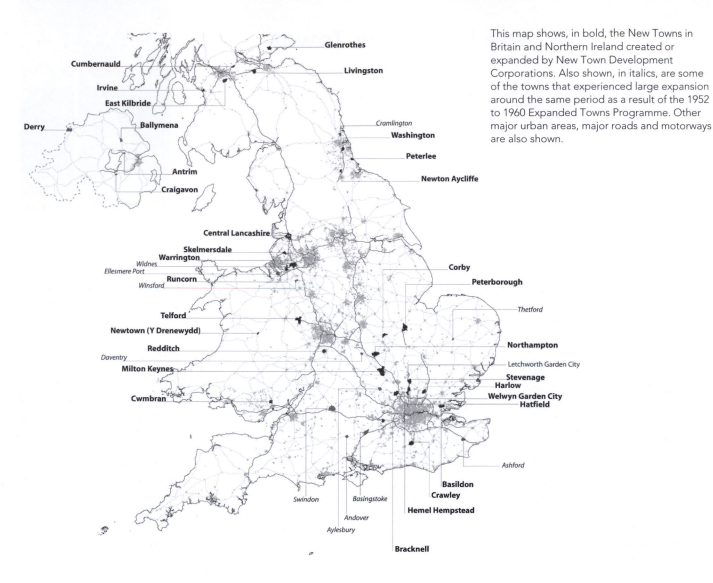

This map shows, in bold, the New Towns in Britain and Northern Ireland created or expanded by New Town Development Corporations. Also shown, in italics, are some of the towns that experienced large expansion around the same period as a result of the 1952 to 1960 Expanded Towns Programme. Other major urban areas, major roads and motorways are also shown.

Glenrothes
Livingston
Cumbernauld
Irvine
East Kilbride
Ballymena
Derry
Cramlington
Washington
Antrim
Peterlee
Craigavon
Newton Aycliffe
Central Lancashire
Skelmersdale
Warrington
Widnes
Corby
Ellesmere Port
Peterborough
Runcorn
Winsford
Thetford
Telford
Newtown (Y Drenewydd)
Northampton
Redditch
Letchworth Garden City
Daventry
Stevenage
Milton Keynes
Harlow
Welwyn Garden City
Cwmbran
Hatfield
Ashford
Swindon
Basildon
Basingstoke
Crawley
Andover
Hemel Hempstead
Aylesbury
Bracknell

Timeline of the 20th century

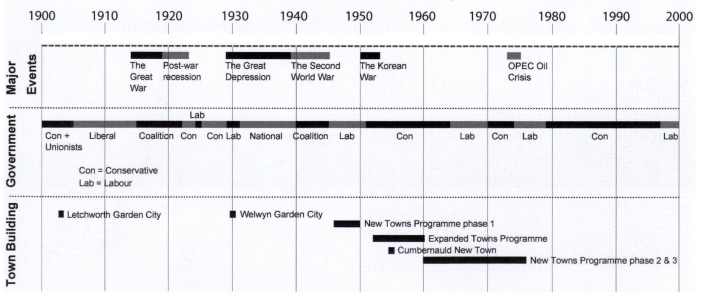

1900 1910 1920 1930 1940 1950 1960 1970 1980 1990 2000

Major Events

The Great War | Post-war recession | The Great Depression | The Second World War | The Korean War | OPEC Oil Crisis

Government

Lab

Con + Unionists | Liberal | Coalition | Con | Con Lab | National | Coalition | Lab | Con | Lab | Con Lab | Con | Lab

Con = Conservative
Lab = Labour

Town Building

■ Letchworth Garden City
■ Welwyn Garden City
New Towns Programme phase 1
Expanded Towns Programme
■ Cumbernauld New Town
New Towns Programme phase 2 & 3

By 1951, the first fruits of post-war rebuilding in Britain, including the New Towns, were unveiled to the public in the Festival of Britain, a cultural and entertainment spectacular on London's South Bank. Marking the centenary of the Great Exhibition of 1851, it proved extremely successful in raising public optimism and showing the reality of a new future on its way. The site of the Festival of Britain included impressive architectural feats, some of which, such as the Royal Festival Hall, remain today.

This physical expression of modernist architecture instantly captured the public mood at the time that the plans for the first New Towns were nearing completion. In the city of Coventry, one of the centres for British mechanical engineering, extremely heavy bombing throughout the war had obliterated its historic centre. The rebuilding, planned from as early as 1941, echoed 'the Festival Style' of smooth, plain surfaces and extensive car-free areas, as did the centre for the New Town of Stevenage. Both Coventry and Stevenage took entirely new approaches to urban design, planned around a different approach to traffic withthe country's first pedestrian-only shopping precincts, which were presented as the most exciting architectural phenomena of their time.

Yet by the time these plans started being built, the politicians responsible for the first generation of New Towns had been swept from office. Mere months after the Festival of Britain had provided a showcase of the new vision of Britain's future, the party that had set out to create it was no longer in power. The Labour Party that had won the landslide victory in 1945 was only narrowly re-elected in 1950. With most of its promises for the post-war welfare state now being implemented, the party was lacking direction and its major players in cabinet were showing their age. Soon into the new government various factors, including the major foreign affairs crisis of the outbreak of the Korean War, prompted a new election in the autumn of 1951. The Conservative Party returned to power under Winston Churchill, and remained there for a further thirteen years.

The New Towns Programme was low on the list of concerns for the new government, and throughout the 1950s development progressed according to existing plans. Instead the Conservatives sought to build housing through partnerships between different local authorities rather than by dedicated development corporations. The so-called Expanded Towns Programme was created by the 1952 Town Development. The ongoing decentralisation of the urban populations was to be

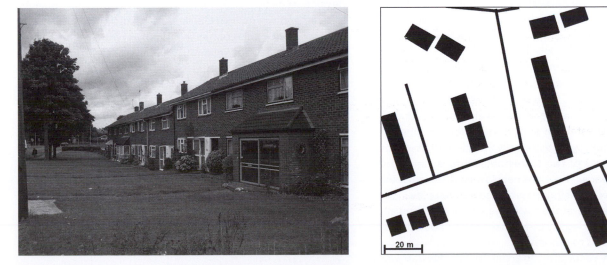

The early housing in the first generation New Towns was built to a formulaic design and low-density arrangement. The above image and figure-ground are of Rockingham Way, Stevenage. This can be contrasted with working-class housing of the nineteenth century, shown on page 54.

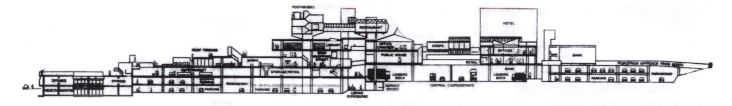

Cumbernauld town centre was conceived as a single superstructure.

facilitated through the expansion of existing towns. Large numbers of Londoners were encouraged to move through arrangements between the London County Council and towns in those regions suffering from declining economic prospects. Towns such as Swindon in Wiltshire, Wellingborough in Northamptonshire, Aylesbury in Buckinghamshire, Andover in Hampshire, Thetford in Norfolk, Bury Saint Edmunds in Suffolk, and Basingstoke in Hampshire, as well as many others had major new housing estates added to them to swell their populations.

Inevitably, there were a couple of exceptions to the clear break from the 1946 to 1950 New Towns Programme and the Expanded Towns Programme of the 1950s. In 1955, Cumbernauld New Town was designated by the secretary of state for Scotland on the grounds that East Kilbride was proving insufficient at fulfilling the decentralisation policy for Glasgow. It also answered a growing criticism from architects and campaigners that the first generation of New Towns had been extremely formulaic in their design. Constrained by shortages of materials and manpower, the development corporations had adopted a standardised book approach to house design; neighbourhoods were created on large scales to essentially the same patterns with buildings that were essentially mass-produced. Despite attempts to establish strong identities for different areas of the towns, they were essentially indistinguishable. The ubiquitous pattern was of two-storey brick terraces arranged on gently curving roads. The extremely low land values at the time, and rationale of reversing the crowded nature of life in the inner cities, also meant that the towns were built to essentially suburban densities. This legacy can be seen throughout the first generation New Towns to this day.

In response, ten years after the start of the New Towns Programme, Cumbernauld gave a new, younger generation

of architects the opportunity to experiment with modernist approaches to housing and urban layout. With the influence of the Garden Cities Movement waning, and bolstered by the emerging plans for the modernist pedestrian centres for the first New Towns, Cumbernauld soon became a testimony to the ideas of Le Corbusier. The town plan by Hugh Wilson aimed at higher densities in order to create a more urban feel. Like the Unite D'Habitation, at its centre the various public and commercial functions of the town centre were to be formed inside a single eight-storey high structure, designed by architect Geoffrey Copcutt. The Institute of American Architects soon voted it the best building in the world (*Telegraph*, 2002).

The other comparable developments of this era were major developments built by city councils in partnership with private developers. In the 1930s, Manchester City Council had planned to build and run its own Garden City in order to decentralise its inner-city population. In the 1950s, Wynthenshawe finally emerged as a new settlement of more than 25,000 homes, eight miles south of the city centre. Similarly, Newcastle-upon-Tyne City Council created North Killingworth and Cramlington, consisting of 10,000 and 30,000 homes respectively, just north of their city in an area designated for 'comprehensive development' by the government. The general principles that shaped the appearance of these three resembled that of the New Towns, and, unlike the Expanded Towns, they were effectively new settlements, although not established via the New Towns Act (Hall and Ward, 2000: 67).

The second generation

By the late 1950s, despite having publicly ruled out a return to the New Towns Programme, Conservative Minister for Housing Henry Brooke privately regarded the eight years of the Expanded Towns Programme as having been a failure. Local authorities had simply been unable to create housing growth on the scale needed to address the housing crisis in the cities. Part of the logic behind the original creation of the New Towns Programme, led by specially empowered development corporations, was that local authorities were not capable of setting up and running major programmes of urban growth. A treasury official vindicated this logic, noting in March 1960, 'It is clear the town development programme is not working, and it would probably never work' (Cullingworth, 1979: 164).

Having increased the housing density of the inner cities by encouraging developers to build high-rises on the land currently available, the only alternative for the minister was the further expansion of existing towns or cities outwards by build-ing on their Green Belts or building a new generation of New Towns beyond the Green Belt. Furthermore, both Whitehall (the civil servants) and Westminster (the politicians) had become increasingly supportive of the idea of a centrally controlled housing programme rather than leaving it to the mixed abilities of local authorities. A wave of studies supporting a second gen-eration of New Towns began to build strength (Cullingworth, 1979: 164).

These studies highlighted two additional factors to justify a fresh phase of New Towns. First was that new economic activity in Britain was mainly booming in the south east of England, and London in particular, whilst the economy in the north was continuing to decline. Consequently, large numbers of workers were migrating from the north to the south, further undermining the economic performance of the north. The ports and indus-trial towns of the north that had been economic boomtowns of the nineteenth century were on a long-term decline, still marked by poor housing and a failure to attract emerging industries. The North/South Divide became ever stronger and the use of planning on a regional level was proposed to deliberately promote economic activity in the north.

The economic concepts of laissez-faire – un-regulated and liberal – and *dirigisme* – where government asserts direct control over the economy – reach a complex inter-relationship in this period. Regional economic planning was central to the second phase of New Town development started by the Conservatives. Conservative Prime Minister Harold Macmillan and, from 1964, Labour Prime Minister Harold Wilson both understood the need for modernisation of the British economy. As the 1960s New Towns came to be built, they were hosts to a resurgence in British manufacturing. Only with the rise of the Thatcher Government in 1979 did deregulation and laissez faire really modernise the British economy, but in so doing, effec-tively cut industry (and the coal mining on which it was built) out of the economic, and thus social, fabric of the country.

The second factor to prompt more New Towns was growing concern over an unanticipated acceleration in the size of the UK population. The immediate post-war period saw birth rates triple from their pre-war levels. Eighteen years on and this baby-boom generation were reaching adulthood and in need of homes of their own. The social, economic and political context of regional economic decline; the baby boom; and acceptance that New Towns were logistically advantageous for central government, meant that in 1961 the Conservatives set in motion a new generation of New Towns. The first was Skelmersdale in Lancashire, originally proposed by planners in 1956 to provide overspill housing for Liverpool. Livingston, near Edinburgh in Scotland was designated in 1962 to accom-modate more overspill population from Glasgow and host a large new car factory for nationalised manufacturer, British Leyland.

Birmingham was to have Dawley in 1963, expanded and renamed Telford in 1968, and Redditch in 1964. The historic port town of Runcorn was designated for growth via a New Town in 1964 to take additional families from Liverpool. Washington New Town near Sunderland was designated in June 1964 to provide new economic activity for the region, later becoming home to the Nissan car factory.

The Conservative rule since 1951 ended in 1964, with the return of the Labour Party under Harold Wilson, four months after Washington had been designated. For the incoming Labour Government, building New Towns in the party's indus-trial heartlands was a logical economic development strategy, epitomised by Wilson's call for the regions to 'embrace the white heat of technology' and develop new manufacturing

Central Milton Keynes, 2008.

This is the only New Town to be built on the coast and was an expansion of a historic port town in a traditional coal mining area. Like Cumbernauld, the town centre featured a central mega-structure spanning the town's river in a manner akin to the service stations being built over Britain's new motorways. The expansion of the town was conceived as new neighbourhoods linked in a line along the coast described as 'beads on a string'.

A further New Town created in this period was the ancient Mid-Wales town of Newtown – given that name by King Edward in the thirteenth century, also known, in Welsh, as Y Drenewydd. This took the logic of economic development to prevent depopulation, which had been applied in the north of England, into the context of Mid-Wales. The town was earmarked for expansion from its base of 5,000 people to prevent wider depopulation of the region by bringing in much needed employment. However, the original target population of 30,000 was massively reduced to around 13,000 when it was suggested the town should take on overspill population from the English West Midlands, provoking instant outrage from the Welsh.

The future growth of the early New Towns was also pushed forward following a Ministry of Housing and Local Government study in 1964 on anticipated growth in the South East. This declared that by 1981 the region would need to house an extra 3.5 million people. It was proposed that 350,000 should be housed in a new generation of New Towns, while existing towns should be further expanded to accommodate a further one million people. Many of the first generation of New Towns were to significantly increase in size, including Harlow and Welwyn Garden City. Meanwhile, Newton Aycliffe, which had long argued that its original housing target had been too low, was targeted for new expansion. These new target populations thereby created new waves of housing growth within the original New Towns, much of it to follow the modernist principles of housing now in vogue, instead of the more traditional architecture of the early phase.

By 1964, an economic argument emerged in the civil service that building a small number of large developments was far better than building a large number of small ones (Cullingworth, 1979). Henceforth, sites for over 150,000 people were sought, provided they could be built without a loss of high-quality agricultural land, could expand in the future if needed, and

sectors, particularly in plastics, electronics and automotive engineering.

A third and final phase of New Town designation began late in 1966 with the New Town of Irvine, south west of Glasgow.

infrastructure provision such as water supply and drainage was adequate. A second generation of satellite towns around London was also proposed, this time of a greater scale and at a greater distance than those in the immediate post-war period.

The 'third generation' started with Milton Keynes in Buckinghamshire, the zenith of the New Towns Programme. This large green-field 'New City' exemplified the radical ideas of urban planning combining ideas of the Modernists with those of the Garden Cities Movement. Milton Keynes is without a doubt the most remarkable of the New Towns. According to architect Peter Phippin of the practice PRP, formed in 1963, 'After the disillusionment with modernism that had set in from the mid-1960s, Milton Keynes was the next major push after Cumbernauld – Derek Walker [chief architect] was desperately trying to make modern architecture popular in Britain' (Phippen, 2008).

New approaches to public consultation were taken. The plan sought a revolutionary, flexible approach to design, declaring, 'no committee of experts should try to dictate . . . the final form of the city should be an expression of people's wishes, hopes, tastes' (cited in Williams, 2004: 57). According to Walker, it turned out that what people wanted was 'cars, trees and evening classes', so that is what they got (*Building Design*, 2007b).

Absorbing a few small villages and the earlier Expanded Town of Bletchley, Milton Keynes was predominantly a blank canvas onto which planners could return to fundamentally rethink the shape of urban settlements. It was seen as a last chance to get modernist architecture accepted in Britain (Phippen, 2008) and the designers were gripped by a sense of purpose and spirit of enthusiasm to build in a radically different way. However, despite the explicit modernism of its architecture, the underlying DNA of Milton Keynes, as with all the New Towns, is fundamentally that of the Garden City. It is the ultimate manifestation of design concepts already seen in the landscaped roadways of Harlow and Washington, and even the block structure introduced in Louis de Soissons' masterplan for Welwyn Garden City in the 1920s.

The underlying contradiction between the self-containment sought by Ebenezer Howard and the Garden Cities Movement, and the high-speed mobility favoured by Le Corbusier and the Modern Movement, was also cast into the fabric of Milton Keynes. The step-change seen with Milton Keynes was for the

UK's most deliberately car-based urban development. This was directly inspired by the ideas of American urban theorist Melvin Webber, who argued that walkable neighbourhoods were

Louis de Soissons' 1920s masterplan for Welwyn Garden City featured a coarse grain block structure.

Howard memorial in Welwyn Garden City central park.

wholly misguided. In California, society was fundamentally about universal car ownership. People used their cars to go everywhere and socialised with people they shared interests with not with their neighbours. The reality of the way of life emerging in the new suburbs of the USA was literally urban disintegration. The nature of the town centre as a historic core and industrial periphery was an anachronism. The rapid mobility of the motorcar allowed people to cluster wherever they chose in polycentric urban forms.

Milton Keynes' renowned concrete cows were created in 1978 from surplus building materials. Canadian-born 'artist in residence' Liz Leyh worked with local school children, who wanted to give a tribute to the cows that had lost their grazing land so the new city could be built (BBC. 2007a).

This large block structure later became common throughout the New Towns – Crawley.

Central Milton Keynes and its high capacity road network

Milton Keynes' unique approaches to urban design, as well as its sheer size, makes it essentially unlike any other British town, New Town or otherwise. This difference was exemplified in the advertising slogan used a decade later when the town was being completed, 'Wouldn't it be nice if all cities were like Milton Keynes?' and the song written for the major TV advertising campaign.

> You've never seen anywhere like it: Central Milton Keynes. You've never been anywhere like it: Central Milton Keynes. You've never seen shopping as it should be until you've been to Central Milton Keynes. Come shopping away from the traffic at Central Milton Keynes. Come shopping and under the trees. Shopping as it should be. Junction 14, just off the M1.'
>
> (MKDC, 1980)

The young architects at Milton Keynes had effectively been given a blank slate to design their new city of the future. The glaringly hip designers were dubbed 'the undertakers' because of their trend for wearing black suits (Ward, 1993: 18). Many now world-famous architects such as Norman Foster and Richard MacCormac did some of their first work for the Milton Keynes Development Corporation.

The remaining, more distant, satellites around London were the historic cities of Peterborough and Northampton. These saw New Town Development Corporations created to work in partnership with the existing local authorities to produce extremely large-scale expansions of the towns. Each saw their populations doubled from around 100,000 to over 200,000. Meanwhile, the existing town of Warrington, just west of Manchester, served to accommodate overspill population from Manchester and Liverpool with a similar scale of expansion. Ipswich had also been considered for similar expansion until a well-orchestrated protest campaign highlighted the quantity of grade one agricultural land threatened, resulting in the plans being dropped.

The final designated New Town to result in anything being built was the strangely named Central Lancashire. This was an area north of Manchester with an existing population of around

The pattern of car-based urbanism is clear from the air.

a quarter of a million spread across several different small towns including Leyland, Preston and Chorley. The New Town Development Corporation was set to increase this population to 400,000 by creating a large number of tiny car-based neighbourhood units of several thousand people each. These would be separated by green spaces spanning half a mile in width and would collectively form larger units, dubbed townships, which would in turn form a new car-based disintegrated urban city. By the time the designation order was put into action, the Central Lancashire New Town had its expansion massively cut back to a housing target of only an additional 23,000 (Osborn and Whittick, 1977: 330). Although the Central Lancashire Development Corporation had already purchased substantial amounts of land in the region, the government cut short the vision of a northern sister town to Milton Keynes.

An additional and generally neglected aspect of the New Towns Programme in the 1960s was the adaptation of the New Towns Act to create new housing in Northern Ireland. The 1965

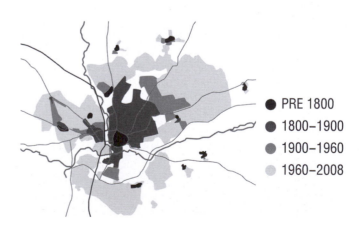

PRE 1800
1800–1900
1900–1960
1960–2008

The 'Partnership New Towns' – Northampton, Warrington and Peterborough – were increased in size by having a New Town Development Corporation oversee their extensions in partnership with the existing local authority. The above illustration of Northampton shows the town's growth from the 1960s onwards, prompted by the New Towns Programme.

Central Milton Keynes, 2008.

New Towns Act Northern Ireland, amended in 1969, designated New Town Development Corporations for Craigavon in 1965, Antrim in 1966, Ballymena in 1967 and Londonderry in 1969.

With Londonderry, Ballymena and Antrim dominated by their historic cores, the Northern Irish New Town of Craigavon is the most significant example of the attempt to build a new settlement, rather than expanding an existing one. Created between Lurgan and Portadown, Craigavon was intended to re-house people from inner-city Belfast and develop a new urban corridor from the city, to the north east, connecting existing towns in the area. Many of the same approaches to urban design seen in the British New Towns were taken, with the town characterised by a shopping mall centre, single-use zoning, low-density housing and extensive pedestrian routes separated from the road network. The neighbourhood units were also designed with a policing angle in mind, with limited entrance and exit points from each neighbourhood making control easy. Many of these estates were built to extremely poor standards of construction and wide spread demolition has since been undertaken. Craigavon remains a half-place, with many residents associating more with the neighbouring towns, than with the New Town as a place. This remains perhaps the greatest failure of the post-war New Towns.

However, another area neglected in most histories of the New Towns are the political consequences of this attempt at centralised house building. Relatively peaceful since the 1920s, in the late 1960s resentment amongst Irish Catholics to British rule and discrimination by the Protestant Unionists in local government erupted in protests followed by riots in 1969. 'The Troubles' led to intervention by the British Army and more than thirty years of urban warfare, preventing social and economic development of the region and seeing violence spread to the British mainland. The protests in 1969 were prompted by local politicians engineering the electoral boundaries of local populations to ensure that political control remained in the hands of Protestants.

In Northern Ireland, the implications of new house building, demographics and cultural identity were so acute as to re-ignite a centuries-old dispute over sovereignty that escalated into a deep and lasting crisis over territory and human rights. As with the mainland New Towns, by the mid-1970s those in Northern Ireland were also curtailed, and by 1973, with the dissolution of the Northern Ireland Government, were formally ended as programmes (Rowthorn and Wayne, 1988).

The end of the New Towns Programme

By the 1970s, the New Towns were regarded with increasing ambivalence by central government. They did not meet with a dramatic halt with any particular politician calling for an end to programme. Nor were any major policy changes enacted, although subsequent, incremental legislative changes did have profound cumulative effects over the long term. However, while construction of the later New Towns was underway in the 1970s, the rationale applied in the early 1960s to justify them was no longer as strong as it had been.

First, the population growth forecasts were abruptly rendered obsolete by the very rapid impact on birth rates of the contraceptive pill in 1965. Redundant forecasts resulted in a failure to predict the massive slump in birth rates brought about by this new era for family planning, bringing the post-war baby-boom generation to an end. This is a key instance of a disruptive technology producing social change in a very short space of time, whilst the speed of urban development reacted more slowly.

The second factor was that all regions of the UK remained at the mercy of international economic forces. No amount of rational urban planning could help the fact that economic forecasts were also disrupted by novel or rival products and services, or political circumstances such as the 1970s oil crisis, which disturbed the existing status quo. Milton Keynes became the culmination of the New Town vision at a time when this uncertainty was becoming increasingly apparent. Inherent within its design was a far greater flexibility and adaptability that, along with its strategic location between Britain's largest city, London, and second largest, Birmingham, proved vital to its becoming the most successful of all the New Towns.

The economic instability in the 1970s made the ongoing construction of existing New Towns more difficult. Interest rates on the towns' sixty-year loans from the Treasury fluctuated unpredictably, causing plans to be continually revised. Additional 'third generation' New Town projects were scrapped, including Llantrisant in Wales, designated in 1972, and Stonehouse, near

Table 4.1 Full list of town development resulting from the New Towns Programme. The original population of the New Towns, before designation, indicates the size of the historic core. The designated area indicates the volume of land purchased for each town.

New Town (in order of designation)	Year of designation (nb, some towns took years before being approved)	Original population	Designated area (hectares)	Original planned population	Current population (2007 est.)
Stevenage	1946	6,700	2,532	80,000	79,400
Crawley	1947	9,100	2,396	85,000	100,100
Hemel Hempstead	1947	21,000	2,391	65,000	81,000
Harlow	1947	4,500	2,588	80,000	78,300
Newton Aycliffe	1947	60	1,254	undefined	29,000
East Kilbride	1947	2,400	4,148	82,500	73,300
Welwyn Garden City	1948	18,500	1,747	42,000	43,300
Hatfield	1948	8,500	947	25,000	27,900
Peterlee	1948	200	1,133	28,000	30,000
Glenrothes	1948	1,100	2,333	55,000	38,900
Basildon	1949	25,000	3,165	103,000	100,000
Bracknell	1949	5,149	1,337	55,000	50,100
Cwmbran	1949	12,000	1,278	55,000	47,200
Corby	1950	15,700	1,791	-	49,200
Cumbernauld	1955	3,000	3,152	70,000	49,600
Skelmersdale	1961	10,000	1,669	73,300	38,800
Livingston	1962	2,000	2,708	70,000	54,800
Dawley / Telford	1963/68	20,000	7,790	135,000	164,600
Runcorn	1964	28,500	2,930	71,000	61,200
Washington	1964	20,000	2,271	65,000	60,000
Redditch	1964	32,000	2,906	70,000	79,500
Craigavon	1965	*	*	*	57,700
Irvine	1966	34,600	5,022	116,000	33,000
Antrim	1966	*	*	*	20,000
Ballymena	1967	*	*	*	28,700
Newtown / Y Drenewydd	1967	5,000	606	11,500	12,700
Milton Keynes	1967	40,000	8,900	150,000	184,500
Peterborough	1967	81,000	6,453	160,000	161,800
Northampton	1967	100,000	8,080	230,000	202,800
Warrington	1968	122,300	7,535	160,000	195,200
Londonderry	1969	*	*	*	83,600
Central Lancashire (Preston City)	1970	234,500	14,267	271,000	300,000
Totals		740,809	87,459	1,963,300	2,616,200

* Data unavailable at time of printing
Source: Various, incl. Osborn and Whittick, 1976.

Glasgow, designated in 1973. If any single event marks the end of the New Towns Programme, it is the decision in 1976, by Peter Shore, Secretary of State for the Environment for the Labour Government, to pull the plug on Stonehouse. Shore questioned the success of the proposition that the New Towns were supposed to relieve the conditions of the inner cities – and in this particular case, the needs of Glasgow. By cancelling Stonehouse, Shore instead channelled the money directly into the revitalisation of inner-city Glasgow, effectively ending the government policy of decentralisation first formally initiated thirty years earlier in the 1946 New Towns Act.

The background under which this policy had first been formulated was subject to a range of studies by senior civil servants. In hindsight it is significant that the ultimate arguments for the New Towns had been questioned at the time from within the world of Whitehall and Westminster. Douglas Jay, soon to be Economic Secretary to the Treasury, questioned the assumption of Lewis Silkin, Minister for Town and Country Planning, that New Towns were a valid policy. Jay argued that the New Towns Programme sought to pursue two objectives at once. One was to relocate employment away from the cities where demand for labour exceeded supply, to areas where supply of labour exceeded demand. The other objective was to relocate people from over-crowded inner-city slums, where health and quality of life, as opposed to employment, were the main problems. Achieving both these objectives would require careful co-ordination, and Jay argued that Silkin had not outlined how this would be achieved.

Jay described the impact of the creation of recent new towns Letchworth and Welwyn Garden City plus Slough, as directly causing unemployment in North East England and South Wales as employers leapt at the chance to relocate close to London. This presented serious challenges in balancing national economic and social objectives. Firms relocating to a New Town would have to come only from congested inner-city areas, and should not be in addition to those factories. Meanwhile, although it would be possible to control the selection of firms moving to a New Town, it would be difficult to control what would happen to their vacated premises, which would similarly fill with firms wanting to relocate in from elsewhere, leading to further unemployment in those places (Cullingworth, 1979: 40).

The problem was echoed with housing. Balancing the need to relocate employment with the need to answer poor housing conditions did not tally easily. Inevitably both the New Towns Programme and the development corporations themselves were subject to criticism for failing to meet the stated objectives. The ambition was that new settlements beyond the cities would offer a better future for the urban poor. In reality, this problem could not be solved so easily partly because the most impoverished did not have the skills necessary to get a job in a company relocating to a New Town. In reality, the London satellite New Towns drew their populations from the suburban outer boroughs such as Tottenham, Southall and East Ham, rather than the crowded inner-city boroughs such as Camden, Tower Hamlets or Southwark.

Nonetheless, when the New Towns Programme was hastily enacted in the late 1940s, the rationale of decentralising the population to address over-crowding had considerable momentum. Only by the 1960s and 1970s when the towns were still being built did the continuing neglect of the inner cities come to light. The focus on the regeneration of the inner cities that started with Shore's decision on Stonehouse, and culminated in Britain's 'urban renaissance' in the 1990s, is a similar thirty-year-long policy of contraction as opposed to the previous thirty-year policy of expansion. Viewed over the course of many decades, population migration - shaped in part by government policy - can be seen as an attempt to balance extreme pressures facing the inner cities, first at its height in the 1930s, and then at its lowest by the 1990s. The balance between these two forces continues to be debated in planning policy. An October 2008 report into the West Midlands' regional spatial strategy suggested that creating a major, free-standing new settlement would not undermine the goals of urban renaissance, since, as the Garden Cities Movement had always argued, people with families fundamentally wanted to live in good sized houses with gardens, which were simply unavailable in city centres (NLP, 2008).

Despite the top-level policies of government that shaped where people should live and work, shifting over the decades, towns were built. People moved to them and created new lives there. Throughout the thirty-year period of the New Towns Programme, teams of architects, planners, developers and social and economic development experts moved from one New Town project to the next. An informal coherence was thus created between the different New Towns based on the collective practice of that particular generation.

The New Towns thus represent the ideas of post-war British urbanism and the large-scale introduction of planning concepts such as zoning, the neighbourhood unit, and motorisation. The thirty-year length of the programme also reveals changing mindsets of the people involved, and the changing nature of life in Britain. When it began in the 1940s, the planners and architects at the heart of it had been working through the 1920s and 1930s creating places such as Welwyn Garden City. Gibberd was one of the younger and more dynamic designers working on Harlow and Crawley in the late 1940s when he himself was in his forties. Those that built Milton Keynes, however, would have been babes in arms in the time of the Garden Cities, or were born after the war in the baby-boom generation. By the 1970s they were gripped with an enthusiasm to produce something more radical than had been achieved with the earlier New Towns.

The 1960s generation (and not the radical edge of the swinging sixties but the mainstream of working families) were concerned with the new freedoms offered by car ownership, motorways, and employment prospects in a new era of British manufacturing. From the 1950s, when the first New Towns began construction, to the 1980s when the last neared completion, huge social, economic and technological change took place in Britain. This transformation of Britain is manifested in the various stages of development of the New Towns. The New Towns therefore give an insight into the changing decades of the twentieth century, the different problems that design sought to address and the different aspirations for the sorts of places people hoped would be built.

'Back-to-back' workers' housing of the nineteenth century was built to high densities and with little or no outdoor space. Recreation space was provided in municipal parks and public wash-houses provided sanitation, subject to charity and philanthropy. Above: Harold Mount in the Hyde Park area of Leeds, West Yorkshire. Below: Public baths, Southwark, London.

Although the New Towns Programme was a policy of the 1945 Labour Government in direct response to the circumstances created by the Second World War, the New Towns did not come out of the blue. The origin of the campaign for their creation lies some fifty years earlier as a response to the way that Britain's housing had developed in the nineteenth and early twentieth century. The aim of producing homes and places that provided a better quality of life than those built in the Victorian and Edwardian era was a great social cause that mobilised both top-ranking politicians and activists on the ground.

The philosophy and design concepts that characterise these towns were inspired by other urban developments during this time, specifically the Garden Cities in England and new construction in the USA, the USSR and Scandinavia. In terms of their layout, Britain's New Towns were unlike any previous urban development in Britain because of the influence of these new ideas. Their design was intended to solve the problems that had emerged in the old cities including over-crowded housing conditions, neighbourhoods where housing and factories sat side by side preventing expansion and blighting residents with pollution, and traffic congestion from a massive increase of people on the move.

A major concept for defining these ills was 'environmental determinism'. This was the idea that living in an inherently unhealthy and stressful environment in the inner city produced social problems. Therefore, living in new places purposely designed to avoid these problems would give people the opportunities for self-improvement and emancipation. This meant new housing designs and road layouts that would provide a great deal more space and light than the cramped nineteenth-century terraces. Houses were to be set out in airy and spacious, low-density arrangements as a deliberate departure from the gloomy and crowded neighbourhoods of the old cities. The low value of the land where the New Town would be built was the crucial factor that made this possible. Streets could be designed with houses set back from the road with a generous provision of green space. The level of social infrastructure in housing developments, such as open green space and access to shops, markets, schools and hospitals, had been a hit and miss affair in the urban expansions of the nineteenth and early twentieth centuries. Now however, new purposely planned communities would include these from the start as part of the emerging art and science of town and country planning.

By the 1920s and 1930s Britain's suburban housing boom demonstrated new urban planning ideas such as the cul-de-sac and gently curving streets, as deliberate contrasts to the rigid grid patterns of terraced streets. The form of individual buildings was also that of the semi-detached house with front and back garden, built for speculative sale on the open market. In the interwar period of 1919 to 1939 the goal of these house builders and master planners was to produce houses for sale on the open market. In the post-war New Towns, by contrast, the goal was to provide a new form of state-owned housing for working-class communities. Not only were a new generation of architects and planners mobilised to carry out this mission, but also the freedom of designing new places from scratch meant the chance to experiment with new ideas on a massive scale. With two-thirds of Britain's working-class population living in houses with outdoor toilets, in the words of Elain Harwood, 'Planning these new housing areas provided a stirring opportunity for the relatively new professions of town planning and landscape architecture' (Harwood, 2000).

However, the design of housing and the surrounding urban areas were not the only reasons for the social problems in the inner cities. At a political level, the nature of property ownership and the policy of rent control were principal reasons why the traditional housing stock of the inner cities was in such bad condition. At the start of the twentieth century, 90 per cent of the housing in Britain was rented and only 10 per cent owner-occupied (Power, 1987: 19). Since the First World War the government had controlled how much rent could be charged to occupants and, inevitably, this had squeezed landlords' profits and discouraged them from investing in basic maintenance or major improvements to their properties. Houses were condemned for demolition on the basis of lacking decent plumbing, rather than being structurally unsound.

Not only was the condition of housing decaying, but also the pressure for occupation was immense. Since, the latter part of the

nineteenth century the number of people in the inner cities had increased rapidly – far faster than the ability for house builders to cope. As such, the pressure on housing led to conditions of immense over-crowding, where whole families would occupy single rooms in houses rented out by exploitative slum landlords.

Throughout the previous century, Britain experienced large-scale migration of population from rural areas into the cities. Also, driven by political stability and improvements in public sanitation, increased life expectancy and rising birth rates led to substantial increases in the overall level of population. According to the government's first-ever census conducted in 1801, Britain's population was 10.5 million. By 1901 it was 38 million (Jefferies, 2005). Meanwhile, in the same period industrialisation prompted a huge shift from rural to urban living. In 1801, 30 per cent lived in towns and cities but by 1901 it was 80 per cent, a greater proportion than in any other European country (Hennessey, 1992: 164). This meant 30 million people lived in Britain's towns and cities by the dawn of the twentieth century in 1901 compared to just over three million a century earlier. The challenge of this remarkable ten-fold expansion in Britain's towns and cities was met by private enterprise. The centres of the industrial revolution in the West Midlands and the North were the New Towns of their age, seeing huge volumes of working-class housing built in a very short period of time.

A few famous examples of planned communities for industrial workers in locations outside of the existing cities were the so-called 'model villages' built by philanthropic factory owners. These predated New Town rationale, which similarly meant that rural locations provided a nicer environment for the workers, with cleaner air and access to nature for the workers, and cheaper land for the factory owner.

The first was New Lanark in 1785, where factory workers were relocated from Edinburgh to a new factory in a rural location whose community facilities included shops, a school and wash-house. In 1854, Titus Salt built Saltaire, just north of Bradford, consisting of a vast new factory and surrounding village, including schools, a hospital and a church though no pubs. In 1888, on the Wirral, soap baron Lord Lever created Port Sunlight, consisting of 800 homes for 3,500 people (the average family size being 4.3 people per home). Confectionery giants the Cadbury family created the factory village of Bourneville near

Birmingham in 1893 (consisting of 313 homes), while rivals, the Rowntrees, created New Earswick near York in 1901. Meanwhile, within the major cities, housing associations such as the Peabody Housing Trust and Guinness Trust built apartment blocks and public bath-houses for urban workers.

Each of these was a beacon for improved conditions yet were miniscule enterprises compared to the volumes of market housing provision, much of which was produced by small teams of entrepreneurial builders. The majority of Victorian housing was created using standard designs, called pattern books, and street layouts determined by the landowners. Yet this combination of charity, philanthropy and market forces still could not produce the volume or quality of housing that social campaigners argued was necessary and so state intervention in housing slowly emerged as a solution. As the London Trades Council argued in 1884, 'Economic forces and population have out-stepped their endeavours: hence evils accrue. But what the individual cannot do the state municipality must seek to accomplish . . . for it alone possesses the necessary power and wealth' (Hennessy, 1992: 165).

Although state intervention in housing began at this point, the rate of improvement in housing conditions remained painfully slow. Failure to address the conditions of the industrial working classes fuelled the birth of the Labour movement. By the end of the First World War, the political classes in Britain realised the potential for armed revolt from soldiers returning from the Front as had taken place in Russia in 1917. As a result, Prime Minister Lloyd George demanded 'a fit country for heroes to live in', later paraphrased as 'homes for heroes' to finally put this issue on the political agenda.

Government involvement in housing provision begins here. Anne Power's *People Before Property* (Power, 1987) outlines this history in detail. The comparison with other countries' responses is also significant, notably Scandinavia where the government does not build housing but subsidises the rent of low-income families to allow them to live in property provided by the private sector. Before returning to how state provision of housing reached its zenith in the wake of the Second World War, and the birth of the New Towns Programme, the story of the Garden Cities Movement (which outlines the rationale and structural principles of the New Towns) must be told. This movement aimed to address the problems of the urban poor not merely as an issue of housing but by looking at the function of towns as a whole.

The birth of the Garden Cities Movement

The Garden Cities in the early years of the twentieth century were the concept and creation of social reformer Ebenezer Howard. Born in the City of London in 1850, Howard's parents, who ran a confectionery shop, were able to send him, from the age of four, to boarding school away from the city, first in the small rural town of Sudbury in Suffolk and later Cheshunt in Hertfordshire. He thus grew up understanding the contrast between life in the rural countryside and the smoke-filled city. Both suffered from problems that Howard later outlined in his famous diagram of the three magnets (see page 4 in colour plate section). The Garden Cities, and the New Towns that came after them, were thus intended from the outset as a happy marriage between the best attributes of the town and the country.

At the age of twenty-one, Howard travelled to the USA to experience life as a settler on a farm in Nebraska, and then as a shorthand reporter in Chicago. In 1871, the city had been ravaged by fire and was undergoing a large-scale rebuilding programme. Dubbed 'the Garden City', Chicago's rational city plan, as well as that of Washington DC and Adelaide in Australia, provided a vital inspiration. The works of Thomas Paine, Herbert Spencer and T.H. Huxley also influenced Howard on the value of rationality and science. A pamphlet called *Hygeia: A City of Health*, by British social reformer Benjamin Ward Richardson, prompted Howard to think about how health (or the lack of it) can be a consequence of the way cities operate. He therefore laid out the basic concepts of environmental determinism, by reasoning that good design could potentially promote better health. The means by which this could occur was naturally through the creation of new towns that had these principles enshrined in their design from the outset.

Howard was not alone in these ideas and campaigners such as Henry George in North America, and the Land Nationalisation Society in England were arguing that public ownership of land whereby profits could be reinvested to benefit local social causes was vital (an idea first theorised by Thomas Spence in the late eighteenth century). Returning to London in 1876, Howard could see that the 'Social Question' of how to manage the changes wrought by industrialisation was becoming ever more acute.

America in the 1870s had been in a period of recovery after the Civil War of 1861 to 1865. Technological advances that took place as a result of war became commercialised in its aftermath. Whilst Britain had pioneered the industrial revolution in the first half of the nineteenth century, by the third quarter of the century the American economy was industrialising on a far greater scale. Railroads stretched in from the East Coast cities of Boston, New York and Washington to huge mineral resources west of the Appalachian Mountains and the Mid-West cities of Buffalo, Chicago and Detroit. The myth of the Wild West romanticised this period, ending with the completion of the railroad across the continent to tame 'the wild frontier'.

The consequence of rail travel opening up the centre of the American continent was to have a dramatic effect. American grain from the Mid-West flooded onto world markets, and along with the growth of American industry, British industry and agriculture experienced a sudden economic collapse that soon became known as 'The Great Calamity'. By 1879, a terrible British harvest resulted in the total collapse of Britain's domestic agricultural sector. The free-market economic ideas promoted by the Victorian industrialists had spread to farming, with the result being a huge depreciation in the value of farmland. The consequence was a rapid depopulation of rural areas and a mass migration of farm workers into the cities.

In London, labourers from East Anglia and the Home Counties flooded in looking for work. Between 1871 and 1901, the population of London increased by three million, producing a total population of 6.6 million by 1901 (Howard, 2003: 3). This inward migration was in addition to the natural population growth that resulted from political stability and growing life expectancy. The consequence for inner London was the outward migration of the middle classes to the new railway suburbs, eventually including Howard's own family, and increasing numbers of rural working classes moving in to take their place. This transformed the demographics of the inner cities, creating an intense housing crisis.

In the 1880s, these new urban conditions fuelled campaigns for radical reform. Howard joined the ranks of George Bernard Shaw and H.G. Wells in calling for fundamental changes to the way society was run. A Royal Commission on Housing for the Working Classes was created in 1884, yet by the time it had considered the issues the economic crisis had spread to affect not just housing but also jobs, and rioting soon followed. Howard, alongside many others, felt a keen moral duty to campaign for a better world. At the time, now in his thirties, he was working as a shorthand reporter in the Houses of Parliament, and thus was able to draw first-hand insight into the debates occurring and the key players in parliament conducting them.

Another crucial factor of Howard's outlook that was to be of enormous significance later was his aptitude for machinery. With abilities far in advance of the requirements of a reporter, Howard supplemented his income devising improvements to the mechanisms of typewriters. At heart he was an inventor. He began to formulate the notion that improvements to the nature of urban society were a matter of improving them as if a functional mechanism. An early example of his thinking is in a diagram drawn in the early 1890s he called 'The Master Key'. Although not published at the time, it is an indication of the thinking he expressed in the debating societies and political meetings he frequented at the time.

Howard's 'The Master Key' was a set of radical suggestions for improving society, some of which later became part of the twentieth-century welfare state. At the time, these ideas were part of an avant-garde reform campaign of which Howard was to become a leading spokesman. Yet, crucially, it was not in Howard's nature to be a philosopher. Like Karl Marx's famous epitaph, 'philosophers have interpreted the world in various ways, the point, however, is to change it', Howard sought practical progress on the ground. Fundamentally, he was an engineer and an inventor. His dream was, in the words of biographer Robert Beevers,

> to re-draw the map of haphazard industrialisation in a rational and planned fashion by creating totally new cities, each with its own industry and agriculture, but linked together so as to form collectively a new economy and, indeed, a new society.
>
> (Beevers et al., 1991)

The Garden City Association Howard founded in 1898 to develop these ideas on the ground soon led to a practical opportunity for creating a new community away from the dysfunctional industrial city. The political momentum created by this idea meant that over the subsequent years the Garden City concept gained influence, albeit slowly, in the debates on housing policy. By the time the Second World War was over, Howard's arguments and practical achievements in building Garden Cities became the foundation for the New Towns Programme.

The design principles of the Garden City were expressed in a book Howard self-published in 1898, called *Tomorrow: A Peaceful Path to Real Reform*. Here he argued that the efforts of the newly created London County Council to deal with the housing problem via a vast programme of slum clearance and demolition as being expensive and ineffectual (Howard, 2003: 71). Instead, he saw the solution as being the creation of scientifically planned new settlements, Garden Cities, away from the old dysfunctional industrial cities, and in turn revitalising the desperate state of the rural economy.

Howard recognised the low value of agricultural land as an opportunity with natural potential. Three years after the publication of his book, he had convinced a number of wealthy investors in the City of London to support his purchase of 3,800 acres (almost 10,000 ha) of land in Hertfordshire for the creation of the new town of Letchworth Garden City. Many years later, on Howard's death in 1928, George Bernard Shaw, who had gone from criticising Howard's campaigning to becoming an investor in the Garden City project, described him as one of those, 'heroic simpletons who do big things, whilst our prominent worldlings are explaining that they are utopian and impossible' (Beevers et al., 1991).

Letchworth Garden City, some 30 miles from Central London, was to become the first of the twentieth-century new towns. The realisation of Letchworth and its successor, Welwyn Garden City, started in the 1920s, were to come late in Howard's life. He played a significant role in the foundation and building of both but was ultimately disappointed. Neither had realised many of the aspects he thought were fundamental to the Garden City idea described in his book. The land-ownership via a community trust fund had been compromised by the need to attract private investors, who sought a return on investment. Also, the population and industry attracted to move there were not alleviating the urban problems of London. One manufacturer had relocated from the North East, and a significant proportion of the population (nearly three thousand people, some 30 per cent of the total) were Belgian refugees fleeing the Great War (Carr, 1995).

Although the promotional value of Letchworth Garden City was high and it soon gained an international reputation for his theories, Howard dismissed it as merely, 'a poky experiment', akin to a prototype but not the fully realised vision. Aware that the widespread reform intended was not being achieved, one of the young men to work at Letchworth, Frederick J. Osborn, was to take Howard's vision forward into a new generation, ultimately bringing about the New Towns Programme.

From Garden Cities to the New Towns

So what was the Garden City concept and how much was echoed in the New Towns Programme? The entirety of Howard's vision, published as *To-morrow: A Peaceful Path to Real Reform* in 1898, was reprinted in 2003 – Letchworth's centenary – with commentaries by Peter Hall, Dennis Hardy and Colin Ward. It remains a surprisingly pragmatic outline for town building and became a central inspiration for Le Corbusier and the modernist planners of the 1920s and 1930s, as well as for the master planners of the New Towns in the 1940s, 1950s and 1960s (see pages 4 and 5 of the colour plate section).

The first concept was to combine the best elements of the town with the best elements of the country, as described in a diagram of three magnets (Figure 5.1). Two of the magnets represent the pros and cons of town and country, while the third represents the balance between the two. The city offered employment but was gravely polluted and rents were expensive, while the countryside offered no employment but was healthy and rents were cheap. The Garden City sought equilibrium through the provision of employment in a healthy and affordable setting. Parkland was central to the design, and town centres were to be defined by a 'Crystal Palace', a covered space where people could shop with comfort even in the rain. This use of landscaping and central covered shopping arcades were significant parts of the original Garden City concept to persist in the design of the New Towns.

The Welwyn Garden City central park.

The Garden City was also to be of a limited size – Howard thought 32,000 people – and surrounded by an agricultural belt that would make it self-sufficient in basic foods. Forms of building that would benefit from a more rural setting such as convalescent homes, farms for epileptics and allotments were all integral to the layout. The Green Belt was a central concept, limiting the ability of the town to grow unchecked, and creating an agricultural hinterland to provide food for the residents.

A further aspect of self-sufficiency, what would now be called environmental sustainability, was a proposed sewer system that returned wastes to the soil in an ecologically valuable way. This was the opposite of the open-ended sewer system created in London by Bazalgette in the 1850s that flushed the nutrient-rich waste out to sea. Water supply was to be divided into potable and non-potable systems, linked with a canal system. Windmills and pumps would move water to a high-level reservoir from which hydroelectric turbines could produce power. Many of these ideas pre-empt by decades modern sustainable development proposals, and Howard described the physical and economic logic behind these ideas in detail.

Crucially, the residents of the Garden City were to collectively own the land, capturing long-term profits from rents to feed into a trust fund to provide for community needs – essentially a localised pre-cursor of the welfare state. Howard saw the nature of rents in the inner cities as deeply problematic, and made detailed calculations of the economics of providing rented property at a reasonable return based on the value with which land for a garden city could be bought. From this, investors could be attracted, and as the town grew, rents would rise and profits pay back the initial debts and then swell the community fund.

When the town grew to the declared maximum size of 32,000 people, living within 1,000 acres of land (405 hectares), the agricultural areas – that would later inspire the national Green Belt policy – would prevent further growth, and a new city would be started nearby. Together, these Garden Cities would be connected by transport links (principally train and canal) to create a unified family of distinct Garden City settlements linked together as The Social City, with a population of 250,000.

The Garden City Association (later becoming the Garden Cities and Town Planning Association, and, finally, the Town and Country Planning Association) sought to advance Howard's ideas of rational planning and the creation of purpose-built settlements. To create these new towns a series of Garden City Companies were founded. Each would independently take forward the development of the towns as effectively private-sector endeavours driven to act in the public interest of their residents. The first company, the Garden City Pioneer

Welwyn's industrial facilities included Nabisco's Shredded Wheat Factory.

Company, was set up in July 1902 to search for suitable sites. When the site for Letchworth had been found and purchased, a new company, First Garden City Ltd, was created in September 1903. Investors in the scheme became shareholders expecting a return, and although some of the proceeds went into the community trust fund, the Association was at pains to ensure the scheme was more palatable to investors and less radical in its political ideas than Howard had originally intended.

The Association reissued Howard's original text in a toned-down form in 1902, the words 'Real Reform' dropped and the title changed to simply 'Garden Cities of Tomorrow'. Some of the more radical sentiment had been pruned, and along with it some of the underlying philosophy, meaning that the wide circulation of the Garden City idea tended towards the surface issues, rather than its deeper foundations (Howard, 2003: 199). In the New Towns, however, Howard's ideas were to shape both the explicit surface and the implicit foundations, with the New Towns Programme later effectively becoming a major government programme for land nationalisation.

Progress at Letchworth proceeded rapidly, with site surveys soon completed and a masterplan designed by Unwin and Parker. Within ten years, Letchworth had a rudimentary road system, 2,000 houses and 12 factories built. Osborn was employed as the housing manager at Letchworth in 1912, whose responsibilities included collecting rents from residents. The outbreak of war in 1914 horrified the members of the Garden City

Association, whose non-conformist members included many pacifists. The 29-year-old Osborn sought to avoid conscription, or arrest, by moving to London, eventually conducting research in the British Library on the history of community building in the UK. Another of the staff members of the Garden City Association, Charles Purdom, joined the army and was despatched to the battlefields of France. There, Purdom wrote and published a political pamphlet, *The Garden City After the War*, which reinvigorated Howard with enthusiasm for the Garden City cause.

Under the banner of 'The New Townsmen', Howard, Osborn, Purdom and others took over the running of the Garden City Association, now renamed the Garden Cities and Town Planning Association, and set about promoting the vision of Howard's 1898 work through a new publication, *New Towns After the War*, issued in 1918. Here, a practical programme for government, rather than for philanthropic private investors, was laid out. Government, it was proposed, should provide 90 per cent of the investment in the form of loans to local authorities or to trusts who should build 100 new towns. Here, the basic proposal for the New Towns Programme was laid out, but it was to be another twenty years before it would come to pass.

The morale-boosting potential of a new vision for housing was evident in Prime Minister Lloyd George's promise of 'homes for heroes' (Hennessy, 1992: 168). Osborn, Purdom and others sought to capitalise on this context by lobbying the

Addison's 'council cottage', bucolic architecture with extensive green space nearby, inspired by Letchworth, Sunray Park, North Dulwich, London.

minister now responsible for housing, Dr Christopher Addison. With many allies in parliament, Howard and the New Townsmen were successful in getting the Garden Cities Association an audience. Addison's Housing Bill of 1919 proposed the construction of five million homes within three years, and the promoters of the New Towns naturally argued that a hundred of Howard's Garden Cities with populations of fifty thousand each was the only solution that could ensure well-balanced, high-quality and healthy environments for people. The minister disagreed and argued that building wholly new towns would take at least four years to begin to deliver the housing, while he had a housing demand to be met immediately. Instead, the required housing must come from the outward expansion of the existing cities. Thus was Britain's suburbia created in the interwar years. Ultimately, between 1920 and 1939, London was to expand outwards with three million new homes, while a quarter of a million homes were also built around other towns and cities.

Addison's bill also put a new responsibility on government to build council housing, under the auspices of the new Ministry of Health. Local authorities were required to predict their level of housing demand for which the Treasury would provide the funds for construction. This led to the creation of the so-called Addison estates, using cottage designs similar to those created by Raymond Unwin at Letchworth. By this time Unwin had become one of the most influential figures in British housing, having become a senior advisor to government, leading a housing committee that resulted in the hugely influential *Tudor Walters Report* in 1918 and subsequent *Board of Local Government Housing Manual* in 1919 (Hennessey 1992: 168). This set out the principles of housing and layout, using the measure of housing density as a basic measure by which improvements to housing standards could be made. The principle expressed in his 1918 book, published by the then 'Garden Cities and Town Planning Association', called *Nothing*

Chamberlain's legacy in housing was the mass boom in the interwar suburban semi. Green space almost entirely in the private domain of the back garden, often generously sized.

Gained by Overcrowding, was that wherever possible settlements should be built to no more than twelve dwellings per acre (around thirty dwellings per hectare).

As Letchworth amply demonstrates, Unwin loved the English village as much as he disliked the back-to-back terraces of the Victorian industrial cities. Unwin's role in shaping the Addison policy saw the council cottage, designed by S.B. Russell, as the basic design for mass social housing. However, neither central government nor local authorities had any experience in house building or town planning, and had only relatively recently managed to address their new obligations to provide schools. As a result, the programme only managed to see construction start on 170,000 council cottages, rather than the 500,000 Addison had hoped for. The housing standards saw costs of production exceeding the recognised value of the houses and Addison was accused of wasting huge amounts of public money. Economic difficulties in 1920 put the programme on hold until 1923 when Neville Chamberlain replaced Addison as the minister in charge of housing. Chamberlain altered the 1919 Act so private builders as well as local authorities could receive government subsidy. With the private sector paid to build by government, the rate of house building in the UK soon massively accelerated. Rather than Unwin's cottage estates, the mock-tudor semi became the ubiquitous housing type reproduced across the country. Speculative builders quickly expanded the outer edges of Britain's cities in a boom of sub-urbanisation. From Winchmore Hill to Eastcote, Petts Wood to Streatham Vale, the capital expanded outwards across the Home Counties to create Greater London.

Suburban sprawl and the rise of town planning

Over the twenty years up to 1939 some four million new homes were built in England and Wales, a third of Britain's total housing stock of 12.5 million homes, including 1.5 million built by local authorities (Hennessy, 1992: 169). Municipal housing was often built on vast estates such as Manchester's Wythenshawe, Liverpool's Speke and Birmingham's Kingstanding estates. The largest was Dagenham, nearly 18,000 homes built by the London County Council, east of the city. Here, the problems of poor attention to the principles of town planning became acute. There were no social amenities provided, no schools, hospitals or shops. All the working residents would need to commute long distances into work, and families were left stranded in a 'non-place' (Clapson, 1998: 33). Looking at these places today, each ranks highly on the governments Index of Multiple Deprivation (Hall, 2008).

Research conducted on living conditions at Dagenham suggested that poor health was a direct consequence of the high cost of commuting, as families had to buy less food in order to afford to get to work (Clapson, 1998). The solution was a planning system that would prevent this poor-quality urbanism. The Garden Cities Movement thus joined the campaign for the introduction of a government policy for town and country planning, whereby standards for urban development would be created and enforced. For Howard and Osborn, the ideal urban settlement was the Garden City, designed to be self-contained, with a well-planned balance of employment and housing. Only this scale of town, where people did not need to commute to work, could guarantee a decent quality of life for all. Suburbanisation, including the out-of-county council estate, was anathema to this ambition.

The city, London in particular, having grown into a sprawling monster could house its workers in better environments on the suburban edge, yet they still had to commute into the over-crowded centre. Writing in 1934, Osborn directly attacked the homes built over the previous decade on the suburban edges of the cities. Enabled by rapid transport, the old overcrowded slums of the inner cities had been replaced by 'slums on wheels', millions of commuters packed into trains, spending up to twenty hours a week doing nothing but being transported between home and work (Whittick, 1987: 51). These people had been caught between the desire for urban employment and that of the house with a garden in the suburbs. He continued this tirade against suburban expansion and in favour of self-contained new towns throughout his life. Writing in *New Towns: the Answer to Megalopolis*, the same sentiment was expressed.

Within the scope of his personal choice, the average city-dweller is confronted with a dilemma. Either he and his family must live in close quarters and often graceless surroundings near the centre with its varied amusements and cultural facilities, or they must forego these advantages . . . in order to have a single-family home in a pleasant suburb. By the latter choice, the city-dweller cuts himself off from the distinctive down-town advantages, except as things of infrequent resort. The former choice is made by the genuinely urban-minded minority, by those closely tied to down-town occupations, and by the mass of the poor and passive . . . That in a complex economy some people must travel longish distances to work need not be contested . . . What is needless and fantastic is that hundreds of thousands of people should be housed in one situation and travel en masse to a remote situation for work.

(Osborn and Whittick, 1977: 14)

The relationship between the suburban built form created in the interwar years and patterns of personal transport are today brought into focus by climate change. Osborn's critique is now validated by the unintended by-product of all this 'needless and fantastic' mobility, the carbon dioxide greenhouse gas pollution that pours from the tailpipes of cars. The issues of mobility addressed by the New Towns, and the notion of environmentally sustainable urban forms in the twenty-first century that follow Osborn and Howard's ideas have undeniable relevance today.

Although healthier places to live than the smoke-filled inner city, as mere residential appendages connected by railway to employment in the city centre, the suburbs failed to offer Howard's ambition for a fundamental transformation of urban life. The Garden City ideal was really one of radical change in the conditions of the workplace, not just the home. Yet, in the face of inevitable suburban expansion, Howard's response to the unsuccessful meeting with Addison asking for a government-sponsored Garden Cities programme was to press ahead with the creation of a second, privately funded Garden City. Unknown to the young Osborn, Purdom and other members of the Garden City Association, Howard had already entered into correspondence with a landowner with regards to securing a second site. It was one that Howard himself had seen from the window commuting from his home in Letchworth to his work as a shorthand reporter in London.

Howard had long been sceptical of government, famously remarking to Osborn, 'If you wait for the authorities to build new towns you will be older than Methuselah before they start. The only way to get anything done is to do it yourself' (Whittick, 1987: 30). Howard had identified an area of land adjacent to the train line north of Hatfield. By coincidence, a large proportion of his intended site was to be sold at auction within just a few days. Using every means at his disposal, by the date of the auction on 30 May 1919, Howard had managed to borrow £50,000 for the deposit, bar £200 that he managed to convince the auctioneer to lend him. His powers of persuasion had sud-

Only one street away from Welwyn Garden City's town centre, Guessens Road where Howard and Osborn lived is considerably suburban in character.

Howard's house on Guessens Road.

denly secured him a 1,500 acre (600 hectare) site, upon which to build Welwyn Garden City. Howard's biographer, Robert Beevers describes what happened next:

> On his return to London that evening Howard was met by Purdom and Osborn, themselves deeply shaken by the event. They knew that only with their unreserved support and unstinting efforts could the second garden city be founded and Howard vindicated in an act they both regarded as crazy. Instead, by a subtle shift of emphasis they made Howard's initiative at Welwyn seem like part of a major development of new towns on the outer fringes of London. The Second Garden City was to be only the first of a group of some twenty satellite towns to be built within the orbit, as it were, of the metropolis.
>
> (Beevers et al., 1991: 33)

Writing in the Garden Cities Association journal, Purdom outlined the basic concept of what was to later become the post-war New Towns Programme, twenty-five years later. At the time, the idea made little impact. In July 1921, the first post-war economic depression meant a halt to all UK house building, affecting both the government's Homes for Heroes programme and the project for Welwyn Garden City. Howard, Purdom and Osborn managed against the odds to pull together the necessary finance, and took a highly professional approach to organising the venture.

With a remarkable display of enterprise and self-sufficiency, subsidiary companies were founded to carry out all of the practical work required to build Welwyn, and each was independently able to attract investment. Gravel extraction, brick making, infrastructure, house building and commercial development were all undertaken by firms set-up and part-owned by the Welwyn Garden City Company. This meant a monopolistic approach, but it was highly effective in getting the job done, and by 1926, the town had been built.

Howard had been age 52 when Letchworth had been set in motion in 1902. When he bought Welwyn he was 69. He died in 1928 at the age of 78, living his final years in Welwyn. The last years of his life saw him travelling the world lecturing on his ideas and receiving a knighthood for his services to housing. However, his drive to manifest his true vision of the Garden City never left him. Aware that both Letchworth and Welwyn had been compromised by their commercial backers wanting to make profit on their investment and remove a dividend from their stake, rather than keep reinvesting in the town, Howard had sought to raise sufficient funds himself to donate into a trust for building and running a third Garden City.

Howard hoped to raise a staggering £2 million to ensure independence from either private shareholders or support from government. He spent his last years working in his shed desperate to perfect an invention whose patent he hoped would secure these millions. His failed attempt to invent a shorthand typewriter was his last hope for establishing the true ideal of the Garden City, where collective land ownership would create a radically new form of settlement, marrying the distinct characters of the town and the country.

Just a hundred yards down the street, Howard's protégé, Osborn, who had been 34 years old when Welwyn started in 1919 and would be 57 by 1942, dedicated his life to taking the concept of the Garden Cities forward as the only answer to urban development. Osborn's influence in shaping housing policy after the Second World War not only benefited from his stature as an established expert in the subject, but also from emerging evidence of the long-term consequences of suburban sprawl. The mistakes made by Addison's decision after the First World War were now obvious, and these culminated in the plans put forward for reconstruction in the wake of the Second World War. Although the suburban expansion of London and other cities had met the housing need, the prospect that the city might expand indefinitely prompted a change in thinking. The Garden City ideal of new, purpose-built, self-contained towns that promised better living conditions was easily presented as a well-established alternative policy. Together with the creation of the British planning system, Osborn led the creation of the New Towns Programme to fulfil Howard's campaign for a better future, combining the best of an urban environment with the best of the rural.

Part 2

Building the New Towns

Family Group, sculpture by Henry Moore, Harlow Civic Square, 1972. Courtesy of The Museum of Harlow.

The formulation of the
New Towns Programme

Frederick Gibberd outlining his plans for Harlow, 1947. Copyright: Museum of Harlow.

Patrick Abercrombie's post-war reconstruction plans after the 1939–45 war sought to address its housing crisis through a very different form of urban development than that in the aftermath of the 1914–19 war. As described in Chapter 2, the aim was to reduce the urban population density by rebuilding in new, modernist ways, whilst promoting the creation of new self-contained towns in a ring around the capital.

Support for this idea was driven throughout the 1920s and 1930s by the sheer success of Welwyn Garden City. Although the Garden Cities Association delegation to Dr Addison had been unsuccessful in winning outright support in 1919, Addison's successor, Chamberlain, later to be prime minister, had considerable sympathy with the Garden City Movement's objectives. In the Housing Act of 1923, Chamberlain included a clause that permitted the government to make loans to 'authorised associations' that intended to build Garden Cities (Whittick, 1987: 45). With the Welwyn Garden City Company formerly recognised as an authorised association, a government loan contributed to the success of the venture. By 1932, a government review on the Garden Cities noted with admiration how within twelve years,

> a purely agricultural estate, with five farm houses, labourers' cottages and one mansion house, has been transformed into a town of 9,000 inhabitants with 2,500 homes and some forty industries; with shops, theatres, schools, churches, banks, playing fields, macadam roads; with complete drainage and water supply, electricity and gas. It may fairly be said that there is a town in being and that the objectives of the enterprise have been substantially realised . . . the Committee is of the opinion that the establishment of such garden cities is in the public interest, we venture to suggest that some public machinery must be set up which will provide a substantial amount of the loans necessary at any rate in the early days of development, and that the body actually responsible for making the loans should definitely be instructed by Parliament that the object is to establish garden cities.
>
> (Whittick, 1987: 46)

Four years later, in 1936, after fifteen years of working for Welwyn Garden City Ltd, Osborn resigned as secretary and housing manager and took up a post of finance director at one of Welwyn's manufacturing ventures, Murphy Radio. Part of his terms for this new role was that he work part time to allow him to continue campaigning for the creation of more new towns. Taking the role of honorary secretary of the Garden City and Town Planning Association, Osborn soon provided evidence to the Royal Commission on the Geographical Distribution of the Industrial Population, chaired by Sir Montague Barlow, and including Professor Patrick Abercrombie as a commissioner. The resulting 'Barlow Report' added to a rising tide of policy recommendations that were to culminate in the government's post-war New Towns Programme.

The objectives of the commission were to address how industry came to be where it was, what the impact was, and what might be done about it. The social and economic ills that the incremental, speculative development of industry and housing had wrought in Britain's cities were laid out. Here, in 1938, a central government commission sought to address the factors that Howard had campaigned about more than forty years previously.

The evidence submitted to the Barlow Commission by the Garden Cities and Town Planning Association under Osborn's leadership outlined the background to the Garden City campaign and the practical experience gained at Letchworth and Welwyn. The consequences of further intensification in the city centres or suburban expansion were then painted as contributing to long-term problems that should be tackled through the creation of a national planning board. This was to be, 'charged with the duty of determining so far as information is available the directions into which industrial businesses and house-building developments should be guided in the national interest' (Whittick, 1987: 58).

With the outbreak of war in 1939, practically all the functions of British industry came under government control. The origin of the planning system and the nationalisation of industry in the post-war environment cannot be separated from this context. The Barlow Commission, reporting in 1940, thus became the overarching strategy for post-war reconstruction. Osborn, as one of its main contributors, soon found himself occupying an opulent office in Whitehall, providing on-hand advice to Minister for Works Lord Reith. By chance, Osborn had secured greater access to the minister than many senior civil servants had. Thus, through the Town and Country Planning Association and its members, including Professor Abercrombie, plans for how Britain should be rebuilt after the war began to crystallise.

As a former director general of the BBC, Reith's first role in government was as minister for information. The promotion of the vision of a better life for the working classes after the war was a central message. However, by 1942 Reith had been shuffled by Churchill to the Ministry of Works, in charge of establishing plans for the practical business of reconstruction. Reith dovetailed his former role with the new one, promoting the exciting images of post-war modern architecture as part of the morale-boosting communications campaign.

Reith encouraged the London County Council to commission Abercrombie to produce the County of London Plan (described in Chapter 2), alongside their chief architect J.H. Forshaw. This covered central London, but not Greater London, which had been created through suburban expansion in the 1930s. In January 1942, Reith steered an informal conference of local authority leaders from the Home Counties towards approving the creation of a plan covering the whole of the London region – the first of its kind in Britain – and the appointment of Abercrombie to write it. With the local authorities in the Home Counties subtly brought on board, this plan advocated the decentralisation of a million Londoners to various sites, including new satellite communities built beyond the new Green Belts. The idea of urban depopulation became firmly embedded within the political firmament. Osborn thus achieved the goal of Howard to accommodate growth in satellite towns, rather than suburban expansion or inner-urban densification. The greatest change was that these towns were to be government projects rather than the private enterprises of Garden City Companies.

Formulating the New Towns

Reith's tenure in the wartime Coalition Government was brief but influential. By 1943, Churchill had dismissed him from the Cabinet, finding him arrogant and difficult to work with. He spent the rest of the war working at the Admiralty. Yet, the New Towns policy continued to be examined. Reith's replacement as minister for works and planning, Wyndham Portal, supported Abercrombie's plan for the reconstruction but emphasised that the two plans for London, the County and the Regional plan, must not be carried out in isolation. 'The plan for the area surrounding London,' he wrote to the Standing Conference on London Regional Planning, 'and those for the county and the city, although separate and distinct, would need to be closely co-ordinated, so as to form together a comprehensive plan for the whole of the region' (Cullingworth, 1979: 4).

Meanwhile, from December 1942 to July 1945, the minister for the new department of Town and Country Planning, William Sheppard Morrison, fleshed out how the Abercrombie satellite towns might actually be created, but was circumspect on their likelihood in case the incoming post-war government was against the idea. Morrison proposed new legislation for two different delivery vehicles. Both would be publicly owned corporations, but one proposed by local authorities and the other by central government. Where private investment would be utilised, a private company would be set up. Where the entire project would be led by central government, it would be financed by government loans. In both cases the town would ultimately form a new local authority and all assets and liabilities be transferred to them when the corporation created to build the town was dissolved.

Private enterprise new towns had been central to the concept of the Garden City, at a time when the role of the state was far less than it was to become. Until the Labour victory in 'the khaki election' of 1945, both public sector and private sector were seen as being valid contenders for building new towns. Between February and April 1945, the Co-operative Building Society, together with the architect Alistair Macdonald, began inquiries about building a new town at Brickendon Bury in Hertfordshire or Ongar in Essex. Lewis Silkin, then an opposition MP, had been invited to chair a Garden City Company to run the venture.

With the Labour victory, Silkin, a former chair of the London County Council's town planning, housing and public health committees, replaced Morrison as the new secretary of state for the Ministry of Town and Country Planning. He soon appointed Reith to chair a Committee for the New Towns, including Osborn as one of the commissioners. When the architect Alistair Macdonald, this time accompanied by George Gibson, ex-president of the Trades Union Congress, approached Silkin again to find out 'whether he would react favourably to the idea that a public utility society should be formed to develop a satellite town in conjunction with local authorities', Silkin stated that he would wait until the Reith Committee had reported. When it did it was clear that private enterprise was to play no central role in the development of new towns (Cullingworth, 1979: 10).

The brief given to the Reith Committee was to,

consider the general questions of the establishment, development, organisation and administration that will arise in the promotion of new towns in furtherance of a policy of planned decentralisation from congested urban areas; and in accordance therewith to suggest guiding principles on which such new towns should be established and developed as self-contained and balanced communities for work and living.

(cited in Cullingworth, 1979: 14)

The committee thus embarked on determining the fundamental operating logic of the New Towns Programme. Yet many of the essential principles that the New Towns should include were already decided, and were explicit within its brief. Although ostensibly representing a range of views, the opinions of the chairman were strongly reflected in the final product. Far from an open investigation, the New Towns were a foregone conclusion and the committee was merely to focus on the mechanisms for delivering them.

Reith's views were, in turn, shaped by the close counsel of Osborn, who took forward Howard's critique of the old city into the heart of the New Towns Programme. Reith's subsequent evocation of the New Towns was a powerful vision that implied the need for new forms of design to correct the apparent failure of Britain's historic places in light of technological progress:

It is not enough in our handiwork to avoid the mistakes and omissions of the past. Our responsibility, as we see it, is rather to conduct an essay on civilisation. By seizing an opportunity to design, evolve and carry into execution for the benefit of coming generations the means for a happy and gracious way of life.

(Reith, 1946)

The goal of building Garden City satellites, the rebuilding of London and the protection of the countryside from urban sprawl provided by the Green Belt, and the birth of the planning system, thus all came together through this period. In addition, the close working partnership of Osborn, Abercrombie, Reith and others, as well as the huge freedom that Silkin, as minister in charge of a brand new ministry found in the immediate post-war environment made it all possible (Gibberd et al., 1980: 9).

Planning the New Towns

A key recommendation of the Reith Committee was to locate the New Towns far enough away from their parent city to prevent commuting. This was at least 40km from London and 20km from other cities. The intended population of each town was to be 20,000 to 60,000 residents, in family housing built to low densities, the majority of which would be for young families. To prevent the need for inward or outward commuting, every inhabitant was to have a job within the town. Housing was to be organised around the concept of the neighbourhood unit, each self-contained around schools and local shops, and with its own identity. These districts were reinforced by green spaces, echoes of the Garden City boulevards, and connected by traffic-free pedestrian routes.

The vehicle for delivery was to be the publicly owned corporation, independent from direct government control, but granted the powers and resources needed to undertake the programme. This was essentially the same basis as the British Broadcasting Corporation, a publicly funded corporation independent from government. For Reith, this independence from government had been the result of a fierce battle following an attempt by the government to censor the BBC's coverage of the General Strike in 1926. For Osborn, a development corporation supported by loans from the Treasury was an acceptable compromise. Chamberlain's support for authorised privately owned Garden City companies as suitable builders of a new generation of Garden Cities, as reflected in the Marley Commission, was dropped from the final report of the Reith Committee, though private developers and charitable trusts were considered as additional options.

For the government, the definition of Garden City did not entirely tally with the objectives of the New Towns Programme, so although many principles were retained some were not. Howard himself would have objected to the role of the state, preferring total independence. This was a more realistic, indeed, only option, in the Edwardian era, but by the end of the Second World War the state had assumed control over almost every aspect of life, and private sector involvement would have been essentially impossible until rationing was lifted (not for another eight years).

The independence of the development corporation, and its ability to recycle profits in order to further develop the town did, however, ring true to Howard's essential economic basis for the Garden Cities, and would have appealed to his principles of libertarianism. It also achieved what had been impossible in the creation of the Garden Cities of Letchworth and Welwyn – the removal of the demands of private investors. The New Town Development Corporations were essentially private companies with only the Ministry of Town and Country Planning as their sole shareholder, with the Treasury, the bank that provided the loan.

The nature of the project and its scale also made New Town Development Corporations appealing to the fledgling Ministry of Town and Country Planning. Silkin, beyond getting the planning system up and running, had a major delivery project in the New Towns Programme, giving the ministry an important role. A newspaper cartoon at the time caricatured life in the ministry. Pin-striped civil servants lounge around an office, a coat of arms is on the wall with the motto 'Omni Vincta Silkin' plus a blueprint for a state-owned pub (Reith had indeed intended to extend public corporations into the brewery business). One of them, blindfolded, throws darts at a map of Britain whilst his colleagues, lounge around with huge cups of tea complaining, 'It's not fair, you got to choose the sites for the satellite towns last year! It's my turn!' (reproduced in Hardy, 1991a).

In reality, the ministry would select the sites and commission the development corporation. Once the corporation had drawn up its masterplan, either in-house or by subcontracting to private sector consultants, the minister was then responsible for approving it, occasionally with considerable amendments. Once this had been achieved, the development corporation became the planning authority for the area and then got on with the task; acquiring land, hiring staff and labour, and managing the construction and subsequent social and economic development of the town (Aldridge, 1979: 39). As Osborn described it, they were to have, 'all the powers that an ordinary large-scale developing landowner would possess, plus one or two of the powers usually exercised by local authorities' (Gibberd et al., 1980: 9).

Osborn knew what the practical business of building the New Towns would involve, and anticipated that local authorities would not be capable of carrying this out. From conducting topographical surveys, planning roads and sewage systems, to mobilising the designers and contractors, managing the

Public sculpture in Crawley shows a heroic depiction of the independent family in the atomic age.

financial and legal arrangements and carrying out a long-term construction and management programme, specialist skills were clearly vital. These 'obvious weaknesses' of local government meant the need to create this alternative delivery body.

Government money was to supply the entire funding, estimated for each town of 50,000 people (approx 20,000 homes) as £10 million, spread over the period of development of around twenty years, repayable after sixty years. Sixty per cent of this cost would be for housing, 15 per cent for other buildings, 15 per cent for site development and services and 10 per cent for land; £1 million for purchasing land, £1.5 million for site clearance and services infrastructure, £6 million for housing and £1.5 million for all other buildings.

According the Institute for Measuring Worth (an academic research facility), by comparison to modern values this estimates at around £280 million in today's money. Given that today the cost of a single major urban development costs billions in infrastructure alone, it is clear that it was substantially cheaper to get this work done in 1946 than in the early twenty-first century. Clearly the cost of labour and the price of equipment, commodities, and not least oil, are all significant factors above and beyond the scale of investment then compared to now. However, as remarked by the government's official historian of the New Towns Programme, J.B. Cullingworth, these estimates of cost were 'little more than an inspired guess' (Cullingworth, 1979).

With what seemed to many as excessive haste, the Reith Commission reported within months, swiftly turning the long-established arguments of the Garden Cities Movement into government policy. The bill granting the powers needed to create the towns was put to the House of Commons on 17 April 1946. It was voted through with cross-party support and only a single vote in dissent. The debate touched upon questions of when the development corporations should be wound-up and who would make that decision. The atmosphere in the House of Commons was near euphoric. Silkin, quoting Thomas Moore's *Utopia*, took Howard's ambitions to alleviate urban poverty through creating new, rationally planned towns into a declaration for working-class emancipation and social mobility.

Our aim must be to combine in the new town the friendly spirit of the former slum with the vastly improved health conditions of the new estate, but it must be a broadened spirit, embracing all classes of society . . . We may well produce in the new towns a new type of citizen, a healthy, self-respecting dignified person with a sense of beauty, culture and civic pride . . . I want to see New Towns gay and bright . . . they must be beautiful. Here is the grand chance for the creation of a new architecture. We must develop in those who live in the new towns an appreciation of beauty. The new towns can be experiments in design as well as in living.

(House of Commons Debates, vol. 422., col 1091, cited in Aldridge, 1979: 36)

Environmental determinism – the notion that crime and immorality were created or amplified by the urban environment – led to a tacit view that a better environment would therefore produce a better society. The idea that towns should balance jobs and housing implied that they should be self-sufficient, and the Reith Committee, like Howard previously, assumed that the New Towns could be self-sufficient in cultural life too, with their own venues for arts and entertainment. Utopian ideals had been inherent in the attitudes of social reformers of Ebenezer Howard's era. The early residents of the Garden Cities had also been progressive in their thinking, and keen to live in new ways. In the euphoria of victory and alongside the foundation of the welfare state, the New Towns Programme was the fulfilment of a long campaign aimed at creating better conditions for the lives of working-class families.

The tacit assumption was that the New Towns, as the product of the latest scientifically informed thinking, would be so attractive that the middle classes too would be keen to relocate there. In fact, the way that the New Towns came to be built – according to the ideas enshrined in the ideas of Howard and the policies of Osborn, Reith and Abercrombie – produced places that would have been impossible to predict. Writing twenty-five years later in 1970, Silkin confessed, 'despite the pioneering work of Ebenezer Howard and his colleagues, we had no real knowledge of the organisation and finance required nor could we readily see the social problems that might emerge' (cited in Gibberd et al., 1980: 9).

Principles of New Town design

The urban form of central Basildon demonstrates the familiar New Town structure of a modernist town centre and residential Neighbourhood Units separated by major roads. The town's industrial estates are sited to the north, just beyond the border of this image.

The principles of urban design that became central to the nature of the New Towns were the result of a lively debate that had united the goals of the Garden Cities Movement with those of the Modern Movement. Whilst the former were primarily concerned with town planning and the latter with architecture, the ideas of these two groups were synthesised by Professor Abercrombie in his influential role bridging academia, policy-making and professional practice. These ideas, that defined post-war urban development in Britain, became the ubiquitous standard through the creation of the Dudley Report, or to use its formal title, *Design of Dwellings: The Central Housing Advisory Committee Report of 1944*. This was produced by the Ministry of Health to review the direction of council house building in the 1930s, but included an appendix from the fledgling Ministry of Town and County Planning. This proposed that as towns had grown, community had become weaker and hence new housing should be laid out in a planned way to provide for a better quality of life (Ravetz, 2001: 102).

A summary of these recommendations, which soon became a new consensus for urban design, are perfectly summarised by the 1948 government information film, *Charley in New Town* (described in Chapter 2). New communities were to be built by using zoned separation of residential housing estates from industrial estates, the formation of housing into 'neighbourhood units' built around a primary school and other local facilities, and the separation of these from each other by major roads and green spaces to form 'superblocks'. Vehicle movement and pedestrian movement were to be segregated into separate networks, with people moving uninterrupted through under-passes and networks of footpaths, ensuring safe movement from neighbourhoods to secondary schools or town centres.

In Britain in 1948, this seemed like a progressive, futuristic way to build, but these were ideas tried out in other countries during the 1920s and 1930s. Given that the early New Towns took until the 1960s build, these new design concepts were thirty years old by the time they were delivered. Nonetheless, as the first of their kind to be built in the UK, they represented the height of modern development.

Ebenezer Howard's vision of the Garden City unifying town and country meant that New Town housing had an abundance of green space in public places. In the case of Harlow, this fitted into the landscape such that it really did feel like a town in the countryside and at times feeling like one had left the town entirely. A generation later, and Milton Keynes set out to create a 'city in a forest', with low-density neighbourhoods separated by dual carriageways with speed limits of 70 miles per hour. Extensive landscaping and tree planting shielded the housing from the increased traffic noise.

The low-density arrangements that were made possible by the cheap land values meant that space was less valuable than in established urban centres. In response to the high density of the urban slums, the Garden Cities and New Towns were to adopt extremely low-housing densities. Parts of Harlow for instance were at four dwellings per hectare. This meant houses were set back from the road by generous green verges. Services such as water, gas, electricity and sewerage were in places routed through these green verges, rather than under the street as was the norm in established towns, so that introducing or

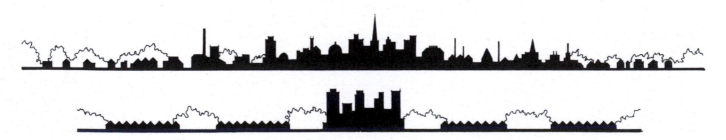

Gibberd deliberately broke with the traditional urban form, inserting green wedges through Harlow to create a union of town and country. Source: Museum of Harlow.

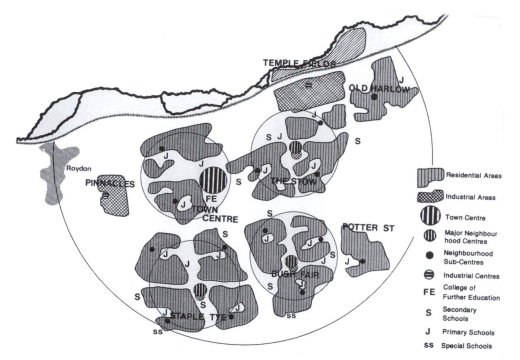

Legend:
- Residential Areas
- Industrial Areas
- Town Centre
- Major Neighbourhood Centres
- Neighbourhood Sub-Centres
- Industrial Centres
- FE — College of Further Education
- S — Secondary Schools
- J — Primary Schools
- SS — Special Schools

Frederick Gibberd's masterplan for Harlow deliberately broke away from the traditional urban form in order to reflect Ebenezer Howard's ambition of a marriage of town and country. Housing is grouped into Neighbourhood Units, each with its own local centre. These are kept apart by expansive 'green corridors', which the major road network runs through. Source: The Museum of Harlow.

The goal of marriage of town and country is central to Gibberd's masterplan for Harlow.

repairing these services would not mean disrupting the traffic. Comparing the arrangement of housing and provision of green space in a typical Victorian working-class terrace with that of Gibberd's first neighbourhoods in Harlow New Town shows the comparative distances between dwellings and the overall levels of green space. The New Towns embodied Howard's town and country hybrid, with housing organised according to the principles enshrined in the Dudley Report. These had been adopted by the new Ministry of Town and Country Planning based on American ideas of town planning, themselves inspired by Howard's Garden Cities a generation earlier.

Each New Town was to be formed of distinct housing estates according to the 'neighbourhood unit concept', as formulated by American urbanist Clarence Perry in 1923. Inspired by Howard and Unwin, Perry formalised the four neighbourhood wards seen in Letchworth and the recent planned suburb of Forest Hill Gardens in New York. These represented well-functioning places because all the essential social facilities such as shops and a school were contained within close proximity. As the author of the New York Regional Planning Survey in 1929, Perry called for neighbourhood units to be implemented to reduce the social isolation emerging from high-rise tower blocks. His ideas were later further expressed in *Housing for the Mechanic Age*, published in 1939. This freshly promoted his definition of a self-contained neighbourhood unit as a distinct area bounded by major roads, with a network of culs-de-sac inside, shops at the edges and a school at the centre (APA, 2004). The Abercrombie Plan and the Dudley Report in 1944 recommended this idea and it thus soon became a new consensus for planning in Britain. The idea that the physical design of a 'neighbourhood' inherently related to the formation of social links was an example of the tacit assumptions of environmental determinism that marked the thinking of the time.

The first half of the twentieth century saw a huge two-way flow between the UK and the USA of such ideas. Parker and Unwin, the architects who designed Letchworth Garden City for Ebenezer Howard, went on to build Hampstead Garden Suburb in north London. This led to a schism within the Garden Cities Movement as it contradicted the principle of self-sufficient communities, but if suburbs were to be built, Garden Suburbs appeared to be the preferable option. This soon became an easily applied buzz-word however, and the notion of 'garden' in front of developments was applied around the world. Today, much the same can be said of the epithet 'green' or 'sustainable' as an all-too-easily applied label for urban development seeking to gain attention in the market.

Parker and Unwin soon came to influence the basic appearance of the whole of Britain's suburban expansion of the 1920s and 1930s (small villas with mock-Tudor detailing, in cul-de-sac road layouts located off access roads from major transport arteries). Their work was to have international influence too. The end of the First World War was a time of rapid urbanisation for the USA, and these new British design ideas were well received. Acting as the main conduit for their promotion was the Regional Planning Association of America, founded in 1923 by Lewis Mumford, Henry Wright and Clarence Stein as a US equivalent of Howard's Garden Cities Association. Their equivalent of Letchworth was the new town of Radburn, in the State of New Jersey, designed by Stein and Wright. Around 12 miles west of New York City, it was designed and built in the 1920s and 1930s as the first 'Town for the Motor Age'. Like Letchworth Garden City, the town was built by a small, privately funded corporation that reinvested its proceeds via a community development trust to further improve the town.

Wright dubbed his design principles, 'Six Planks for a Housing Platform'. These planks were:

1   Plan simply, but comprehensively. Don't stop at the individual property line. Adjust paving, sidewalks, sewers and the like to the particular needs of the property dealt with – not to a conventional pattern. Arrange buildings and grounds so as to give sunlight, air and a tolerable outlook to even the smallest and cheapest house.
2   Provide ample sites in the right places for community use: i.e., playgrounds, school gardens, schools, theatres, churches, public buildings and stores.
3   Put factories and other industrial buildings where they can be used without wasteful transportation of goods or people.
4   Cars must be parked and stored, deliveries made, waste collected – plan for such services with a minimum of danger, noise and confusion.
5   Bring private and public land into relationship and plan buildings and groups of buildings with relation to each

The principles of traffic segregation developed in Radburn, New Jersey, were a fundamental design principle applied across Britain's New Towns. Left: grade-separated route under Londsdale Road, Stevenage. Right: grade-separated route under First Avenue Mandela Avenue, Harlow.

other. Develop collectively such services as will add to the comfort of the individual, at lower cost than is possible under individual operation.

6   Arrange for the occupancy of houses on a fair basis of cost and service, including the cost of what needs to be done in organizing, building and maintaining the community.

(Cited in Gatti, 2008)

Zoning, the neighbourhood unit and new, unconventional layouts thus extended the vision of the UK Garden Cities into the design of Radburn.

The new design principle that Radburn introduced was the separation of vehicle traffic from pedestrian movement. It was the first example of segregated movement within a neighbourhood unit, where houses would all connect to the road network on one side, with service rooms facing the garages or parking bays connected to the road system. The other side of the house, where the living room and bedrooms would be located, faced onto gardens and beyond to a pedestrian walkway. These networks of walkways linked to every other part of the neighbourhood via parkland areas. Underpasses and overpasses connected to surrounding neighbourhood super-blocks, so that travelling from home to schools, shops or church could be done without ever crossing a road. The Radburn layout provided

safe spaces for children to play, in the communal grass areas in front of houses. The traditional street, however, saw cars parked in front and a garden at the rear fully enclosed. The goal of safer and healthier spaces, seemed to have been successfully answered by the approaches pioneered at Radburn, and the recommendation of the Radburn model made by the Dudley Report in 1944 meant that vast amounts of Britain's post-war housing adopted these principles.

Radburn had been intended as a community of 25,000 people, but became a victim of the Great Crash of 1929. By 1932, after having acquired 149 acres, and built 430 detached, 90 terraced and 54 semi-detached houses, plus a 93-unit apartment block, the development corporation was forced into bankruptcy. Radburn amounted to just twelve culs-de-sac backing onto a central park area containing a school, plus a further seven backing onto a smaller parkway immediately to the south across an access road, called Howard Avenue. The Radburn Association survived however, remaining as a trust fund for the existing inhabitants, which meant that over the years the shops and parks were augmented with substantial sports and other community facilities.

Despite being uncompleted, the progressive approach of Radburn's design received huge support from architectural theorists and practitioners, who saw it as a great advance. It was

The Altham Grove estate in Harlow, built to the Radburn principles of the front of the house facing a car-free area, and cars parked at the rear of the house.

described by journalists and luminaries as 'the most significant development in 20th century urban development', 'the first major advance in city planning since Venice' and 'a kind of planning that recognises that the growing edge of civilisation is in the human and not the mechanical direction'. Ronald F. Gatti, manager of the Radburn Association from 1969 to 1989, described its impact by saying, 'Radburn is unique because it was envisioned as a town for better living, and it was the first example of city planning which recognized the importance of the automobile in modern life without permitting it to dominate the environment' (Gatti, 2008).

Although Radburn itself had stalled, the principles were soon to be replicated in an American government programme as part of President Roosevelt's New Deal in 1935. The US Resettlement Administration was part of the US government's response to the Great Depression that saw Stein contribute to new 'garden towns' to provide construction jobs and housing. Out of an original eight towns proposed only three were built: Greenbelt, Maryland; Greenhills, Ohio; and Greendale,

Wisconsin. They were 'utopian co-operative communities' espousing the principles espoused of the Regional Planning Association, the American sister to Howard's Garden Cities Association. Although they eventually only housed a couple of thousand residents, these towns, and the government programme for their creation, are the bridge between Letchworth and Welwyn Garden Cities and Britain's post-war New Towns. Their 'humanistic' combination of the Garden City town plan and modernist car-based urbanism had emerged from two-way dialogue across the Atlantic. Design features such as segregated pedestrian routes crossing the road system through grade-separated tunnels transferred directly from here, as did government-sponsored compulsory purchase of land and planning that bypassed the existing local planning authorities.

The British New Towns Programme that commenced a decade later was the largest implementation of these design principles. As soon as the Stevenage Development Corporation was established, Clarence Stein was brought over from the USA as a design consultant. The 'garden town' ideas of zoning,

Planning to provide amenities within walking distance of homes meant each 'neighbourhood unit' had a 'neighbourhood sub-centre' generally including retail units such as a small super-market, takeaway food outlets, hairdressers, dry-cleaners, and sometimes a pub or a church. Left: Furnance Parade, Weald Drive, Crawley. Right: The Glebe, Chells Way, Stevenage.

An example of the Radburn layout from the Londsdale Road area of Stevenage. Top right (A): The 'front door' of the house is accessed by a car-free walkway. Bottom left (B): Cars arrive in a separate garage area at the 'rear' of the houses, accessed through the back garden gate. Bottom right (C): The 'front door' as viewed from the pedestrian-only 'street'. See also Stevenage image on page 77 for another view from the same location.

the neighbourhood unit and the transport segregation thus transferred directly into the design of Britain's New Towns. The neighbourhood unit was to reinforce local identity and cater for day-to-day needs, while the town centre would provide facilities such as banks and major shops that required a larger number of people to support them.

However, two significant changes were made to Stein's original Radburn concept. First, New Towns houses were built as terraces instead of detached or semi-detached villas. Second, garages were grouped into courts, often a short distance away from homes with poor surveillance. Abandoning the conventional arrangement of houses facing onto a street in order to accommodate car access to the rear meant the houses on Radburn-style estates often lacked clearly identifiable fronts or backs. A houses would have its 'front door' face onto a footpath, offering little privacy, while the back of the house, accessed from the car-port area, increasingly became the door used more often by an increasingly car-using population (Ravetz, 2001: 103).

The final new design concept came from a similar post-war New Town Programme being enacted in Sweden. A planned development at Vällingby, just west of Stockholm – also inspired by the Garden Cities model, intending to create a balance between employment and housing to reduce commuting – developed the first car-free, pedestrian-only town centre. In aesthetic terms, this development, with its modernist public realm, is the clear precursor of the New Town centres (Downie, 1972b).

Liberty and consumerism

The British New Towns sought these fundamentally new approaches to urban design in order to address the problems of the old cities. Evidence of the new design ideas were quickly picked up by the national and professional press as proof of the new society being delivered in the post-war era. As the design of Stevenage progressed, the designers looked to ensure new innovations were picked up quickly. As one of the senior architects, Ray Gorbing, recalled,

we persuaded the Development Corporation board that . . . it should be the pioneers in England for a pedestrian

shopping centre. The estates department were really anti . . . pedestrianising the centre. They used to say 'It will never work'. They said, 'You can't have a shopping centre without a street' . . . without traffic going along and all the rest of it. And in fact, if I remember rightly, having produced our scheme it was then put up to the Ministry and in fact it was thrown out.

(Stevenage, 2005a)

The architects, determined not to give in easily, presented their ideas to the public, who voted in favour of the idea. The corporation and the ministry then approved the scheme for Stevenage town centre, which took some fifteen years until 1967 to be completed. The response from the intelligentsia when the plans and models were first displayed in the 1950s was profound. The town centre was held up, as the town architects had hoped, as a perfect example of new, exciting, modern thinking being put into practice. For the TCPA's Frederick Osborn and Arnold Whittick, the pedestrianised centre rapidly became the justification of why the New Towns were an improvement on the towns and cities of the pre-modern age.

The Stevenage scheme was followed by Gibberd's comprehensive design for Harlow town centre – intended as a series of piazzas in the spirit of Venice or Florence. For Crawley, Hemel Hempstead and Corby the circumstances were different because of the scale of the existing, traditional street pattern. Hemel Hempstead's original town high street, containing a wide variety of building types and a mix of housing, retail and commercial uses, was subject to major demolition so that the new vision could be built. Just as Le Corbusier and the Modern Movement had objected to towns designed in the era of the horse and cart, the Garden Cities Movement view, as expressed by Osborn and Whittick was also deeply disdainful of the historic high street. Reviewing the design of Hemel Hempstead, they wrote,

The long central shopping street resembles more the old haphazard development than the precinct conception as realised at Stevenage, and partly at Crawley . . . it has the disadvantage of an important through road in the centre of the shopping area . . . It would be a considerable

Broad Walk, The High, Harlow town centre, under construction in 1956. Source: Museum of Harlow.

improvement if the central stretch . . . could be changed to a pedestrian way or at least a bus-only route.

(Osborn and Whittick, 1977: 161)

The critique of the problems of the inner city had extended into a critique of all traditional urban forms whatever their scale. The problem was not the car, but the failure of the urban form to accommodate it. The town centre for Corby, the last of the first phase New Towns, received similar criticism of its 'traditional arrangement', revealing some of their fundamental assumptions about the nature of movement in the new, modern world,

The shopping centre, with a wide street as the main feature and shops on either side, follows the traditional arrangement resulting from the haphazard grouping of shops on either side of a main traffic thoroughfare. It was, however, a bad tradition to follow for a modern shopping centre, as it perpetuated the mixture of traffic and

pedestrians, which is one of the serious disadvantages of modern urban life. Corby centre could not, therefore, have been regarded as a good example of a modern town or shopping centre. Traffic should only move to, and not through, a centre, and car parks are provided on the periphery for this need.

(Osborn and Whittick, 1977: 341)

The notion that mixing traffic and pedestrians was a 'serious disadvantage of modern life' illustrated the conundrum posed by the obvious utility of motor transport, but the obvious disadvantages in terms of physical safety and local air pollution. The ability for traffic to move at speed was part of its utility, which urban design should accommodate through wide roads, roundabouts and pedestrian underpasses. The interplay between town planning and transport planning, and ultimately between the property and retail industry and the motor industry, was the single greatest influence in shaping urban

The block structure of Stevenage shows the impact of the design principles on the resulting urban form. The industrial estates are on the far left, composed of large factory structures. The town centre is next, composed of large blocks with pedestrian-only streets between them. Neighbourhood units can clearly be identified elsewhere, separated from each other by large green spaces crossed by the major road network. Stevenage Old Town can also be seen at the top left, in line with the left-hand edge of the New Town centre. Buildings fronting onto the old coaching route clearly mark out the historic urban grain.

settlements in the late twentieth century. As such, the post-war New Towns form the starting point in the UK for the car-based urbanism that has since become the norm. The urban environment often found at the edge of many of Britain's towns and cities – the more recent elements that are the most adapted to rapid vehicle movement with dual-carriageway slip-roads and wide junctions or extensive guard-rails and pedestrian under-passes – are found throughout the New Towns.

Just as the neighbourhood unit concept came to dominate the approach to housing in the New Towns, the pedestrian precinct dominated the approach to the town centres. The idea that vehicles should move to but not through the centres meant that they needed to move round them, and major road infra-structure separated the town centres from the neighbourhood units, just as the neighbourhoods were separated from each other. Besides being self-contained pedestrian areas, the buildings forming the pedestrian areas were large, essentially single block-scale structures, first seen in protean form in Louis de Soissons' design for Welwyn Garden City in the 1920s.

Stevenage had rapidly picked up on the idea produced for Vällingby, as had the plan for the reconstruction of the exten-sively bombed city centre of Coventry. Both were held-up as the two most significant pieces of urban planning of the immediate post-war era for creating car-free areas and were dubbed as being in 'The Festival Style' because of the focus on the public spaces between the buildings created for the 1951 Festival of Britain on London's South Bank (Osborn and Whittick, 1977: 128). The Swedish government had intended Vällingby to be a showcase for what could be achieved through a socialist welfare state – a sentiment readily adopted by the practitioners and policy-makers working on the New Towns Programme in Britain. The political changes taking place in the 1950s meant that by the end of the decade Britain had linked its future not to the progressive socialism of the Swedish welfare state but to the liberal consumer-culture of the USA.

The pedestrian precinct developed at Stevenage and Coventry were to be the precursor of the fully enclosed shop-ping mall. These were to come to the fore in the era of the

The Howard Centre in Welwyn Garden City opened in 1990, reflecting Howard's ambition for Garden Cities to feature glass-covered shopping arcades.

second generation of New Towns, such as Runcorn, and famously be applied on a massive scale in the centre of Birmingham on the site of the old Bull Ring. Intriguingly, the indoor shopping mall had been one of Howard's original ideas for the Garden City, inspired by the Victorian arcades of cities such as Paris and Leeds, and taking the name Crystal Palace from the eponymous glass and steel structure created for London's Great Exhibition in 1851. In Howard's design for the Garden City, first expressed in 1898, the civic centre was to include,

a wide glass corridor called 'Crystal Palace.' This building is in wet weather one of the favourite resorts of the people . . . Here manufactured goods are exposed for sale, and here most of that class of shopping which requires the joy of deliberation and selection is done.

(Howard, 2003: 34)

This arguably links the Victorian arcade to the modern indoor shopping mall, many of which have glass roofs resembling to a greater of lesser extent the shape of the Crystal Palace. Today, the train station in Welwyn Garden City opens directly into a shopping mall named The Howard Centre.

The impact of these retail centres and their separation from the surrounding areas has become one of the most unique and contentious factors of the design of the New Towns. Naturally, the radicalism of this new approach to urban movement produced places that behave differently from historic towns. For the New Towns that were built on substantial existing settlements, such as at Hemel Hempstead or Crawley, this effect was less pronounced, compared to the largely 'greenfield' developments of Harlow, Washington and Milton Keynes.

The Co-op supermarket in Stevenage in 1958 ushered in a new form of 'self-service' super-market shopping. Copyright: Stevenage Museum.

Accommodating the needs of the motor age

For the partnership New Towns of Warrington, Northampton and Peterborough, the existing historic town centres supported populations of over 100,000, but even here the creation of large-scale road infrastructure around the centre, the insertion of shopping malls over existing streets and the conversion of traffic streets into pedestrian streets had similar results. In the case of Peterborough, the town centre's extensive shopping mall sits adjacent to a historic market square. The inner ring road creates, as Osborn stated, the means by which traffic could move to, but not through a centre, and multi-storey car parks surround this centre.

The presence of a substantial amount of existing town was instrumental in blurring the coherence of these design philosophies. The long-term view of development of an existing town such as Peterborough or Crawley shows how waves of adjacent activity over the years rather than comprehensive redevelopment mean the place has evolved differently. The contrast of the New Town street pattern compared to the historic street pattern illustrates the way the town's essential functioning was changed.

Towns such as Stevenage and Crawley originally formed around coaching routes out of London. Market town high streets were defined as places that people moved through. Throughout history, anywhere in the world, a market town on a crossroads is one of the fundamental reasons for towns to form. With motorised traffic extending the distance one could travel in a day, and blighting the historic centres with traffic congestion, towns such as Crawley built bypasses so that people would then move round instead of through the town centres. By contrast, the centre of the town then needed to attract people in who did not need to travel through on the grounds that it was their route to their ultimate destination.

The fully enclosed shopping malls first pioneered in the New Towns replaced traditional high streets as the centres of activity. The Antonine Shopping Centre, Cumbernauld. Courtesy of North Lanarkshire Council.

In the original New Town design, a spacious pedestrian precinct sat just to the east of the old market square, with civic buildings, town hall and library, to the north, and a public park to the south. A dual-carriageway road then circumvented this centre to link the surrounding residential neighbourhoods. Today, Crawley's central retail area is characteristic of the New Towns pedestrian precinct. However, to the south a large indoor shopping arcade, The Pallisades, dating from the 1980s, complete with multi-storey car park, shows the evolution of the car-based urban environment continuing with single large structures. The final part of this evolution in Crawley is seen with the even later addition, a short drive north west of the town centre, where a leisure park provides cinemas, a bowling alley and restaurants, shifting the essentially functioning of a town centre once again.

In Stevenage, a similar development in part of its original industrial zone west of the railway line, pulls activity away from the town centre, into an area of 'big-box' leisure functions such as nightclubs and restaurants, which have considerable capacity for car parking, and essentially mirror the car-dependent urban sprawl developed in America and since exported worldwide.

The relationship between car ownership and the nature of the urban form is central to the story of the New Towns. As described in the film *Charley in New Town*, at its start the New Towns Programme built neighbourhood units on the basis of people being able to walk or cycle to work. Before the war, Professor Abercrombie, the leading proponent of Britain's post-war urbanism, had never expected car ownership to ever be more than a luxury purchase for the wealthy. He anticipated that car ownership in the UK would not rise above 16 per cent of the population (Plymouth, 2005: 22) and planned communities on that basis. However, by the 1960s levels of car ownership in Britain were rising fast. Between 1949 and 1966 the number of households in the UK owning a car went from around 7 per cent to more than 53 per cent (Clapson, 1998: 48). After the austere and unstable 1950s, economic stability meant rising wages, and cars soon became one of the most desirable purchases. The consequence of these rapidly rising levels of car use meant a growing crisis for the design of towns across the UK.

In 1940, in line with Abercrombie's thinking, the view of the Ministry of Health (then in charge of housing) was that new housing should be built with one garage for every ten homes.

Crawley's medieval market square lay on the major north-south movement route running through the centre of the town.

Queens Square, the post-war pedestrian precinct forming the heart of Crawley New Town lies around 150m to the east of the original town high street and market square.

Opening in 1992, The County Mall is a large indoor shopping centre with multi-storey car park, located a short distance to the south of Crawley New Town centre, and easily accessed by car.

The Crawley Leisure Park continues the car-focused model of urban development, with chain restaurants, bowling alley and multiplex cinema, located north of Crawley town centre. This development, and similar ones elsewhere, draw economic and social activity away from previous locations.

For the first generation New Towns, these assumptions, plus the principle of self-contained, walkable communities originating in the Garden City concept, was out of date by the time construction started. Working on the masterplans for Harlow and Crawley, Frederick Gibberd campaigned against this restriction,

> By the time the first quarter of the town had been built demand was already at 20 per cent and we had to go back and build blocks of garages wherever space could be found. It was a slow, laborious and frustrating experience, particularly for the housing and architects' departments . . . The whole process went on for some

years and the only people to get any satisfaction out of it were those who obtained garages.

(Gibberd et al., 1980: 183)

It took until 1967 for the government standards to accept the need for one garage or parking space for every new home (Gibberd et al., 1980: 183). This delay is remarkable given that the promotion of private car ownership was a deliberate policy of central government. In the immediate post-war years, Stafford Cripps, Minister in charge of the Board of Trade, began reshaping the country's military industrial capacity to form the British motor industry (Hennesey, 1992: 105). New British cars such as the Mini, were affordable and immensely popular, and became icons of Britain in the modern world. The resulting effect that rising car use had on Britain's towns and cities came to a head with the publication of Professor Colin Buchanan's influential 1963 report *Traffic in Towns*. This established the principles that major infrastructure such as bypasses, underpasses and ring roads were needed to ensure that traffic could continue to circulate freely.

Early New Towns such as Harlow separated their neighbourhood units by roads running through green landscaped areas, in accordance with the principles of Perry and Stein and in tribute to Ebenezer Howard's vision of marrying town and country. These wide carriageways came to be the prototypes of the later major roadways that became common in many other towns. The later generation of New Towns designed in the 1960s were to develop the concept of 'full motorisation'. Washington New Town was designed around a grid of roads forming squares half a mile long, into which would be the neighbourhood units, renamed 'village areas', which were supposed to accommodate public transport, but assume most people would use private cars (House of Commons, 2002b).

The changing perception of the role of public transport compared to the private motor car is clearly seen in the evolution of the masterplan for Milton Keynes. Following the development of a segregated busway in Runcorn New Town, Milton Keynes was originally proposed as a series of neighbourhood units linked by a high-tech monorail system. However, new theories of urban development from America were to prove immensely significant in having this public transport system dropped. What resulted at Milton Keynes was the Washington model recreated on a vast scale.

Professor Melvin Webber, at the University of California at Berkeley, argued against the fundamental logic of the neighbourhood unit concept. Car ownership fundamentally undermined the principle of locality at the heart of the thinking of the Garden City pioneers. In his 1963 paper, *Order in Diversity: Community without Propinquity*, he argued against anti-car rhetoric: 'By now almost everyone knows that low density developments on the growing edge of the metropolis are a form of "cancerous growth", scornfully dubbed with the most denunciatory of our new lexicon's titles, "urban sprawl", "scatterisation", "subtopia"' (Webber, 1963).

Instead, citing the evidence of Herbert Gans' book *The Levittowners*, about life in America's post-war suburbs, Webber pointed out that people who live in suburbia like it. The car gives them total freedom of movement and so people socialised less with the people they happened to live next door to, as they had done in the 'friendly slums' of the cities. Instead, people socialised with people they shared common interests with in a 'non-place urban realm'. By 1965, in the book *The Urban Place and the Non-place Urban Realm*, Webber argued how 'automobility' allowed people to choose to be wherever they wanted to be, and thus traditional formation of urban places was inflexible for progress. Later, Webber argued that urban designers and planners had tacitly adopted, 'the concepts and methods of design from civil engineering and architecture' (Webber, 1974) and that since society was an inherently complex and unpredictable phenomenon, the approach of the engineer was entirely incorrect. Instead, urbanists should attempt to enable development in a bottom-up, responsive manner, rather than provide urban developments on the basis of predicting the nature of a future settlement.

Richard Llewelyn-Davies, leader of the Milton Keynes planning team, agreed. The monorail was scrapped and the design of the New Towns was instead based around the private car. The result was to produce an urban form that exaggerates the earlier ideas of the New Towns into a pattern resembling the suburban sprawl that the British planning system had been created to counter (Clapson, 1998: 49). As one of the consultants contributing to Milton Keynes' masterplan, Webber could put his arguments into practice just as Clarence Stein had at Stevenage some thirty years earlier.

Just as car ownership represented freedom of choice, an inherent flexibility in the approach to urban design taken at Milton Keynes meant that it pioneered community involvement in planning through a flexible approach that responded well to the economic instability of the 1970s and 1980s. The wide, grid-structure of Milton Keynes that lay in extensively landscaped road cuttings and embankments took the design principles developed at Harlow and Washington and applied them on a grand scale. But the greatest influence on the final form of Milton Keynes came from a single decision late in the design phase. The road network had originally been intended for a speed of 35 miles per hour, common with other urban centres.

Each intersection would thus be a signalled junction with conventional sidewalks. Such a pattern would have produced a conventional street pattern of main streets and side streets, in the manner of the classic grid cities such as Glasgow or New York. With the roads forming the centres of neighbourhoods, areas could overlap and change, and the junctions between blocks could in future become new local centres.

However, a high-level decision was taken that the roads should become highways. The dual carriageways in Milton Keynes, now designed for a top speed of 70 miles per hour, meant a dramatic change in the nature of the town. The distance between each neighbourhood increased to accommodate the larger roads. Each intersection became a roundabout instead of a signalled junction and the sides of the road became landscaped and forested banks to contain the increased traffic noise. Despite the desire on the part of the designers to make a radical break from the designs of the early New Towns that used Stein's neighbourhood unit super-blocks separated by landscaped roadways, Milton Keynes instead implemented the early New Towns model on a giant scale (Edwards, 2001).

As one of the masterplanners, Mike Macrae, described it,

When we designed the masterplan for Milton Keynes it was intended that the kilometre main road grid would provide local activity centres with bus-stops within 500 metres of every home. There would be opportunities for local shops and employment to develop, with a sense of specific locale . . . The 'vision' of [chief architect] Derek Walker of the city as a forest has been extremely damaging . . . The grid was designed for speeds of around 40mph not 70, with computer-controlled traffic lights operating a green-wave system. Unfortunately the Walker vision played into the hands of the highway engineers and estates department, and encouraged them to parcel up isolated housing sites off spike roads as elsewhere. Which is why there is no there there, and the buses don't work. Sadly the architects were never set the brief of place-making.

(*Building Design*, 2007d)

Milton Keynes' grid of four-lane freeways produces insular neighbourhoods separated from the surrounding areas. As with Harlow and parts of Peterborough, it is possible to drive through the town without ever really having a sense that there are buildings present on either side, since they are so well concealed by the landscaping. The centre of Milton Keynes encapsulates the character of the urban fringe and suburban sprawl developments that Webber defended, but does so in the heart of the urban area (Clapson, 1998: 205). The peculiar character of Milton Keynes is that the centre of the New Town resembles the edge of a typical town or city. Yet residents who live there find these qualities of high-speed roads and wide green spaces crossed by dedicated cycle paths part of its appeal as a place to live.

Ebenezer Howard's dream of unifying the best qualities of town and countryside, in the wake of rising car use, meant that the wide green spaces that lined the roadways of Harlow, or the freeways that criss-cross Milton Keynes, have little of the tranquillity of the real countryside. By trying to accommodate the rise of car use, the New Towns would never be free of the presence of traffic. A swishing drone of traffic washes across the edge of Milton Keynes Campbell Park, entirely unlike the busy rumble of traffic in a conventional town. Perhaps it should come as no surprise that the first car-based urban environment in the UK, the New Town of Stevenage, would be home to future Formula One racing world champion Louis Hamilton.

Building modern Britain

In the post-war era, the British car industry, centred round the West Midlands, was to be joined by a growing aviation sector, with the development of the commercial jet engine centred round the De Havilland factory at Hatfield. The parallel development, to have immense significance for the future urban development of the UK, was the building of the motorways in the late 1950s, as Britain's equivalent to the German autobahns and American interstate freeways, built during the 1930s and 1940s.

The construction of commercial airports around London, at Heathrow, Gatwick, and later Stanstead, was then a further instance of military transport technology applied to commercial ends that was to have a huge impact. For the New Towns, their strategic location in relation to these new transport routes played a significant role in their long-term success (to be discussed later), and the growth of the related industrial sectors were closely tied to the employers of some of the New Towns.

The early New Towns designated between 1946 and 1950, and built over a period of around twenty-five years from 1950 onwards, and the later New Towns, designated from 1961 onwards, belong in two camps. The first assumed the neighbourhood unit of several thousand people would form clear communities, built around the local school, local shops and other essential amenities. For these early New Towns, adapting

to the rise of car ownership meant reviewing the original designs. For the later New Towns, car ownership was assumed from the outset. Residents and employers appeared to benefit from designs that put easy movement by car first.

In terms of their overall location, the proximity of the early or later New Towns to major transport infrastructure such as the motorways or airports became a major factor affecting their long-term success. The presence of Gatwick airport was later to grant the residents of Crawley Britain's lowest level of

Milton Keynes' high-speed dual carriageway road system forced each neighbourhood to become inward facing, and suburban rather than urban in character.

Highway-scale roads next to Bracknell town centre create severance.

Segregated and grade-separated pedestrian and cycle routes were intended to be safer, but lack 'natural surveillance' and have proved expensive to maintain.

unemployment. Bracknell, near Heathrow to the west of London, and located between the M3 and M4 motorways, became a hub for emerging industries such as office supplies, kick-starting the Thames Valley Corridor as a major growth region. Hemel Hempstead, Stevenage and Milton Keynes to the north of London, and Warrington in the north west, similarly benefited from their close proximity to the motorway network. In contrast, other New Towns such as Peterlee and Redditch lacked this connection.

For Harlow, the overall strategic location was positive, but the town's layout was to be deeply undermined in 1964 by a lack of joined-up thinking between the government department in charge of planning the New Towns and that planning the motorways. When Harlow had been planned, the Ministry of Transport had proposed to send the route of what was to become the M11 between London and Cambridge to the west of the town. Gibberd thereby built the industrial estates on the west. However, when the location of London's third airport was determined for Stanstead to the north east of Harlow, the route was changed to pass Harlow to the east. Gibberd was furious, declaring the impact on the Harlow masterplan was like

building a seaside town and then finding they had moved the sea (Gibberd et al., 1980: 155). The Harlow Development Corporation expressed its feelings to the ministry saying,

> The Corporation recognises that new considerations may have arisen which would make a major change in the line of the M11 road desirable. But it feels bound to point out that such a change might well destroy the fundamental traffic basis of the carefully executed Town Plan.
>
> (cited in Aldridge, 1979: 68)

Indeed, to this day, the subsequent result has been that all commercial traffic drives through the centre of town to reach the M11, creating a daily gridlock at peak times. The degree to which planning decisions and new design concepts intended to produce better communities, inevitably produced unintended side-effects. At the level of the internal structure of the towns, both as a reaction to the historic towns and cities in terms of the relative location of workplace and homes and as a reaction to the new realities of the motorcar, the future evolution of the New Towns was inescapably linked to the nature of the design decisions and the constant change in society wrought by changes in prosperity and new commercial realities.

The problems of the historic towns and cities had been answered by adopting the principles of the neighbourhood unit, the industrial estate and the central shopping area, surrounded by extensive landscaped roadways. Yet, the radicalism of this departure from the historic street pattern of British towns and cities was subject to enthusiastic declarations from their promoters. These design concepts soon became a dogma, and deviation from them was at times attacked by advocates of the New Towns, such as Frederick Osborn and Arnold Whittick, in this review of the emerging masterplan for Peterlee New Town,

The built form of Telford shows the residential neighbourhood units and the shopping mall centre. Industrial sites are visible to the right. However, the form is more dispersed than the earlier New Towns. The empty space to the south is that formed by the town park, while that to the north of the centre is caused by the major road infrastructure of the M54.

The design for the town centre in the masterplan of 1952 was not a very progressive one and was planned on stereotyped traditional lines before the value of the pedestrian precinct as exemplified at Stevenage and Coventry was fully realised . . . later plans were made, completely different from the first plan. They incorporated several pedestrian areas and shopping ways on two levels.

(Osborn and Whittick, 1977: 280)

Traditional urbanism of market centres formed around historic movement routes and crossroads were seen as a 'stereotype', but the New Towns also soon displayed a 'stereotypical' form. The value of the pedestrian precinct model was also assumed without the benefit of any empirical understanding. The central shopping areas were all the last aspects of the New Towns to be built, since they needed sufficient population present to attract major retailers. The small shops provided in the neighbourhood centres supplied people's basic needs (Aldridge, 1979: 54). The clear and immediate benefit of the innovative pedestrian centre for Stevenage was its promotional value, sending a clear message to the world – that Britain was driving forward in the aftermath of the war.

The old urban form was subject to rhetorical language to drive home the point about social progress that the architecture and urbanism of the New Towns was manifesting, as shown by this quote from the *Architects Journal* in 1972 describing a pioneering new housing development in Crawley New Town,

The dirty urban street, the basement area with its rotting coal in dark vaults, the cracked backyard overawed by sawtooth brick housebacks and fouled by cats – they seem an age away. But so for that matter, does semi-land with its garden wastes, its harsh displays of domestic competition.

(cited in PRP, 2007: 32)

For all the credit due to Osborn for getting the New Towns Programme up and running, the zeal with which he promoted the new and discredited the old became a dogma that resonated with the 'progressive' spirit of the age. Yet this attitude disguised a lack of understanding of the functional properties of existing places and buildings, which had evolved over time to serve various uses. The common ground shared between the Garden Cities Movement and the Modern Movement to reinvent urbanism had ultimately become a living experiment that would take decades to be proven. It was, as the minister ultimately in charge, Lewis Silkin, later confessed, 'A leap into the unknown' (Gibberd et al., 1980: 1). Each of the design decisions that shaped the New Towns – described so concisely by the film *Charley in New Town* – produced places that were uniquely new in order to answer specific problems of the old urban forms. But in so doing they created new problems of their own. The academics and practitioners working on the New Towns laid out their ideas in brick and concrete. The remarkable scale of construction initiated throughout the thirty years that these ideas were in vogue has left a lasting legacy on Britain's urban landscape.

Housing adjacent to the nominal centre of Skelmersdale is to a low-density design, surrounded by an expanse of green space. Image courtesy of West Lancashire District Council.

A leap into the unknown

Building the New Towns

John Profumo MP (third from left) Secretary of State for War, visiting the English Electric missile development facility in Stevenage in 1960 (later British Aerospace). Copyright: Stevenage Museum.

To understand how the design concepts for the early New Towns were built in reality, the national context in which the development corporations were working must be appreciated. Britain had spent six years fighting the Second World War, and the aftermath saw economic instability and a shifting of international priorities with the drawing of the Iron Curtain. The war had meant that central government had taken control of virtually all aspects of the national economy. Private industry became entwined with public service, with a civil servant appointed to the executive boards of major firms, and military manufacturing established within existing commercial factories. From the front line to the home front huge numbers of people were directly involved in the war. As such, the first generation of New Towns were built by people coming directly from military roles.

The chairmen of the development corporations were invariably senior commanding officers. From 1955, Stevenage Development Corporation produced a quarterly publication delivered free to all new residents covering news of the progress in town building. This included profiles of people 'making outstanding contributions to the development of Stevenage', always referencing their military service record along with other personal details.

Chairman of Stevenage Development Corporation, Sir Roydon Dash DFC LLD FRICS FAI, is the sixth distinguished person to have held this appointment in nine years . . . In the 1914-19 war . . . he was well known for his successful combats over the Western Front, and was awarded the Distinguished Flying Cross. At 67 years of age he is still an ardent golfer and motorist, driving himself to and from his home in Guildford on his weekly visits to Stevenage.

(Purpose, 1955: 13)

The outlook, attitudes and expectations of the staff and residents, and the management style of their superiors, were all to play a part in the way the corporations carried out their tasks. The culture was naturally authoritarian and less consultative than in later years. The planning system took a command-and-control approach, which sought to confirm that what had been specified on an approved blueprint was what got built. Plans were based on predictions that were scientifically determined. The public were compliant because of a broad social assumption that the state simply got on with things that were for the public good, informed by the best experts available (CLG, 2006).

In contrast to the background of the chairman, the first issue of Stevenage's magazine also provided this profile,

Alfred Luhrman . . . escaped from the shell-torn beaches of Dunkirk . . . is now working as a general foreman on one of the building sites in the town . . . Chairman of the General Purposes and Civil Defence Committees of Stevenage Urban District Council and a vice-president of the Stevenage Rangers football club. However, he still finds time to devote to his two young children Alan and Maureen, at his home in Brox Dell, Stony Hall.

(Purpose, 1955: 13)

As a new career after the war, the job of building New Towns was extremely attractive, and a new generation of architects, planners and civil engineers were among the first people to be hired. Ray Gorbing, later to become one of the main architect planners working on the Stevenage masterplan, described how he qualified as a planner after serving in North Africa, Italy then Greece.

During my time in Athens, when the war was virtually finished, we didn't have very much to do. I studied planning then as . . . a correspondence course . . . when I got home I got onto . . . a crash course in London attached to the university there, to take the final exam for planning . . . at the end of four months . . . so by '47, I was a qualified Associate of the Town Planning Institute . . . So my first job was in planning in Nottinghamshire . . . just after the war, the government didn't have very much idea what planning was all about, I don't think we did really, but we at the school of planning were the only people who could really produce structure plans . . . the director of planning, who was an engineer, said I don't know anything about planning . . . go up there and sort yourself out, fix yourself up with an office . . . go and buy equipment, drawing boards or what ever you want and get your staff together.

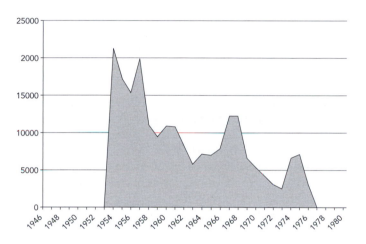

The housing completion rates for Harlow show the phases of growth of a single town. The initial spike of construction is followed by sharp declines in response to national economic downturns. The spikes in the late 1960s and mid 1970s show the town's waves of new expansion.

This was ridiculous, I mean this was my first job, you know . . . I got a chap to help me who was a colleague of mine at the school of planning so between two of us we recruited local staff, student planners up there and we produced one of the first plans I suppose that were produced in this country for North Notts . . . we finished it in about a year . . . and sent them down to Nottingham and they sent them down to the Ministry of London. They didn't know what to do with them and they just sort of sat on them there you know, so it really meant that we were sitting up there, without any work to do . . . and it was at that time after about 18 months up there that the job in Stevenage was advertised, so I applied to come down to join the staff in the new town.

(Stevenage, 2005a)

In January 1950, Gorbing moved to Stevenage and began work on producing the masterplan for Stevenage, while also working on the detailed plan for a housing neighbourhood. When money finally started to come through to allow construction to start, the conditions of post-war Britain continued to cause delays. Small details, such as being able to get hold of

door locks or handles or sanitary ware, could easily hold up the completion of housing. Throughout this time the government also maintained very strict financial restraints on the development corporations, stipulating tight budgets for the creation of each batch of housing (Stevenage, 2005a).

Construction in the New Towns really only got underway in 1952 and soon reached a rate, across all of the towns, of around 10,000 houses per year. In 1955, all towns experienced a dip in productivity but this recovered within a year and by 1957 had reached a peak of 12,000 house completions per year across the whole New Towns Programme. In this year Crawley achieved the highest number of completions of 2,484 homes, while Harlow came second with 1,994 homes. In 1958, however, the total number of completions slumped, recovering only slightly before declining to its lowest point of around 7,000 completions in total, around the time of the 1964 election. From then, with

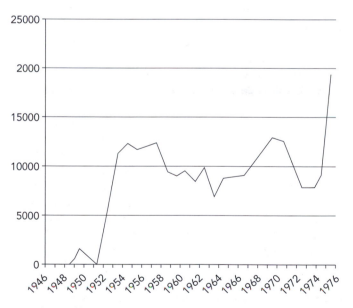

Annual rate of housing completions in the New Towns from 1949 to 1976. Although the New Towns Programme officially started in 1946, it took five years before volume house building got underway. Around 1958, 1963 and 1971 production slumped due to the impact of economic recessions. From 1975 onwards, total house completions accelerated significantly as the larger scale third generation New Towns were built out.

the creation of the second generation of New Towns, and the expansion plans for the first generation, the number of housing completions rose to reach a new high of over 12,000 homes per year in 1970. Between 1972 and 1975 a similar slump in output occurred, then rising to a new high as the plans for the third generation started construction.

From the start, the early New Towns can thus clearly be seen as a post-war public works programme, where the new discipline of planning was given the opportunity to build new communities on a vast scale. The design principles adopted for the New Towns (described in Chapter 7) were applied without any questioning of their validity as Leonard Vincent, one of the senior architect-planners at Stevenage, recalled in 1987,

> The idea of the neighbourhood plan came out of the Greater London plan 1944, where Abercrombie suggested the 10,000 neighbourhood was a good idea as a residential base, and that was adopted. We saw no reason at the time to do something differently, I suppose primarily because of no experience. To be quite frank about it, none of us had any experience in those days of building new towns – I mean huge communities – lots of experience in building estates, residential estates, but that is a different thing altogether.
>
> (Stevenage, 2007a)

With hindsight, Vincent's experience of how the neighbourhood units worked in reality made him challenge Abercrombie's figures – and the assumptions, ultimately, of Clarence Perry.

> My general view now is that the neighbourhoods are too big. Their areas are all right, where they are located [but] they are too big to be called neighbourhoods and they should have been possibly split down into residential areas or units, probably about a third of the size . . . [because] many years ago we had a social survey done . . . and they found, quite rightly . . . the people that lived at one end of a neighbourhood had no connection whatever with the people that lived at the other end of the neighbourhood. They were like strangers. But the neighbourhood next door – the other side of the road – they had a lot of communication. So the physical idea of

the neighbourhood as a social or community wouldn't work in that sense.

> (Stevenage, 2007a)

The new legal process of planning, whereby a blueprint was approved by a public servant, and its subsequent compliance checked against the approved plan, made the basic assumption that experts had calculated what was needed, and that is what should be built. By the end of the Second World War, the prevailing ethos was of a new age of reason. Since the Charge of the Light Brigade and the trenches of the Somme, old ways of warfare had been cruelly and abruptly disproved. Besides the essential matters of military strategy, manpower and resources, victory in the new industrial circumstances of the twentieth century depended on the ability to invent and manufacture new technologies of warfare faster than the opponent could. A thousand secret projects from the Mulberry Harbour to radar, the computer, the jet engine and ultimately the atom bomb, all established the new right-to-rule of the scientific elite. The boffins that won the war through physics and chemistry were then expected to be able to turn their talents to achieving the objectives of peace in the post-war period. In the New Towns, the commanders asked the experts to provide the answers. The experts, who tended towards the philosophical belief that social matters were in principle as open to rational inquiry and predictability as chemistry, mechanics and ballistics, went ahead and gave their best shot.

A further element where the New Towns development corporations were acting in essentially new and unchallenged ways was that previously, landowners, architects and builders had all been separate players, with a client–service relationship. Under the new structure of the New Town Development Corporation (following the pioneering example of the Garden City Companies), a single organisation owned the land, approved the plans and hired the architects and builders. Practically every aspect of the organisation of construction was completely new and the nature of outside relationships had to be established in entirely new terms.

Despite having an unprecedented scale of operational independence from government, the development corporations arguably had less freedom than the Garden City Companies had, simply because the world of the 1950s was so different from that of the 1900s or the 1920s. The complexity of relationships between the development corporations and central and local government was often troublesome.

Local councils were to represent the local population and had responsibility for some aspects of development such as roads or schools. In Crawley this was particularly complex as the designated area of the New Town overlapped three different existing county council areas. Some relationships such as at Basildon, Corby or Peterlee, were at the more positive end of the scale because the New Town had been designated in response to the request of the existing local authorities. At the other extreme, the relationship between the New Town and the local council members was antagonistic. As Leonard Vincent, at Stevenage described it,

> the Development Corporation and the then District Council never saw eye to eye on anything. It was a bit like 'Big Brother': the Development Corporation with its special powers (I have every sympathy with them) which the indigenous population of Stevenage, as it was then, viewed with great suspicion. Being mainly recruited from the Old Town, because that's all there was at the time, the Council just didn't like 'Big Brother' telling them what to do with the area. Right from the start they had this basic suspicion.
>
> (Carruthers, 1996: 31)

Following the objections to the designations of the New Towns, many local people, who formed the council members of local government, were naturally hostile to the development corporations. From the very start the concerns of local residents not wanting new housing on their doorsteps was acute. The New Towns Programme started with vitriolic criticism from local residents in the Conservative-voting heartlands of the English Home Counties against inner-city Labour voters entering their constituency en masse. In Stevenage, once the first factories and housing started to be built and people from London began to relocate to the New Town, the reactions from the original population were mixed. 'There were quite a few delicatessen – high-class shops as they called themselves – in the town, which weren't amenable to us of course as we were "dirty Londoners", as we were spoken about', recounted a Mrs Cotter. Meanwhile,

according to a Mr Udell, 'I can recall when my wife and I were in the bread shop in particular, which was called Edwards, the assistants would deliberately ignore you and serve the Old Town people first' (Carruthers, 1996: 23).

However, before too long, as the numbers of residents started to increase, the traders in the old town started to benefit. As a Mrs Hampton recollected, 'The Old Town was doing marvellously, because on a Saturday morning . . . queues all the way down the High Street. All the shops, people were queuing for their goods because that was the only place where you could get things' (Carruthers, 1996: 24). Eventually, accepting that the city dwellers needed to relocate and that there was an economic benefit to the local traders, attitudes started to soften on a personal level. Eventually, as the New Town grew larger, the slow, rural way of life of the old village began to give way to a more urban life, with all the benefits, such as better shops and new jobs.

However, at the political level, relations often remained frosty. As Richard Crossman, Housing Minister in 1960, described it, some of the local county or district councils, 'felt the usual hate of the development corporation, with their brand new offices, their big salaries, and their air of being feudal masters' (Aldridge, 1979: 70). The decision taken by the Reith Committee to adopt the model of the development corporation was at the expense of the work being carried out by local authorities, enhanced to carry out the work. Once the New Town development corporations existed, local authorities would then find it hard to attract staff with the necessary competence to begin to offer these services. As Ray Gorbing described, 'any architect worth his salt . . . wouldn't get a job at a borough council [but] at a development corporation because they were doing all the exciting stuff' (Stevenage, 2005a).

Disputes over transport infrastructure regularly took place between the corporations and the local authorities. Through-routes were a county responsibility while estate roads fell to the corporations. Various deals were created between the two groups as a result of lengthy negotiations over the relative contributions of what was all, ultimately, public money. The persistence of this state of affairs until 1967 was later seen as evidence that there was no cross-government commitment to the New Towns that would have prevented this waste of manpower and tax payers money (Aldridge, 1979: 68).

It is ironic that although the development corporations may have seemed faceless and all-powerful arms of the state for resident tenants and the nearby local authorities, they in fact had little power or influence at the national level. The New Towns were always a creation of the fledgling Ministry of Town and Country Planning, who had failed to establish specific cross-government support for the New Towns Programme. Rushed into being in the turbulence of the immediate post-war years meant a lack of cross-government support that hampered the co-ordinated delivery of vital infrastructure. Some towns suffered delays in construction until sewers could be provided by the Water Board or telephones installed by the Post Office. Provision of education and medical services continued to be a problem for many years, affecting each generation of the New Towns.

A Commons Select Committee study in 1974 was surprised to find that in building a New Town, there was no guarantee whatsoever that social facilities such as schools or hospitals would receive funding. The development corporations had to bid for such facilities but were treated the same as any other part of the country, and furthermore would receive no special support from the New Towns Division of the (then) Department of the Environment in promoting the needs of the New Towns to the other government departments. The Department for Health and Social Security, responsible for hospital provision, would consider the needs of all areas with no special consideration to the growth of the New Towns, and would allocate their resources on a national basis according to their own priorities and forecasting models. In 1975, Milton Keynes Development Corporation's annual report stated baldly, that the town was, 'disgracefully under-provided with health facilities . . . We should not be asked to build houses without . . . the assurance of proper supporting services' (Aldridge, 1979: 67). Regarding the Department for Transport, the example of Harlow serves as an exemplar of the lack of co-ordination between central government and the activities of the development corporation (see Chapter 7).

Attracting employers

In terms of employment too, the national economic strategy operated by the Board of Trade, and later Department of Trade and Industry, could not achieve a long-term link between the national economic development strategy and the means for attracting new employers into the New Towns.

In the English New Towns, the policy objective of decentralising industry and population from the cramped and polluted inner cities was managed through a process called the Industrial Development Certificate scheme. Companies wishing to relocate could not do so unless they met the criteria imposed by the Ministry of Town and Country Planning. This process inevitably became too prescriptive and incapable of opening the doors to all firms wanting to move in. New sectors, such as distribution and warehousing, service industries and white-collar work, were often outside the remit. For those firms that passed the criteria, the economic model of the development corporation to use rental income to invest in future construction meant that firms could not buy the land outright, but only lease it on a long-term basis. Many private firms may have been discouraged by the prospect of having to pay rent to the development corporation (Stevenage, 2005a). This factor ceased to be a concern in the later New Towns designed in the 1960s, when a more liberal approach to businesses was taken and a new focus emerged for attracting companies in from abroad.

A major early boost to the New Towns Programme therefore came when, in the early 1950s, English Electric (later the British Aircraft Corporation, then British Aerospace) selected a 70 acre (28 hectare) site in the town to develop new sectors such as surface-to-air missiles and aircraft components for the military. This soon prompted other companies, acting as sub-contractors, and Stevenage increasingly became a town dominated by this sector. Other firms attracted to Stevenage and the other first generation New Towns show that Britain's growing industries were predominantly in engineering, for machine tools, car manufacturing, clothes manufacturing, food processing, and the emerging high-technology manufacturing.

In the first New Town, Stevenage, the first new factory to be completed was in 1952 for Bay Tree Press. Existing firms already based in Stevenage also relocated into larger premises, including George W. King and W.H. Sanders (electronics). Alongside English Electric, incoming industries included Amoco Industrial Laboratories, Associated Bowater Industries, British Aircraft Corporation, British Visqueen, Ether Ltd, Flexile Metal Co., The Furniture Industries Research Association, Hawker

Siddley Dynamics, Hilmore Ltd, International Computers and Tabulators, International Exhibition Co-operative Wince Society Ltd, John Lewis & Co., Kodak, Mentmore Manufacturing Co., Shunic and Taylor Instrument Companies. Neighbouring Hatfield was home to De Havilland Aircraft Co., pioneers of the jet engine (later merging with Hawker Siddley Aviation), while Hemel Hempstead was home to Lucas Aerospace. This regional focus on aerospace, built up by the post-war demands of the Cold War, rapidly led to extensive job losses in the region in the wake of the disintegration of the Soviet Union in 1992. Many of the professional workers in those companies moved to other parts of the country, where similar firms were based, such as Bristol.

In Corby, a company town built by a private steelworks, Stewarts and Lloyds Ltd, in the 1930s, later becoming the nationalised British Steel, the Development Corporation's mission was to ensure a wide mix of employment to avoid over-reliance on this single industrial sector. This proved extremely hard to achieve in practice, and as late at 1974, the British Steel Corporation employed 50 per cent of the workforce. In Runcorn, the chemicals and brewery industries dominated with ICI, Guinness Breweries and Bass Charrington Ltd being the prime employers.

The dominance of a particular sector, either by virtue of size, or by clustering arising from strategic location or local skills base, created an inevitably brittle situation. A clear example was seen in Skelmersdale, with the abrupt closure of the town's two major employers, Thorn Colour Tubes and Courtaulds, in 1976. Similar problems arose in Redditch and Peterborough. By contrast, a more healthy mix emerged in Bracknell, where growth of the town catalysed the creation of the 'M4 corridor' west of London, beyond Heathrow airport. The strategic value of the location, and focus on the office services industry that evolved into the telecoms and computing sectors meant that Bracknell came to host the headquarters of over forty blue chip companies, including 3M, Panasonic, Waitrose, Cable & Wireless, Boehringer Ingelheim, BMW, Dell and Hewlett Packard.

In the 1950s, Glenrothes in Scotland was one of the most successful of the early New Towns where a deliberate strategy was developed to avoid dominance of a single industrial sector. Designed as a coal mining community, it had a parallel master-plan for alternative employment to take over when the local coalfield was exhausted. With the Scottish New Towns coming under the more comprehensive remit of the secretary of state for Scotland, the co-ordination difficulties between different ministries that plagued the English New Towns was avoided, and Glenrothes subsequently became a major centre for Britain's emerging electronics industry.

Looking at the names of the companies that relocated into the new sites being built in the New Towns, there are many familiar household names, and others now forgotten, that sound deeply old-fashioned today. In nearby Welwyn Garden City, factories and offices built by the Garden City Company in the 1920s hosted Murphy Radio and Nabisco. By the mid-1950s, the development corporation included other familiar names including ICI (Plastics division), Rank Xerox, Roche Products, Smith and Nephew, Smith, Kline and French (later Smith-Kline-Beecham) and G.K.N. Lincoln Electric.

In Basildon, to the east of London, the major employer was the tractor factory for the Ford Motor Co., and other employers included Ilford, Teleflex Products, Carreras, Marconi Wireless and Telegraph, York Shipley Ltd, Carsons Ltd, Standard Telephone and Yardley & Co. In Wales, Cwmbran's employers included British Nylon Spinners Ltd, Girling Ltd, Guest Keen & Nettlefolds, Alfa Laval Ltd, Saunders Valve Company, Quality Cleaners Ltd, Monmouthshire Co-operative Bakeries, Cambrian United Dairies, Atlas Copco, Perry Tool and Guage Co., Eylure (Erida) Ltd, Redifon Telecommunications, Siebe Gorman Ltd and Gwent County Council.

In East Kilbride in Scotland, the engineering focus was underpinned by the presence of the National Engineering Laboratory and the Building, Fuel and Road Research Stations. Major employers included Rolls Royce (aerospace), Sunbeam Electric, Mavor & Coulson (mining), John MacDonald & Co. (pneumatic tools), W.D. & J. Bain, Lansing-Bagnall, Perma-Sharp, Hayward-Tyler, Cooper & Co. Stores Ltd, Scotbeef Ltd, Kirriemuir Gingerbread, Kraft Foods, Schweppes (home), Laird-Porch Fashions, Lerose, Standard Telephone and Cables, Metal Box, Motorola Electronics and the Inland Revenue.

As chief centre of electronics industry in UK, Glenrothes, besides existing employers, The National Coal Board, Tullis Russell and Co. (est. 1809) and Fife Paper Manufacturers (est. 1816), major new firms included Hughes Microelectronics, Beckham Instruments Ltd, Brand Rex, GEC Telecommunications,

General Instrument Corporation and the Burroughs Corporation. In engineering, employers included Anderson Strathclyde, Intercobra Ltd, Robertson and Ferguson Ltd, Sandusky Ltd, Cessna Industrial Products Ltd and Thomas Salter Ltd (toys), and in food processing, Union Cold Storage and United Glass.

Co-ordinating delivery and building communities

The collective result of the mixed relationship between the New Town Development Corporations and external organisations from local and central government and the private sector was that life was extremely difficult in the early years. The resulting development of the towns may have seemed at times the worst of both worlds. Despite the appearance of being a government programme, the New Towns lacked full cross-government support directed from the Cabinet Office. The varied aspects of a town naturally cut across the specific remits of government departments. The first minister for town and country planning, Morrison, had foreseen this when scrutinising the proposals for the New Towns Programme before the end of the war. As the government historian J.B. Cullingworth describes, Morrison had,

> emphasised the need for a large scale effort from the government as a whole – the Board of Trade for assisting the synchronisation of movement of industry and population; the Ministry of Health for the programming and allocation of housing, and for the problems of water supply and sewerage; the Ministry of Agriculture and Fisheries for the orderly withdrawal of land in farming use and for drainage problems; the Ministry of Fuel and Power to facilitate arrangements for gas and electricity; the Ministry of Education for schools; the Ministry of Works for allocation of building permits; the Ministry of Labour and National Service for assistance in the supply of building and civil engineering labour; the Ministry of War Transport for improvements in communication; and so forth.

(Cullingworth, 1979: 12)

Not only did the New Town Development Corporations struggle to get the support they needed, but they also failed to benefit from the fully liberal, laissez-faire system that the Garden City Companies enjoyed in the 1920s and 1930s, whereby space could be offered to any employers interested in moving in, and social infrastructure such as hospitals were paid for privately, as at Letchworth and Welwyn.

This was, of course, a consequence of the post-war context. For much of the nineteenth century, schools and hospitals had been either private or provided by churches or charitable institutions, and business had a relatively free rein. The expansion of the state into the management of all of these areas of life, via the centrally controlled wartime economy and then via the welfare state, meant a transformation in the relationship between society and government. In pursuit of equality and social welfare, the size of the state increased and new ministries and departments were created to administer provision of these social amenities.

However, although the New Towns Programme suffered from often unfair criticism from the press, in order to attract employers to relocate into the New Towns, the Development Corporations became adept at promoting an invariably positive image. In this, they pioneered the application of marketing principles that are commonplace in urban development today. The difficulties of co-ordination that did exist were generally short-lived, and once the initial construction was complete life could go on.

The promotional magazine of Stevenage Development Corporation, called *Purpose*, provided a 'brickbats' section, where residents could write in with questions or complaints.

> Are we ever to have the playgrounds so desperately needed to prevent the children from playing in the streets and straying on to the main roads? When will the Corporation do something about it?
>
> Something should be done to limit the speed of traffic in Shephall Lane. It is becoming exceedingly dangerous for adults let alone children.
>
> Is it true that the Corporation will not allow residents to put up the new aerials for Commercial Television?

(*Purpose*, 1955: 8)

The publishing of these gave the Corporation the opportunity to showcase the actual playgrounds, traffic-calming measures or best methods for attaching TV aerials. As the towns started to gain critical mass of population, their success started to become apparent. By 1959, *Purpose* magazine was filled with adverts for local employers and new products. Huge numbers of houses were built (at a rate far greater than that achieved in the 1980s, 1990s or 2000s), jobs were created, employers were able to expand into new premises, investment was attracted in from abroad, new schools and hospitals did get built. When considering the combined challenge of delivering housing, social infrastructure and employment, it is clear that the New Towns did not evolve as smoothly as expected, but neither were they the disasters that some thought them to be (Aldridge, 1979: 71).

Because the underlying concept of the New Towns was to ensure a lack of outward commuting or internal unemployment, housing was to be balanced with employment. As such, migration to the New Towns was initially promoted at companies, for whom the offer of cheaper running costs, better transport connections, modern office buildings, and happier workers was extremely appealing. Firms that were to relocate would offer their staff a house as part of the package, and the message, as seen in the promotional film *Charley in New Town* was that quality of life would be vastly superior to that in the cities. Mary Tabor, housing officer at Stevenage New Town, describes the experience of promoting the towns to potential new residents,

> They used to come down in coaches with their wives on a Saturday. They used to be driven round the town . . . and I used to have a microphone, say 'this is where the factory is going to be', in a wide open space . . . We used to go to schools – as soon as there were any schools built. That was a tremendous carrot always – that they were going to have these wonderful schools built for the children. That was what they were concerned with.
>
> (Stevenage, 2005b)

Firms relocating to the New Towns would build their factories and ideally want their workers to move en masse the moment they were finished. In reality this was extremely difficult, so workers relocated in phases, the rest commuting via factory shuttle buses until they could move house. However, with the first new residents satisfied with their housing, their colleagues were invariably keen to follow them. Another of the first generation, Michael Cotter, later a town councillor, recalled moving to Stevenage on 15 February 1952,

> I can remember my wife standing now, with a four bedroom house in Rockingham Way – still there – standing at the bottom of the steps and looking up the stairs and saying 'is it all mine?' Yes, and the kids were having a great time. The two eldest ones running in the front room, through the dining room, through the kitchen and back in the front room again. Round and round in circles. Couldn't believe it, the freedom you know. And that was it for the hard grind ... We had very little furniture because you lived in one room and we didn't have the money to buy it.
>
> (Stevenage, 2005c)

The social impact of everyone moving into a new community had a range of effects. For many young women, with their husbands enjoying the social atmosphere of the workplace, their early experiences were less positive. As Mary Tabor recalls,

> I think when you talk to people who came in the early days, a lot of the wives say, 'oh it was pretty awful to begin with'. I mean it's thrilling to have a new house. They're absolutely thrilled at it and it's their first home and so on, but that wears off and then they could be desperately lonely . . . most of them either had children or were going to have babies. They weren't working on the whole, they were at home, they were far away from friends and of course if they had lived in town all their lives, it was pretty ghastly to have to walk two miles to the shops and something like that.
>
> (Stevenage, 2005b)

Sufficient essential amenities and services for new incoming residents were of course vital, and failure to provide these helped fuel emotive media stories about 'New Town Blues'. However, this was not a new phenomenon, and had been widely experienced on the interwar municipal housing estates, new suburbs (where it was dubbed 'suburban neurosis') and in the new housing estates of the expanded towns (Ward, 1993: 50). But where developments such as Manchester's Wythenshawe or London's Dagenham had lacked facilities because of poor design, the New Towns represented better provision, once it had actually been delivered. Delays in provision of services such as public transport, street lighting, telephones and hospitals were all frequently mentioned as causing concern for residents. These concerns remain familiar in new development today.

Throughout the initial building of the New Towns during the 1950s and 1960s, these problems were well understood by government and the quality of provision varied on a site-by-site basis depending on the exact circumstances at any given time (Clapson, 1998: 145–7). In the case of the Stevenage, which as the first New Town was the first to experience many of these issues, the formation of residents' associations helped bring pressure on the development corporation. Examples included houses that lacked paths to their front doors or gardens with no topsoil. The residents' groups were instrumental in addressing these problems and getting shops, telephone boxes and post boxes installed (Carruthers, 1996: 31).

The largest cause of the so-called 'New Town Blues' was not so much the experience of living in the chaos of a major construction, but that people simply did not have the social support networks they had in the cities. In London, people had enjoyed regular bus services, long-established local shops and other amenities, as Mary Tabor, recalled, 'People used to talk about missing the bright lights of London . . . but what they were missing was their families' (Carruthers, 1996: 22).

Most of the first generation relocating to the New Towns were in their mid-twenties and either had or were expecting babies. The New Towns thus soon gained the nickname of pram towns. Having moved from long-established communities where they would see their parents and relatives on a daily basis, this sudden lack of support meant obvious difficulties – although naturally a similar phenomenon exists whenever anyone moves to an unfamiliar area away from family, and this had been widely reported in the 1920s as the phenomenon of 'suburban neurosis'. In fact, people in the New Towns soon turned to each other for support, and a strong sense of community emerged.

The range of experience of early residents was captured in a number of sociological studies that debated various aspects of this issue (see Clapson, 1998).

For the development corporations, ensuring that the experiences of newcomers was positive became part of the remit of housing officers and public relations managers, who soon started to redefine themselves as community development specialists. One problem was that since the New Town would have none of the normal informal social events and networking opportunities such as clubs or societies already in existence, there was a need to actively encourage their creation. In Stevenage, amateur dramatic clubs became common, and in Harlow, music groups from skiffle bands to string quartets achieved a wide reputation. Balancing the need to take community development seriously while avoiding a paternalistic attitude was a complex issue for development corporations and was addressed differently in different places (Ward, 1993: 54). Only in 1967 did the government produce a report, *The Needs of New Communities*, to outline some of the issues. Janice Scott Lodge recounted the experience of moving to Cumbernauld in the mid-1960s, revealing the reality for New Town residents,

Although there are yet few social amenities like cinemas, dance halls and tea shops, the social life in Cumbernauld is thriving. The young women, housebound by young families, are intellectually starved and grasp eagerly at any opportunity for mental stimulus. A lecture course in almost any subject can expect to be oversubscribed within hours of being announced, local women's groups have enormous memberships, and the further education classes received such an overwhelming response that the Board of Education was forced to advertise frantically for extra teachers.

(*Town and Country Planning Journal*, 1967a: 68)

The masterplans for the New Towns completed by the corporations and their consultants focused on physical delivery more than any subsequent social development. Throughout the development of the New Towns, changing social circumstances and spontaneity were not as successfully addressed as perhaps they might have been. Social change was happening faster than

Early residents of Cumbernauld New Town. Copyright: North Lanarkshire District Council.

the process of physical development. As Gerald Brooke-Taylor, Community Development Officer at the Hemel Hempstead Development Corporation and later the Dawley/Telford Development Corporation, described in the mid-1960s,

Fashions and needs are now changing at such a pace that public demand expressed today indicates what was needed yesterday. In the 1950s, the public were slow to grasp the changing pattern of teenage behaviour. Commercial experts created the coffee bar as a venture into the unknown. And few people in 1953 would have asked for the bowling alley, which later in the decade was to prove such an attraction. It was only the minority of young people who started the beat groups, which later made millions and altered the basis of popular dancing and light music.

(cited in Ward, 1993: 56)

With elements such as venues for dances or drama seen as a lower priority than commercial properties, the social demand was met by grassroots action. In one instance, an architect of Stevenage Development Corporation created a factory with a sloping floor supposedly for public meetings, but also to serve as an unofficial theatre.

What gave the New Towns spirit was the collective will of residents to make the towns work, and to provide whatever they felt it needed. Despite indifference from central government and the public at large, the New Towns ultimately succeeded because their residents wanted them to work. As early resident and later town councillor Michael Cotter describes the early days,

I would say that was the best time from the point of communal living that Stevenage has ever enjoyed. We were all together, we are all in the same boat and we hung together . . . And that was how we came to live in Stevenage, the family have grown up here . . . we love it. The best town in the world.

(Stevenage, 2005c)

The first phase in the life of a New Town was when construction was still ongoing and residents moving in for the first time had the lives of pioneers. What it felt like to move to a New Town must be understood in comparison to the circumstances that people had left behind. For most new arrivals, the majority young couples, the reality was that moving out of a home shared with parents and in-laws in the overcrowded inner city was a blessed relief.

People's personal attitudes clearly affected whether, in the long-run, they found the experience positive. Some felt bad at leaving their wider family behind, others were glad to get away, and others even felt guilty at having got a better life for themselves. Some researchers even noted that a certain percentage of people were likely to be dissatisfied by virtue of their psychological outlook alone, not as a result of the conditions of life in the New Town (Clapson, 1998).

Over time, some people moved on to live in other towns. Others had their elderly relatives or other family members move to join them. Overall, the feelings associated with moving to a New Town were the same as those felt by moving anywhere unfamiliar.

These feelings could be ambiguous, and viewed positively, the fact that all residents were incomers meant a strong feeling of camaraderie and a shared purpose in making the town successful. Viewed negatively, the conditions of moving to a town

that was to remain a building site for years meant obvious inconvenience. As another early Stevenage resident, Thelma Sultzbach, recalled:

While I was grateful to have a home of our own after five years of living in other people's, I am sure if you spoke to any of the pioneers of those early days, one would find their outstanding memory is of dust and mud. We had no gardens, no roads, no pavements or footpaths, no telephones . . . and we were surrounded by construction. It doesn't take much imagination to picture the outlandish conditions in which we lived.

(Ward, 1993: 50)

Creating balanced communities

The balance of jobs to residents succeeded in ensuring extremely low unemployment and also a lack of commuting. The nature of the communities in the New Towns was forged, inescapably, by the demographic of the workers of the companies that chose to re-locate to the New Towns. These companies were those that were encouraged by the selection process, whilst others, put off by the paperwork, could still relocate elsewhere, such as to sites in the existing towns and cities, and new sites being built as part of the Expanded Towns Programme in the 1950s and 1960s. In the New Towns, housing was initially offered to companies to distribute to their workers, but this was not as prescriptive as may be imagined since if someone quit their job and chose to commute elsewhere, they would not be prevented from doing so, they simply continued as tenants of the development corporation.

However, it was assumed by the policy-makers of the New Towns Programme that the towns would acquire a broad balance of people. The Garden City model at the heart of the New Towns Programme aimed to create a well-balanced society, representative of society at large. Such efforts can be seen at work in colonial cities such as Adelaide in Australia and Christchurch in New Zealand. However, as with these nineteenth-century cities, attracting this range of people was extremely difficult. The challenge of obtaining a social mix hinged on providing a broad range of housing types. Whereas

Table 8.1 Estimated housing completions by 31 December 1966 for all UK New Towns. Source: *Town and Country Planning Journal*, 1967a: 38.

Development Corporation	134,122	84%
Local Authority	14,643	9%
Private Sector	10,557	7%

the development corporation architecture departments soon became adept at producing large volumes of mass-housing to be rented to workers, producing high-quality homes for purchase that met the expectations of the middle classes was beset by a number of problems.

First, the development corporations tried to attract owner-occupiers by selling plots to private developers or in some cases to individuals wanting to build their own homes. However, since construction in the 1950s was extremely expensive there were few takers, especially in the New Towns further from London. The sluggish economic conditions of the 1950s meant that uptake was in single or double digits only (Aldridge, 1979: 47). Although the corporations realised there was a need for more high-income housing in the new towns, market forces had made this almost impossible to provide. Public policy had failed to conduct what would now be called the necessary 'stakeholder engagement' to get the private sector investors on board. Mortgage lenders had little interest in navigating the new legal territory of development corporation freeholds and without them the home-owning aspiration of the middle classes could not be met. The New Towns were therefore regarded as a working-class rental sector demographic.

By the second generation of New Towns, and the expansion of the first generation, in the 1960s, the situation had not got any easier. Building societies were still reluctant to provide mortgages, unsure that modernist housing designs with their radical layouts would hold their value. In the end, some corporations themselves became mortgage lenders (Aldridge, 1979: 97). Private developers did build housing, as did local authorities, but by the end of 1966, the total number of completions for the whole of the UK New Towns were 134,122 homes built by the development corporations for rental, 14,643

as council housing by local authorities, and 10,557 by the private sector.

By the end of the 1960s, more than 90 per cent of the New Towns' housing stock was publicly owned and rented to their occupiers. Meanwhile, the managers of the companies based in the New Towns often commuted in from elsewhere. As the New Town Development Corporation at Glenrothes noted,

> one of the most intransigent problems with which the New Town is faced is the five o'clock executive exit . . . In the surrounding county of Fife . . . with its cosy villages and little pan-tiled seaports, there are within easy reach of Glenrothes numerous attractive places in which to set up home. This appeals to many executives who have come to work in the town; yet socially, there is need to encourage such people and their families to live within its boundaries.
>
> (Osborn and Whittick, 1977: 415)

The housing stock of the New Towns was thus unique compared to that of other towns and cities in the UK. The wider economic instability of the British economy in the Macmillan years meant that despite a desire otherwise, the New Towns really had become predominantly left-wing enterprises. The large-scale public ownership also became hard to dislodge, as the significant gap between mortgage repayments and corporation rents meant that no existing tenants had any interest in buying their homes. By the early 1970s, under the Conservatives, they sought to increase levels of owner-occupation in the New Towns up to 50 per cent by offering New Town homes for sale at levels of 20 per cent below their market value (Aldridge, 1979: 97). This became the precursor to the highly significant 'Right to Buy' policy for council housing under the Conservative Government of 1979–97. By 2005, Harlow had a mix of 62 per cent owner-occupiers, 30 per cent rented council, 4 per cent housing association and 5 per cent private rented (Harlow, 2005) – the second highest proportion of council housing in England. Ultimately, the attempt to shift the demographic profile of the New Towns to create a more socially balanced community failed. This failure to create a 'social balance' was to shape the long-term character of the New Towns, and their success as places.

The Birdcage, Harlow, 1960s. Copyright: The Museum of Harlow.

Part 3

Living in the New Towns

Criticisms of the New Towns

Photographer C.J. Clarke (www.cjclarke.com).

Throughout the early years, the progress of the New Towns Programme and its the apparent success or failure was never far from the newspaper headlines. Such short-term perspectives were extremely politicised with many on the right keen to tar the reputation of the New Towns as a failed socialist experiment. Against this was the view that the New Towns were providing crucial sites for British industry to expand and giving around a quarter of a million working-class city dwellers substantially improved living conditions. Establishing the truth of either position was in reality highly complex.

On the one hand, creating all the functions of a town required cross-government co-ordination. The territorial nature of the different Whitehall fiefdoms, each competing for Treasury funds, put the Ministry of Town and Country Planning, in charge of the New Towns Programme, at a disadvantage. Suffering from being a young department, it had yet to establish its credentials or influence. The development corporations, who bore responsibility for successfully creating their towns, were also brand new organisations that had to constantly negotiate with various local authorities as well as the central government departments in order to co-ordinate delivery of necessary infrastructure.

The development corporations also had to promote an image of progress and opportunity to attract employers. The public image of the New Towns Programme was vital to its success since this would act as a self-fulfilling prophecy. If people started to believe that the New Towns Programme was a failure, its failure would be guaranteed; employers would not wish to relocate to the towns and the critical mass of population would not be met. On the other hand, if people believed the New Towns were successful, people would move there, and their success would be guaranteed.

Establishing whether the New Towns were in fact being well planned and developed was another matter, however. In practice, the failure to answer basic questions about the success or otherwise of the design principles and construction process can be understood through the story of the New Towns research programme. In 1946, the New Towns Committee, chaired by Lord Reith, had stated that a research element was an essential part of the New Towns Programme (Reith, 1946, paragraph 283). To ensure impartiality, this should be managed neither by the government department nor the New Town Development Corporations but by an independent organisation, co-ordinated by a central advisory committee.

When the first development corporations were established, Monica Felton, a member of the Reith Committee (and later Chairman of the development corporations of Peterlee and then Stevenage), was called on to oversee the creation of the research programme. She sought the services of the London School of Economics to investigate relevant issues. The Ministry of Town and Country Planning readily accepted that they would pay for the work, but progress stalled over whether such research should be entirely independent. Would its authors be free to publish the results, or would the research belong to the ministry, who may choose not to make the results public if they thought it expedient (Cullingworth, 1979: 350)?

By May 1948, ministry civil servants had instead been appointed to answer general questions for the benefit of the development corporations, but all material generated was to be confidential, not to be published or disseminated. The ministry set up a library that certain development corporation staff members could visit but in practice this served to bring documents from each development corporation back to the centre rather than distribute findings outwards to benefit progress in the different towns.

In addition, the research conducted in-house by the ministry itself suffered from having no access to relevant research undertaken by other departments. The Ministry of Health was in charge of national housing policy and the Board of Trade was in charge of the national industrial strategy. Both held relevant expertise in housing and industrial issues. If independent bodies such as universities were to carry out the work, it was feared that they would have even less chance of gaining access to crucial government documents. The contribution of sociologists was also regarded with suspicion, their findings thought likely to fail tests of objectivity and suffer from political bias. The commissioning of any original research therefore failed to get off the ground.

After long-running controversy, including the failure to record basic information, the research section was abandoned in December 1950, barely eighteen months after its first formal meeting. As historian J.B. Cullingworth revealed, 'Research had clearly been shown to be a dangerous matter which was far more likely to give rise to embarrassment and indeed acrimony than to produce useful guidelines for policy' (Cullingworth, 1979: 358).

The resurrection of the New Towns Programme in the 1960s saw a repeat of the same discussions on the need for research. Again, for identical reasons, these came to nothing. The proposed new research programme had identified ten main points to investigate, commenting, 'It seems incredible that after fifteen years there should be so many basic questions about which we are still speculating – very largely in the dark' (cited in Cullingworth, 1979: 367). These questions, which remain immensely relevant today, were:

How big should new towns be?
How far from their parent cities should they be sited?

How much land should they occupy?
How valid is the neighbourhood concept?
What sort of town centres are called for?
Could the existing industrial layouts be improved?
What had been learned about communication and traffic?
What kind of housing layouts do people prefer?
What social provision should be made, and when?
Are new towns really profitable as investments?'

(Cullingworth, 1979: 367)

These questions had the potential to act as political dynamite; answering them threatened to make or break the New Towns programme. So they were quietly put to one side and the experimental design concepts remained tried but effectively untested.

Poster for June 1967 TCPA conference on the New Towns.

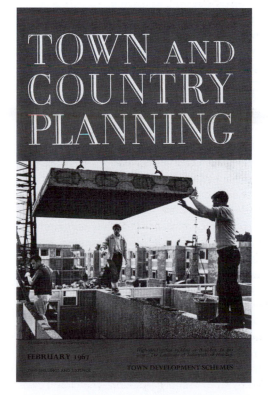

Cover of the *Town and Country Planning* journal in 1967 shows 'industrialised housing' in Basildon.

In the absence of any formal, centrally co-ordinated research programme, the only published analysis on the New Towns was provided in *Town and Country Planning*, the journal of the Town and Country Planning Association (TCPA). As the campaigning organisation originally founded by Ebenezer Howard, the TCPA had become the chief lobbyists for the New Towns Programme. Every year, they published information collated from the annual reports of each New Town Development Corporation accompanied by articles on various interesting aspects of progress in the New Towns. Yet, like the development corporations and the chief politicians responsible – many of whom were members of the TCPA – there was a cultural bias towards promotion of success and away from criticism. More than twenty years after the New Towns Programme had been created the vice-presidents of the TCPA included Lord Reith and Lord Silkin, as well as Sir Frederick Osborn, whilst the TCPA's director was Wyndham Thomas, then chairman of the Peterborough Development Corporation (*Town and Country Planning*, 1967a). As Birmingham University's Meryl Aldridge, described in *The British New Towns: A Programme without a Policy*,

> On the new towns, [the journal] Town and Country Planning remains resolutely propagandist and even missionary – and why not? The Association is, after all, one of the most effective pressure groups operating openly in this country. Given its vested interest, though, it has been to the detriment of constructive criticism of the new towns that the systematic production of statistical data, articles and even books has been left almost entirely to the Association. Such is the commitment of many prominent members of the TCPA to the new towns movement, that detached comment or attempts to clarify concepts have been interrupted as at best irrelevant, or even as destructive criticism.
>
> (Aldridge, 1979: 189)

The chairs and other staff members of the development corporations regularly met each other and held conferences to share their experiences and air concerns. Only from 1970 did these arrangements lead to an official organisation, The New Towns Association, which, as Aldridge described, 'is a shoestring operation not, apparently, equipped for or geared to research,

nor to sharing information with outsiders' (Aldridge, 1979: 188). Naturally, this too was not a forum for challenging any fundamental assumptions. The New Towns Programme was subject to clear political and economic momentum. And the context of post-war reconstruction meant delivering houses and jobs was more important than testing design principles. The first great phase of rationally planned town building thus avoided any rigorous scrutiny.

The architects' critique of the New Towns

With the absence of any independent critique of the New Towns Programme, the first major objections came from outside. The professionals most qualified to scrutinise the emerging plans were architects and their first major critique was published in the *Architectural Review* in July 1953. Gordon Cullen, later to found the 'Townscape' movement, wrote an article 'Prairie Planning in the New Towns' highlighting the impact of the low-density approach to housing. An accompanying article, 'The failure of the New Towns' by J.M. Richards, furthered this criticism. Richards said that rather than living in an urban streetscape with a sense of enclosure, as with a historic market town, the first New Town housing being built at Harlow was located in a scattered arrangement, so that residents 'found themselves marooned in a desert of grass verges and concrete'. Only in the neighbourhood shopping centre, The Stow, was a sense of urban place achieved (Bullock, 2002: 135). Gibberd responded saying there was no concrete in Harlow's housing. The plans were deliberately turning against the pressure of the city and seeking instead the marriage of town and country, as Howard had intended.

The arrangement achieved at Harlow was of course in deliberate contrast to high-density working-class housing in industrial cities such as Leeds and London. This meant no gardens – just a yard – and municipal parks meeting the needs for green space. Gibberd encouraged the emergence of 'landscape architecture', eulogising the new English School of Landscape as, 'probably the country's greatest contribution to art' (cited in Elwall, 1999: 15). In partnership with landscape designer Sylvia Crowe, his designs for Harlow aimed to create a *genius loci* – sense of place – that met Ebenezer Howard's vision of a union between countryside and town. Housing density was at a level set deliberately low by the Reith Committee to counter the overcrowded conditions of the inner-city slum. In Harlow's early phases these were as low as four dwellings per hectare (today's standard is over thirty).

Low density had only been possible because the economics of building on agricultural land made this affordable for the first time. In cities the value of land meant buildings were crowded together and had to rise upwards to gain space. The New Towns offered a new beginning where the health benefits of open countryside were to be incorporated within the borders of the town. Gibberd made this break with the traditional urban form explicit in cross-sections that compared Harlow to a traditional town.

Yet, for Richards and Cullen, this low density and landscaping meant Harlow and the other New Towns were not towns at all, but merely suburban housing estates isolated from each other by functionless green space and large-scale road systems. Ignoring the provision of social amenities, they thought Harlow had not improved on the pre-war suburban sprawl or London County Council housing estates. Richards directly blamed Osborn and the Garden Cities/Town and Country Planning Association for this state of affairs. The New Towns Programme, he maintained, had squandered the opportunity provided by post-war reconstruction to build towns, and had experimented with these new ideas with little appreciation for the character of place that would result.

In the immediate post-war years virtually all available architects were working either for development corporations or government departments on reconstruction. For the next generation of architects emerging in the 1950s, the evidence of what was being built in the New Towns was deeply uninspiring. The housing produced on a mass-production scale, with pre-war ideas of urban planning, prompted a new generation of architects to lobby for change. Leading this were Alison and Peter Smithson, who in 1955 attacked both the Garden Cities Movement and the Modern Movement for their failure.

Each generation feels a new dissatisfaction and conceives of a new idea of order . . . The Garden City Movement has mothered the New Towns . . . the careful provision of amenities, has reached its ultimate anti-climax.

(cited in Bullock, 2002: 137)

The criticism that the New Towns lacked the qualities of an urban place prompted a new approach for the design of Cumbernauld. Designated by the Conservative Government in 1955, the initial plans submitted for approval in 1958 set density deliberately high at sixty-five dwellings per hectare to produce an inherently more urban feel. Its great architectural innovation, however, was to create the town centre as one vast, single building.

Across eight levels, it attempted to include all the facilities needed in a town within a single structure. Architect Geoffrey Copcutt had designed the megastructure according to Le Corbusier's ideas of the Radiant City. Corporation executives were to live in penthouses on the top, able to leave in their cars on a high-speed road network that ran right under the centre. Pedestrians meanwhile would traverse open green spaces through car-free routes. Professor Colin Buchanan's influential government report, *Traffic in Towns*, in 1963, had also praised the town, even though only in its planning phase, as, 'the first example in this country of a serious attempt to elucidate the relationship between activities and traffic . . . the whole town is, in a sense, a gigantic Radburn layout' (Buchanan, 1963: 166). Radburn had become an icon of traffic segregation; the design qualities of the original (and incompleted) New Jersey town, became ever-more distorted with each new application in the UK.

By this time, the second generation of New Towns such as Skelmersdale, Redditch and Dawley (Telford) had started, with vast covered shopping centres, large road networks, extensive green spaces and woodland, and pedestrian-only routes. When Cumbernauld's first phase was actually opened in 1967, TCPA's Osborn and Whittick commented, 'It is premature to judge the architectural effect until the centre is completed. It promises much that is unusual and impressive . . . One virtue of the town, and it is no mean one, is that it has a more complete segregation of vehicles and pedestrians than in any of the earlier new towns' (Osborn and Whittick, 1977: 425–6).

The Institute of American Architects had given the town its highest accolades and the residents too were initially happy. Compared to the housing in run-down Glasgow, which had been the worst in Europe (Parker, 2008: 72), Cumbernauld offered a clear improvement in quality of life. The comments of the McCluskie family, who moved there in 1974, echoed those

The town centre of Cumbernauld was designed as a single mega-structure. Copyright: North Lanarkshire District Council.

Cumbernauld's centre was built on top of a steep hill. Copyright: North Lanarkshire District Council.

of the earliest New Town residents twenty years earlier: 'We had a garden and our own front door. We had neighbours who were like ourselves, families with children. And it was safe for our 12-year-old son' (*Telegraph*, 2002).

Once occupied, however, the reality of life in the town diverged somewhat from the assumptions made by the architects and planners. *Washington Post* journalist Leonard Downie Jr summarised the situation in his 1972 article, 'The Disappointing British New Towns':

In Cumbernauld . . . planners met head on the problems of the automobile and the sterile suburban atmosphere of most of the new towns . . . Like the center of a medieval town, Cumbernauld's center was to be bustling with almost around-the-clock activity . . . It was thus expected that the project's layout would compel residents to walk to the center, and that the spatial, commercial and social variety they would find would keep them there . . . But Cumbernauld has not fulfilled these expectations . . . The steep climb from all directions to the town center is too difficult to make with baby carriages or laden grocery carts, and often is too dangerously slippery without encumberances in bad weather. Although the stores, offices and apartments were put right into the first stage of the center, relatively few social facilities, outside several

bars in a new hotel, were opened. So, while the world's architects visited, studied and debated the unusual Cumbernauld center, the community's new residents got into their cars and drove elsewhere to shop and play. Cumbernauld now has the highest rate of car ownership and use in Scotland. Its residents have turned their backs on its famous center to live most of their out-of-home lives elsewhere in nearby suburbs of Glasgow.

(Downie, 1972a)

The residents had little complaint about the town centre, except that it was dull. The principal leisure activity was staying at home watching television. With rising mobility, the pedestrian routes were unused, except by the town's children. The second generation New Towns starting with Cumbernauld led to a reaction in the third generation of New Towns, culminating in a super-sized Garden City model in Milton Keynes, and a largely suburban development model in the 'partnership' New Towns of Peterborough, Northampton and Warrington. Downie's summary read,

In many ways, Britain's new towns do not offer a view into the future of urban development, but rather a reflection of the past and present of American suburbs. In fact, the curving, tree-softened streets and segregated residential,

115

commercial and industrial zones of the early garden cities like Welwyn are the ancestors of suburban subdivision 'planned communities' in the United States. Stevenage's shopping center is the forerunner of the countless shopping malls that dot American suburbia, and its 30-year-old land use plan is much like that for the suburb-like Columbia, Maryland 'new town'. As Britain and the United States have gradually traded places in recent years as model and imitator, the freeways, interchanges and sprawling drive-in shopping, service and cultural center planned for Milton Keynes are copies of the latest in California exurban development.

(Downie, 1972a)

Like the American suburbs, the New Towns were also economically stratified, and the process of decentralisation from the British cities to the New Towns produced exactly the same effect as suburbanisation had in the USA. The employers relocating out to the new locations brought skilled workers with them, meaning that the working-class communities of the inner cities lost their most economically active members. With the predominantly white, skilled workers leaving areas such as the East End of London and depressed suburban areas of Walthamstow, Tottenham and Southall, 'mostly low income and jobless Pakistani, Indian and black immigrants remain today, trapped in ever worsening ghetto-like conditions' (Downie, 1972a).

The awareness of the state of the inner cities rose sharply in the 1970s, leading to criticism that the New Towns policy had failed. Wyndham Portal had warned in the 1940s that the objective of urban depopulation required simultaneous and co-ordinated urban regeneration in the inner cities. As Downie identified, one of the unintended side effects of the New Towns was that the areas that were depopulated of their historic white populations then became centres for migrants arriving from the British Empire to work. From Notting Hill to Brixton, Tottenham to Southall, the inflow and consolidation of Asian and Caribbean communities forced London to embrace cultural diversity and, ultimately, equality.

Richards' critique of the New Towns was that they were doing things differently, but in a way that was essentially anti-urban. Downie's critique, however, was that the New Towns had embraced car-based urbanism without properly considering the consequences or possible alternatives. Despite repeatedly returning to the vision of Ebenezer Howard, the unintended result of the New Towns Programme was therefore an increase in essentially suburban ways of life. Osborn and Abercrombie's campaign against the railway suburbs creating a 'nation of straphangers' (Abercrombie, 1944) led instead, ultimately to car-based, suburban lifestyles.

The desire for a balance between housing and employment had been a success. All the New Towns easily secured minimal commuting distances, but for everything else, the car was the default option. As a promotional brochure from Cumbernauld Development Corporation proudly proclaimed,

> Cumbernauld has the good location, communications, distribution network and working conditions that industry needs. It also has the good housing, trees, schools, fresh air, shops, countryside, clubs, pubs, sports facilities – in a word, the good environment – that people need. To work well. To live well. And the distance between the two, between home and work 'just three minutes drive' – and that's when the traffic is busy!' (reproduced in Aldridge, 1979)

Between the first generation of New Towns such as Stevenage and Harlow and the second, starting with Cumbernauld, the car received greater attention. The television, too, allowed people to be entertained at home, reducing the need for daily socialising. This had a subtle influence on the provision of community activities affecting the appeal of the urban centres as a focus for the life of a town. Some towns, such as Harlow, were proud of their Playhouse theatre and music groups. Stevenage's amateur dramatic clubs and arts centre were extremely popular. The relationship between local social activity and freedom of movement via the private car is a complex issue, and clearly the first New Towns were defined by walking and neighbour relations.

With the second generation, modernist designs came to the fore, including better provision for the car. However, in the Swedish new town of Vällingby (which Downie heaped praise on), the modern architecture and urbanism was centred on a strong public transport link provided by the local rail service to nearby Stockholm. The apparent success of Sweden versus the apparent failure of Britain must consider its smaller population, different social attitude and, ultimately, different tax and administrative arrangements. The place therefore appeared to have a different quality than in Britain.

In 2005, six thousand people voted Cumbernauld the 'Most Dismal Town in Scotland', describing the town centre building (which was never, in fact, completed as intended) as 'a rabbit warren on stilts', 'the Lego fantasy of an unhappy child' and 'abysmal: dark oppressive spaces, blocked routes and mess' (Welch, 2007).

Yet, although the centre had failed because it was hard to walk to, unappealing when you got there, and frankly simple to drive anywhere else, many basic aspects of the New Towns were clearly successful. There was employment, and it was easy to get to. As Tim Abrahams, Deputy Editor of *Prospect Magazine*, said in response to Cumbernauld's tarnished reputation,

> Reading between the lines, people in Cumbernauld and the surrounding regions are rightly annoyed. Cumbernauld is an affluent town that is failing to live up to its potential. According to the Information & Statistics Division of NHS Scotland, and Communities Scotland, in 2004 the Average Gross Household Income in Cumbernauld was higher than the national average. The number of children in workless households and the number of income support claimants was lower than the national average. And yet the average house price in Cumbernauld is £357K a full ten grand less than the mean cost of a house throughout the country' (cited in Welch, 2007).

Strategic planning and urban design in the New Towns

In the 1950s, Richards' criticism was ostensibly architectural, but was really about urbanism, as was the Smithsons'. Downie also criticised the way the towns had been designed as a whole, but from the perspective of the early 1970s could see how the towns operated in reality. Understanding the long-term consequences of strategic planning decisions meant a better assessment of

The original megastructure of Cumbernauld centre is now accompanied by the Antonine Shopping Centre, opened in 2007. Copyright: North Lanarkshire District Council.

the relative success or failure of the New Towns. The economic success of a New Town then feeds all other aspects of its success. Economic decline inescapably means social and physical decline. With the hindsight of several decades, the following categories are clearly of great significance. Their location, mix of employment and intended size – all of which were decided ultimately by central government – have been fundamental to their relative long-term success.

Firstly, location. Access to major transport corridors is a prime consideration. Cumbernauld, for instance, is located conveniently between Glasgow and Edinburgh. Glenrothes is located on the route from Dundee across the Tay Bridge to Edinburgh. Warrington lies between the M6, M56 and M62 linking Manchester, Liverpool and North Wales. Milton Keynes lies on the M1, midway between London and Birmingham. Peterborough is at the centre of a road and rail network linking north and south, east and west. Bracknell is between the M3 and M4 and close to London's Heathrow Airport, while Crawley is adjacent to London's Gatwick Airport. Telford is somewhat isolated but benefits from its own motorway, the M54 linking it directly to Britain's second city Birmingham. On the other hand, Redditch, Peterlee and Irvine are less well connected, and

Skelmersdale, whilst adjacent to a motorway, is not really on an existing route as, say, nearby Warrington is.

The employment mix can then also be clearly seen, with the towns that are most reliant on single major employers or certain industrial sectors being the most vulnerable. Those with the greatest variety are better able to adapt to shocks. The dominance of the defence and aerospace sector in Stevenage, Welwyn, Hatfield and Redditch, or the British Leyland plant in Livingston, or Corby's vast steel works, serve as examples of problems resulting from this imbalance. Whereas Glenrothes, with its post-coal mining strategy or Milton Keynes, with its broad provision of employment types, have proved more resilient.

A further, highly significant, element affecting the long-term success of different New Towns relates to the way central government revised their housing targets. From the first generation, Newton Aycliffe was initially too small to be viable. Its target population was thus increased midway through its construction. In the second generation, changing economic circumstances meant Skelmersdale's target population was revised downwards, depriving the town of the critical mass to ensure various social amenities its original planners intended (House of Commons, 2002a).

The questions originally posed by the shortlived research programme remain fundamental. How big should new towns be? It would seem the bigger the better. The most obvious amenities of a secondary school, estimated at needing a population of around 10,000 people, is a minimum so that children up to the age of 16 are not forced to travel by bus everyday to another town. To have choice in the sorts of school available a population of 50,000 could give around three to five of them. Triple that population up to 200,000 and social and commercial amenities can extend to arts, further education and major centres.

The question of where towns are best located is no longer seen in relation to the desire to decant population from the terrible conditions of the inner cities. Nonetheless, the role of a large nearby city can help underpin the economic life of a town. And as for how much land should they occupy, factors such as density, the relationship between land value and property value, provision of local amenities and the exact conditions of the local site can all play a role. The extent to which the social provisions made in community building for the New Towns, and the economic model utilised by the development corporations can clearly provide lessons. How these developed in reality is discussed in more detail later.

Questions of the long-term impacts of the urban design features of the New Towns became increasingly clear over the years. The validity of the neighbourhood unit as a design concept, and the nature of town centres, industrial estates and housing design will be addressed in more detail later. However, in general, in the wake urbanists such as Jane Jacobs, responding to the consequences of Robert Moses in *The Life and Death of Great American Cities* (Jacobs, 1961), twentieth-century urbanism has been reassessed. In Britain, the evidence is provided by the long-term development of the New Towns, the Expanded Towns, the rebuilt cities and the provision of highway interventions in and around historic towns and cities. Zoning solved the problem of noise and air pollution spilling over workers' homes, by creating dedicated industrial estates and housing estates, but created a new problem of these 'monotone areas' effectively becoming dormitory housing estates, quiet in the day, and commercial zones abandoned at night – and expensive to keep secure. Traffic congestion and air pollution resulted from the persistent shuttling back and forth.

Meanwhile, large-scale road infrastructure increased the volume of traffic that could flow through the network, but created 'severance', thousands in cities such as New York had found themselves on the wrong side of the tracks. Starved of the vitality of being a through-route, neighbourhoods atrophied. In the dedicated neighbourhood unit superblocks of the New Towns and contemporary developments, locating neighbourhood centres away from the main transport routes could leave them economically depressed.

Finally, the networks of pedestrian and cycle routes segregated from the vehicle routes – all inspired ultimately by Radburn – have produced a number of problems. Milton Keynes' redway cycle network means that cyclists can travel traffic free, but have less road sense than cyclists in conventional towns. The extensive networks of paths are expensive to maintain, not least because it is often hard to get mechanical plant for repairs, normally delivered by road, down onto the routes. In addition, the lack of natural surveillance has in some instances made them into unsafe routes, either actually dangerous, or merely creating the impression of danger.

In Britain, new approaches to contemporary urbanism have emerged from a debate between the previous approach of putting the car first in planning, and between focusing first on a more human scale. Since 1997, a political drive to achieve better quality of design in towns and cities, driven by increasing levels of house building around the turn of the millennium, led to formal guidance from the government over principles of urban design and masterplanning. The government-appointed Urban Taskforce report *Towards an Urban Renaissance* in 1999 was intended to, 'identify causes of urban decline in England and recommend practical solutions ... [and] establish a new vision for urban regeneration founded on the principles of design excellence, social well-being and environmental responsibility within a viable economic and legislative framework' (DETR, 1999: 1).

This was followed by the Department for Environment, Transport and the Regions report *By Design: urban design in the planning system: towards better practice* in 2000, *The Urban Design Compendium* by the government regeneration agency, English Partnerships and the social housing agency, The Housing Corporation, in 2003, and the Commission for Architecture and the Built Environment's *Creating Successful Masterplans* in 2004. Approaching the same issue from slightly different perspectives, these add up to a new consensus on urban design principles being implemented in contemporary developments. Where the New Towns story began with the desire to design better places, these recent guides point to how things went wrong. With such similar ambitions, there is a danger that, in time, these new guides from the turn of the millennium will also produce unforeseen side effects.

Taking the 2000 publication, *By Design*, as an initial introduction to this new paradigm for design, the basic principles it outlines for shaping urban development are:

Character: A place with its own identity.
Continuity and enclosure: A place where public and private spaces are clearly distinguished.
Quality of the public realm: A place with attractive and successful outdoor areas.
Ease of movement: A place that is easy to get to and move through.
Legibility: A place that has a clear image and is easy to understand.
Adaptability: A place that can change easily.
Diversity: A place with variety and choice.'
(DETR and CABE, 2000: 15)

The built form is then defined in the following terms

Layout: Urban Structure . . . Urban Grain . . . Landscape . . . Density and Mix . . .
Scale: Height . . . Massing . . .
Appearance: Details . . . Materials.'
(DETR and CABE, 2000: 16)

The Redways, traffic-free routes for pedestrians and cyclists.

These images of Harlow show how the New Town's commercial and civic centres, ringed by large-scale roads, are cut-off off from the surrounding residential neighbourhoods (left). Access includes grade-separated pedestrian underpasses (right).

Broad conformity exists between the New Towns in terms of layout and scale, and with appearance of buildings changing subtly with each decade of development, the following example covering Harlow expresses issues shared with many of the towns. Harlow enjoyed one of the most considered designs of all the New Towns, under the dedicated eye of Gibberd, Britain's leading architect-planner of the era. Nonetheless, an Area Action Plan, prepared for the Town Council in 2005, contains deep criticisms based directly on the recent paradigm shift in urban design.

> A particular characteristic of Harlow is the lack of human scale in its road design, with a similar approach taken to the design of many of the buildings in the Town Centre . . . The Town Centre is surrounded by a dual carriageway – effectively a 'collar' – which severs the centre from the neighbouring residential areas and restricts pedestrian movement into the town centre . . . The internal road system . . . exhibits an arbitrary network often going nowhere

With the service areas around the outside, Harlow town centre is inward looking, and does not provide attractive entrances.

. . . the majority of primary routes end in 'nowhere place' roundabouts.

(Harlow, 2005: 22–4)

Some of these factors were not Gibberd's fault, such as the upgrading of the road network to handle greater capacity, creating greater severance. Others, such as the way the relationship between neighbourhoods and the road network, clearly were. Gibberd was a keen advocate of 'civic design', yet the report is damning on Harlow's public realm,

the design and layout of the Town Centre organises parking/servicing around the edges. Though this creates a quiet pedestrian inner space, the dual carriageway around the centre does not feel like a street 'fronted onto' by development but has an appearance more like a service road with 'back doors' into this most important part of Harlow.

(Harlow, 2005: 32)

A weak public realm with areas of unclear ownership, poor relation between buildings and streets, open green space that buildings face away from. Overall, there are many attributes of success such as still comparatively low levels of outward commuting. Only 10 per cent of the population commute to London, 20 per cent within Essex or Hertfordshire and 10 per cent elsewhere, so 60 per cent of residents work in the town (Harlow, 2005). The reduction in its original high level of self-containment reflects changes in the life of the town, and the urban character has also drifted from the goals of its original plan. As the 2005 report describes, these goals are still worthy. Future alterations should work with the true character of the place, and furthermore, there should be caution over whether ambitious goals today may suffer a similar fate,

Planning and building in Harlow was a heroic and idealistic endeavour . . . Even if we now conclude that aspects of it were misguided, or now need radical change, we should approach it with due respect. The original motives of Harlow – to house people in the South East in genuine communities with good services and amenities and high design quality while protecting and enhancing

environmental quality – are amazingly similar to those that motivate the [Government's 2003] Sustainable Communities Plan and current housing growth targets. Amazing because our assumptions and responses to essentially the same challenge are in some ways so different. This should make us pause to consider whether our 2004 orthodoxes are any better founded than those set out so confidently by Gibberd and his collaborators half a century ago. We must ensure that they fare better when looked at in another 50 years time.

(Harlow, 2005: ii)

The huge exercise in getting the construction of the New Towns off the ground after the Second World War was highly demanding, and must be recognised for the enormous achievement it was. However, a similar rush to apply radically new ideas in urban design or architecture today runs just as great a risk of creating places that fail the criteria of meeting future needs. In this, the New Towns mirror exactly the contemporary concerns of designers and planners seeking long-term quality. The New Towns suffered from the unintended side effects and unanticipated social and technological changes that undermined the basis of their design decisions.

As Richards had said, experimentation had been undertaken with little understanding of the nature of place that would result. There had also been a compulsion to adopt new arrangements and abandon conventional ones. Given the demands for zoning, low density and new, landscaped, housing layouts, even designing new places on old patterns was anathema, as Osborn and Whittick's views on the design for Peterlee makes clear. The 1952 plan showing a conventional pattern of streets was dismissed as, 'not a very progressive one . . . planned on stereotyped traditional lines before the value of the pedestrian precinct as exemplified at Stevenage and Coventry was fully realised' (Osborn and Whittick, 1977: 280).

Then, the reactions to rising levels of private vehicle use were to alter the plans for the first generation towns, and design the second and third generation by making the car the first consideration in design decisions. For the first generation, the design concepts had been devised in the 1920s and 1930s, yet only completed construction in the 1960s. By this point, rapidly rising levels of car ownership meant that traffic management was seen

The car-free centres of the New Towns have suffered over time. Once the shops close, covered shopping malls exclude the public completely and pedestrian precincts become desolate and lifeless places. The large-scale block structure and inward-looking nature of shopping malls means public routes between buildings often lack active frontages. More recent developments in the New Towns seek to change this adding shops facing the street and introducing restaurants, cinemas, bars and nightclubs to increase activity in the public realm during the evenings. Images taken from Harlow town centre. A: Top Left. B: Top Right, C: Bottom Left.

as crucial to the functioning of towns and cities. Professor Colin Buchanan's 1963 report *Traffic in Cities* provided the key justification for large-scale highway engineering, segregation of pedestrian and cycle movement and widespread adoption of pedestrian precincts in response to 'the impending motor age'. The report celebrates American approaches to urban traffic management, led by the interventions of Robert Moses.

The result of this engagement with the needs of the motor car at all costs came, of course, at the cost of the town. As Downie's criticism noted in 1972, residents of a New Town such as Cumbernauld could as easily drive out of their local neighbourhood, onto a road network that would lead them out to another town, or out-of-town mall, with better shopping. The

New Town centre, now essentially possessing little besides an old shopping mall, would have no appeal and no other function as a centre. Car-based urbanism was anti-urbanism. Melvin Webber, in support of this, argued that, as in places such as Los Angeles or Atlanta, the result was dis-integration of the urban form; and people who lived in suburban America liked it that way.

The only downsides to this are first the contradiction that the New Towns were intended to be 'towns' and all that implied. Richards' critique in 1953 was that towns meant more than that provided for in the New Towns. The second problem with car-based urbanism is of course the more general point, that it means inevitable traffic congestion as levels rise beyond planned capacity, local air pollution damaging lungs, greenhouse gas pollution causing climate change and dependence on foreign energy suppliers.

The final point, now addressed in the principles of *By Design* (DETR and CABE, 2000) is adaptability. The context of post-war reconstruction meant the New Towns were designed faster and built on larger scales than were possible before or since. As a result, they produced large volumes of reasonably identical buildings, and town centres that used new techniques in structural engineering for creating large blocks in the centre. The implication of these planning and construction approaches in the New Towns meant the structures of the towns fundamentally lacked adaptability.

Whereas the traditional street with its fine grain of different buildings could be modified incrementally to whatever desires a building owner may consider. The modern shopping mall was hugely inflexible to changing circumstances, and as they became out of date, alternative, newer, more attractive options for shopping would further exacerbate the worsening economic status of the New Town centres. Despite relatively low levels of in and out commuting in Corby (79 per cent of the population worked in the town), Corby Council had noted that by 2001 around 73 per cent of residents' disposable income was spent outside the town. In Bracknell, only 20 per cent of those living within ten minutes drive of the town centre actually chose to shop there, the remaining 80 per cent spent their money elsewhere, in places such as Reading. Even if successful for retail, these centres lacked sufficient civic amenities. In Telford, its member of parliament described the town centre as,

[an] extremely successful out-of-town retail centre built in the middle of the town. At present it does not operate as a town centre as intended in the original new town concept. The centre closes down at 5.30pm and does not provide any night time economy of merit.

(House of Commons, 2002a)

Having gone down the route of the pedestrian precinct, and then moved towards the covered shopping mall, the New Town Development Corporations had given themselves a challenge. The dilemma was either to maintain control locally and struggle to compete against more powerful competition from elsewhere, or sell-off control of the shopping centres and have the town's retail assets managed by a distant investor. The latter meant the development corporation or subsequent town council might remove their liability but also their opportunity to exert influence. As part of a large portfolio of shopping centres, those in the New Towns risked being a low priority for their new owners.

The most successful of all the retail centres in the New Towns was that of Milton Keynes. Here, its location on the M1 Motorway, its catchment area and sheer scale were the main elements for its success. It aimed to make a big impact by being Britain's first one million square foot shopping centre. It sought to out-gun its competitors and by and large succeeded. Failures, however, were severe. The long-term social costs were summed up in bald terms in 2002 by Torfaen Council, now responsible for Cwmbran New Town, 'Poorly designed and badly lit shopping areas in Cwmbran have led to perceived unsafe or no-go areas, attract anti-social behaviour, provide areas for alcohol and substance misuse, criminal damage and burglary' (House of Commons, 2002a).

Lifestyle in the New Towns: Basildon and the state of the nation

The status of the New Towns as places – their successes or failures – cannot be separated from their urban design. The contradictions of self-containment and mobility, of urban concentration and dis-integration, are there in the built fabric. The implications of this are not just an issue of academic interest but have shaped the lives of every New Town resident. Contemporary lives in a New Town were captured in a 2006 exhibition by photographer C.J. Clarke. As a lifelong resident, his critique of Basildon is informed by direct, daily experience. His personal perspective and photographs are an artistic take on the town and the fundamentals of the New Towns as a whole.

I grew up in Basildon – I'm 25 now – so most of my life has been spent living there. I've always been fascinated by the architecture of the Basildon and how it influences the daily life of the town's inhabitants, how it has influenced my life. Moreover, I'm interested in the disconnect between the stated purpose of new towns . . . and, how this actually manifest itself in reality.

Over the years the town has been expanded and developed – what is now called regeneration – however, no wave of rebuilding or expansion seems to get to grips with the fundamental architectural or institutional problems that prevent the formation of a coherent community. I'm old enough to remember what it was like before the first wave of rebuilding, before the new council offices were built, or the new theatre. I remember the grey concrete of the 1980s. It felt different. Now it's a bit more slick, though fundamentally nothing's really changed. It's still a suburb of nowhere. It's a nowhere place. People don't have a strong sense of belonging to Basildon. All roads lead out. There's nothing in the centre other than a shopping complex, which closes at half past five, six o'clock. In the absence of shopping the town centre is deserted; there is no cultural or civic life that takes place on a town-wide level and is underpinned by some collective civic identity or sense of tradition.

(Clarke, 2008)

As one of the towns in the Thames Gateway Growth Area identified in the government's 2003 Sustainable Communities Plan, Basildon has substantial investment planned. The transformation of the town is ongoing – as it is in many other New Towns – but the fundamental layout of the place, enshrined in the design principles cannot be re-engineered easily. Nor can its people. C.J. Clarke, as an artist seeking to document Basildon, realises the contradictions at the heart of the New Towns, and seeks to capture it in photographs.

The documentary process, which rather than being simply concerned with recording 'truth' actually blurs the line between fact and fiction, so that what you end up with is a strange, magic and highly subjective reality that is created through the collaboration between photographer and subject . . . Basildon is also a fragmented town, with a fragmented sense of community. People live in individual cantons, living within themselves and their own homes and family. This decline in community affects the whole of the UK but in Basildon this is exacerbated by the

architecture. Despite the architects' intention to create a new community this ended up as just a fiction. They were designing a community for their present; they were forgetting that society is in a constant state of flux; thus, they were designing a town for a specific community right at the point when this society was changing: this was their fiction.

(Clarke, 2008)

Yet this view of the town does not undermine his attachment to it. Although familiar with the criticisms that have been levelled at them, many residents are naturally defensive about their home towns, keen to point out that people who live in the New Towns like them. On the one hand, this is self-selecting since people who do not like a place are more likely to move on. This is especially true in a place where the population is largely composed of people who already moved from somewhere else. Ultimately, there is strong connection between person and place.

Despite my critique of the town and what's wrong with it, I don't hate Basildon. I still like it and like the people who live here. I will leave one day, but then I will also come back because I've got family and friends here. That will always be the street I walked down on my way to school, etc. My grandparents lived here from when it was built. Both sets of grandparents worked at the Ford factory. One side moved from Beacontree and the other from Dagenham, relocating when the factory moved out here. Both knew each other by sight and passed each other when they cycled into work, then their kids ended up marrying each other.

(Clarke, 2008)

This sort of story is repeated across the New Towns. Those who moved in the early years felt personally involved in the creation of a new community. These first residents saw the New Town in comparison to the housing conditions they were leaving behind. The state of the pit towns of County Durham, inner-city London terraces or the ill-planned developments such as Dagenham are largely forgotten today. As is the fact that the new designs showcased at the New Towns directly helped to promote a progressive image of Britain abroad. With businesses

Segregated pedestrian routes were designed to increase traffic flow, but at the expense of the human-scale experience. Photographer C.J. Clarke (www.cjclarke.com).

Photographer C.J. Clarke (www.cjclarke.com).

relocating into spacious, purpose-built premises, new British industries such as electronics could develop. People moved in and lived their lives.

Yet the long-term social change that resulted from this population migration is ambiguous. Although branded as 'failed socialist utopias' (Booth, 2006: 108), the New Towns are not necessarily staunch Labour heartlands. Basildon was marked out in an influential report from the think-tank Demos in 2001, *Basildon: Mood of a Nation* (Hayes and Hudson, 2001a), noting that it is a barometer for the national political mood. Its voting habits represent a useful forecast on election nights. The

report's findings challenged the conventional and stereotyped view of the working class. As C.J. Clarke describes, the defining characteristic, amplified by the circumstances of the New Towns Programme, is of aspiration,

Basildon is a manufactured community with a statistical breakdown that perfectly aligns itself with the national average . . . Like my family most people's roots are in the east of London and their decision to move to Basildon was purely voluntary and born out of a desire to improve their standard of living. Consequently, Basildon is a

Photographer C.J. Clarke (www.cjclarke.com).

ruggedly individualistic place where most people see the increase in their standard of living as being purely as a result of their own efforts; they ignore the tremendous impact that local and national government has obviously had on their lives.

(Clarke, 2008)

The result of both this demographic and the urban environment into which they moved is that people socialise mostly in other people's houses. As the Demos survey found,

social activity in Basildon is skewed fundamentally towards individualised activities – to the practical exclusion of communal or even joint-interests . . . They have less allegiance to all political parties than before and no discernable identification with other institutions such as church, monarchy or trade unions.

(Hayes and Hudson, 2001b: 26)

In itself, this individualism is not a problem, and reflects the changing role of social attitudes during the late twentieth century. The authors identified that,

In the early days, the first wave of inhabitants felt themselves to be at the forefront of the hopes and challenges involved in the reconstruction of post-war Britain. Their hopes and aspirations did not go away; but over 30 years

their belief in the welfare model for Britain was eroded by the experience of second-rate and shoddy services.

(Hayes and Hudson, 2001b)

Their fear was that the lack of social bond meant that the inherent aspiration was turning to disillusionment, reflecting growing cynicism and dislocation in the political process by people throughout Britain. The shift that took place in Britain in the 1950s from Swedish welfare state to American consumerism, taking until the 1980s to become dominant, is clear in the New Towns. As C.J. Clarke, concludes,

In many ways Basildon perfectly represents the consumerist society that we have become. In place of significant civic and cultural institutions we have a shopping centre. Indeed, you could argue that Basildon is the perfect expression of the [Thatcherist] reforms pushed through in the 1980s. Society takes time to change, for the results of policies crafted in Westminster to become apparent; perhaps, this is Thatcher's Britain . . . where we are consumers and not citizens, business is everything, the community is fragmented and social contract is disregarded.

(Clarke, 2008)

The contradiction that Clarke seeks to highlight in his photographs is between the aspirations for the place and the aspirations for way of life. The former was defined by socialist

With the town centre failing to act as a focus for social activity in the town, people generally socialise in local pubs in their neighbourhood, or in each others' houses. Photographer C.J. Clarke (www.cjclarke.com).

politicians such as Reith and Silkin and planners such as Osborn and Abercrombie. They had a vision for the sort of place they wanted to create and the way of life they expected people there would lead, and the designs that followed reflected these hopes. The actual aspirations for the people who lived there and the way of life they were to lead would, however, change with each generation.

The Garden Cities Movement and the Modern Movement sought to reinvent the way that places worked. The New Towns were the hybrid of their ideas. Yet the planners and designers were unable to prevent wider social changes following in the wake of technological progress. Consumer society meant that the way of life resulting was not that anticipated by the planners. Howard's formulation of the Garden City concept, that led to the New Towns Programme, was for a balanced town that matched housing with employment to prevent outward commuting. But although Howard had placed the 'crystal palace' shopping arcade at the heart of his Garden City plan, the significance of shopping was not fully understood. Welwyn Garden City had an impressive general store (now John Lewis) but it ran a monopoly for years. The cultural change in the UK between the start and end of the 1950s, from looking to Swedish welfare socialism to American consumer capitalism partly explains this. The New Towns were planned in an effectively pre-consumerist age. Liberal capitalism inherently drove

technological and thereby social progress. The Garden City/ New Town model was founded in an age that still expected stability.

By the late 1950s, the television meant that people could be entertained in their own homes and the car meant they could go wherever they wanted to. The unified society of the early New Town pioneers ebbed away. Yet, the expectation of future change means that perceived problems in urban design or demographic mix may turn into advantages. For instance, the prevalence of subway areas means many dark and empty spaces. Fine to race through on a bike, and in Milton Keynes, where they are broader than most, people linger in them – their edges make for impromptu seating for traffic wardens to fill in their forms or for teenagers to congregate. Perhaps in the future these designs will be turned to new uses? As climate change brings regular summer heat waves, these spaces, sheltered from the burning sun may become centres of activity; the shadowed spaces providing relief from the hardscaped areas of the centre that may hold more heat than the trees or prevailing wind can comfortably disperse.

The New Towns are all cycle-friendly places, though the segregation of modes of transport has not been without problems (Franklin, 1999). The need for sustainable transport may mean these cycle routes and their extensive grass verges will find new life. In Peterborough recently an unprecedented

Photographer C.J. Clarke (www.cjclarke.com).

Photographer
C.J. Clarke
(www.cjclarke.com).

shift out of cars and onto bikes resulted from a pilot scheme to promote sustainable travel (Peterborough 2004). Even this too may be subject to unpredictable change. If fossil fuel transport is radically curtailed and zero-emissions alternatives such as electric vehicles take over, the argument to shift away from private cars on grounds of sustainability (though less so for congestion or traffic accidents) means that the New Town's large-scale roadways may shift from being seen as environmentally unsustainable ways of moving to environmentally virtuous.

The New Towns are testament to an era in history where mobility was a liberating force and the fuel to run it was plentiful and cheap. In the future, everyone may be subject to strict controls over their carbon footprint. It must be remembered, however, that car culture was promoted in Britain and America because it meant a quick return on investment in manufacturing built up to fight the war and the fastest way to get industry back on its feet. Second, mobility played an ideological role; the right of free travel was an explicit liberty that communist dictatorships behind the Iron Curtain denied their people. The freedom of the open road, from American road movie to caravan holiday, was just one of the freedoms the West had been fighting for.

The curse of the New Towns was that the new ways of building towns meant people lived in different ways. The circumstances of the New Towns are almost certain to change again. The story of how they evolved over time is that changes in the political climate were also to have hugely unpredictable impacts on the New Towns. Seemingly small decisions resulted in profound challenges for the New Towns as they faced their first phases of renewal.

How the New Towns grew old

Basildon centre. Photographer C.J. Clarke (www.cjclarke.com).

The critics of the New Towns point to their break with the historic pattern of British towns. The urban design considerations created a new type of place, rationally planned and designed to provide a better quality of life in an increasingly motorised, high-tech age. These new urban ideas affected places across Britain and spread around the world. Besides the physical designs, the more strategic economic planning of towns – their location and transport connectivity, their employment mix and, crucially, their approach to shopping and leisure – had a central influence.

These factors have to be understood in terms of their change over time. How did the New Towns fare over time? Were they any better or worse at adapting to changing economic circumstances than anywhere else? One issue is certainly that they grew rapidly over a short period of time. This is a quality they share with British towns that experienced major expansion in the nineteenth century. Another factor relates to how the New Towns were managed. Practically all the construction in the towns was centrally controlled.

However, the story of how the New Towns aged is open ended. The situation in the 1980s, 1990s and 2000s is not an end, but just another phase. Perhaps their recent ageing has been a period of adolescence on the road to maturity. Recent programmes of regeneration and renewal in the New Towns are ongoing, and they too will be delayed and altered by economic turmoil, changing government policies and targets, and changing lifestyles prompted by inescapable technological and social progress. Understanding the past is helpful to achieve a perspective on the New Towns, first in terms of the scale of their problems, and second to see how things have changed over time.

The nineteenth-century equivalents of the New Towns were the Spa Towns (such as Leamington, Cheltenham, and Droitwich), Mining Towns and Industrial Towns (mainly around the coal-fields of the north of England, South Wales and central Scotland) and the Seaside Towns (linked to the Industrial Towns by rail). Each experienced rapid growth in a short period of time, often from a small existing settlement. Each had a housing stock reflecting the overall purpose that the town was built to serve. For the Spa Towns this included town house villas with generous room sizes, though often built cheaply; for the Industrial Towns it meant dense terraces of workers housing,

and often impressive civic buildings and municipal parks; for the Seaside Towns, guesthouses, hotels, entertainment venues, promenades and piers.

When the underlying reasons for these towns being built changed, inevitably their fortunes changed too. The Spa Towns boomed in the first decades of the nineteenth century in response to the Napoleonic Wars of 1803 to 1815, which discouraged the wealthy classes from holidaying in Europe. Their decline began around the middle of the century. Industrial Towns, Mining Towns and Railway Towns grew in the wake of the industrial revolution between 1830 and 1850 and started their slow decline when foreign competition from countries such as the USA and Germany began to bite in the latter part of the nineteenth century. The Seaside Towns that followed brought holidaying to the working classes but declined in the mid-twentieth century with competition from dedicated holiday camps in the 1930s. Abrupt decline in the post-war decades resulted when commercial airliners made foreign package holidays more compelling destinations. Competition, opened-up by new technology or wider political changes, has always shaped the fortunes of towns and cities. The towns that perform best when their fundamental foundations shift are those able to reinvent themselves. Having a built fabric that is easily able to accommodate change in use is a vital attribute for success.

Looking back on around fifty years of aging in the twentieth-century, post-war New Towns, their ability to adapt to changing circumstances can clearly be seen. Some have fared well, with their strategic location a crucial factor. Milton Keynes is perfectly located between the major conurbations of Birmingham and London to north and south, and the leading university towns of Oxford and Cambridge to west and east. Its range of employment reflects the balanced approach that the New Towns planners had as a main objective. Outward commuting is relatively low, yet its connection to London means that the major facilities of the capital such as museums and galleries are easily accessible. The shopping centre of Milton Keynes attracts people from a wide area.

To the south of London, Crawley is also a regional shopping destination and its position next to Gatwick Airport ensured high employment even during the recessions of the 1980s and 1990s. Perhaps in a future where the carbon emissions from transport massively curtail the viability of airports this will cease to be the case. Over-reliance on this single employer may mean an abrupt fall in the town's fortunes. In which case, alternative employment must be developed that builds on new strategic advantages. Each of the New Towns can be subject to such analysis in terms of their fundamental strengths and strategic location, and such conditions will inevitably change over time. With the major growth areas identified in government plans containing many of the New Towns, they are likely to experience change over the first decades of the twenty-first century (ODPM, 2003).

The regeneration issues facing the New Towns not only relate to their mix of employment, and their range of building types but also to the unique nature of how they were built and managed. Certain problems that have emerged with these designs have been seen across these other places. The post-war urbanism of zoning, neighbourhood units, large-scale road infrastructure and new construction methods for housing can be seen across the UK. Monotone demographics and poor urbanism have led to problems that government guidance such as *By Design* (DETR and CABE, 2000: see Chapter 9) aimed to eliminate in the future, and which recent regeneration programmes across the country have aimed to fix. The New Towns, although sharing some of these features with the Expanded Towns and the inner cities, lie in a different context from these places by virtue of the manner in which they were created, and in this lies their most interesting lesson. The development corporation model was the greatest contributory factor behind their success, but was never truly free from government influence. A clear example of influence can be seen in changing government housing targets and the introduction for new standards for higher-quality housing design, which were to have long-term consequences.

Changes in building design

In the post-war era, the New Towns were at the cutting edge of urban development and, as such, new ideas were often applied in the New Towns before being applied elsewhere. Despite radical approaches to urban design, such as the neighbourhood unit, the demands of the 1950s meant shortages of materials.

With the large volumes being specified by development corporation architecture departments, although new demands for space and light were met, homes and other buildings were basic in construction and essentially conventional in design.

With the need for the government control of building and the rationing of materials withdrawn by the mid-1950s, by the 1960s much of the essential first stages of the New Towns were largely complete. Many development corporation architects then set up in private practice. Private developers and housing associations working on limited plots of land in the New Towns were becoming more experimental with housing design. The complaints of the new generation of the Modern Movement, such as the Smithsons, had led to more experimental designs at Cumbernauld, which were now starting to be built. Throughout the New Towns, architects were being freed from the guidelines and material restrictions that faced the very first house builders. PRP Architects was one of the leaders of the new generation. Their book, *Place and Home: The Search for Better Housing*, details housing developments in the New Towns from the 1960s onwards,

> thanks to a succession of enlightened clients, borough and New Town architects as well as the development directors of housing associations, we were able to explore and utilise the whole gamut of possibilities open to us in house design: courtyard houses, terraces which by their design allowed completely private, not overlooked gardens; houses with interchangeable living spaces and inverted dwellings, with the living room on the first floor to take advantage of good views. We pushed flat design to the economic limits in order to provide generous balconies and terraces with large built-in planters, allowing civilised high-density living. This approach led to a string of projects winning accolades for Good Design.
>
> (PRP, 2007: 42)

New estimates of housing demand in the early 1960s prompted the second generation of the New Towns and also resulted in the expansion of many of the first generation towns. To increase the level at which Harlow, Basildon and Stevenage could re-house more people from London, a 1963 expansion plan aimed to increase the target populations to around double their original levels. This meant substantial opportunities for this new generation of architects in all of the New Towns. However, this expansion was seen as conflicting with the fundamentals of the original town masterplans. As Gibberd described it, 'I and others, like the Town and Country Planning Association, were unhappy about the expansion because Ebenezer Howard's fundamental principle of containing the growth of towns by a Green Belt would be violated' (Gibberd et al., 1980: 153).

Howard's Garden City idea was founded on there being a limit to urban expansion. Once town building had reached a certain intended level, of around 50,000 people, building should stop, and a new Garden City should be founded elsewhere. These were eventually to form a network, and create a 'social city' cluster of around 250,000 people.

Set against this was the government view that there was no optimum size for towns, and that previous targets, outlined by the Reith Committee, had merely been an informed guess. The changes in intended population numbers meant plans had to be hastily redrawn. Changing demands from government, lack of clarity for future growth, and new neighbourhoods being added to the original plans meant a considerable headache for the development corporations.

The reality was, of course, that towns never really stop growing. They are never 'completed', as Howard had thought. Different waves of development are inevitable over the decades. Even Paris, with its grand Naopleonic plan by Haussmann, effectively expands outwards with post-war housing estates and new business districts. London, by virtue of having been subjected to the Great Fire of 1666, Regency suburban expansion in the 1700s, ad hoc slum clearance and infill in the 1800s and ultimately the Blitz in the mid-twentieth century, has left the heart of the city belonging to no particular historical age. London is a montage of more than 1000 years of urban change. Smaller towns show similar waves of development, and there is no reason to assume the New Towns, too, will not be subjected to many future phases of growth and redevelopment.

New government policy on housing was the main factor in altering the planned trajectory of development in the New Towns. Initially, in the 1950s, attempts to massively speed up the rate of house completions resulted in smaller homes being built and to lower standards. By the start of the 1960s, a reaction to this resulted in the Parker–Morris Committee report *Homes for*

Today and Tomorrow (published in 1961). This set out new minimum space standards that by 1967 became mandatory for all housing in the New Towns. The impact of these new and improved internal space standards displaced existing budgets and spending plans. So to meet high volume and large sizes, new construction methods were employed in order to lower costs and delivery times. Le Corbusier's vision for 'Industrialised housing' became a mainstream way to meet the new targets and guidelines. The positive goal of aiming to provide better homes with larger rooms and internal storage pushed the house builders towards new forms of construction technology. The government was enthusiastic since this involved nurturing new products and services for British business. Its specialist agency, the Building Research Station (today known as the BRE), advanced the study of new techniques.

Prefabricated concrete panels could be manufactured in factories and then assembled on site far quicker and far more cheaply than conventional housing built by hand with bricks and mortar. Leonard Vincent, chief architect at Stevenage, recalls the impacts of the government's new policy,

the development corporations were obliged to build 15% of all the dwellings in system building . . . We devised our own system in conjunction with Mowlem's mainly, which was a poured concrete job and it was a monolithic thing and it was clad with bricks on the outside and it suffered none of the problems that we have seen in system building in other places. In fact, I still maintain they are the best built houses in Stevenage – it takes something to shift those.

(Stevenage (2007a)

These examples suggested system build was clearly no bad thing, but the challenge of maintaining high-quality standards, while implementing new procedures on a vast scale, was incredibly difficult. Over time, changing conditions, a push to increase the speed of delivery and the desire for innovative designs created complications.

In Peterlee, the original housing of the 1950s was created with good space standards and with generous gardens. Housing added in the 1960s was more radical. At the Sunny Blunts housing estate designed by Victor Passmore in 1962, damp became a chronic problem that the landlord, the development corporation, had no understanding of or remedy for. Brian Morris, journalist for the *Northern Echo* described the housing, 'brave and imaginative in their general design . . . wretched and shabby in their details and practical execution' (Ward, 1993: 16). Meanwhile in Runcorn, world-famous architect James Stirling produced a radical new house design with a brightly coloured striped façade and circular windows, built between 1975 and 1977. The brief for the Southgate Estate stipulated formal squares and streets to reflect the standards of the Georgian city of Bath. Yet, tenants found it grim and the circular windows were extremely expensive to maintain. The view of the chair of the residents association, Margaret Davies, was 'The architect either had a brainstorm or was suffering from acute depression' (*Building Design*, 2007a). Stirling's estate was demolished in 1990 to be replaced by conventional housing, brick clad with pitched roofs. Renamed Hallwood Park, some of the new properties doubled in value from 1997 to 2005, while the mortgages from the original housing were still being paid off by the housing association.

Stirling's response in the trade paper *Building Design* was that it was 'a little unfair that the architects' input should today be considered as being primarily responsible for the lack of quality'. The developers and contractors responsible for building did not share the architect's passion for quality. Budget restrictions meant that creating innovative architecture, using innovative methods and high-build quality was impossible.

In Milton Keynes housing designed by eminent architects was promoted as offering 'tremendous variety of solutions and creative approaches to design' (Clapson, 1998: 101). Yet as the only major post-occupancy research conducted during the New Towns Programme, the Milton Keynes Development Corporation 'Residential Design Feedback' studies showed that the industrial housing turned out to be poorly insulated against the cold and against noise. The economic conditions of the 1970s meant cost-cutting on production for radical new designs by star architects. As Edward Jones, one of the designers of Milton Keynes' Netherfield estate recalled,

Netherfield was built too quickly and expediently, almost as emergency housing. Its components of walls and floors, realised by platform timber mass production, were trucked in from Harlow. Visits to the factory, where the

production method of nail machine guns occasionally missing the 2 × 4s, was truly alarming. The houses have since been occupied by 'problem families' . . . Norman Foster's housing at Beanhill, a grid square to the west of Netherfield and contemporary with it (design by Birkin Haward and Frank Peacock) was to suffer similar ignomies. All very depressing really.

(*Building Design*, 2007c)

Many of these modernist housing approaches applied in the later New Towns descended into sink estates. Besides the poor build quality, the unfamiliarity of the designs made them difficult to refurbish or repair. Meanwhile, conventional housing designs created by the development corporation's architecture department, and built using well-understood methods, such as Halton Brow in Runcorn, despite being unimaginative in their appearance, proved extremely popular with tenants. Research into resident satisfaction conducted in Milton Keynes found that – tragically – housing built by highly respected architects ended up being the least popular, whilst housing that appeared traditional and conventional was liked the most (Bishop, 1986). A key exception to this depressing state of affairs was Milton Keynes' Eaglestone estate, designed by Ralph Erskine using an imaginative resident-led design process.

The tragedy of Milton Keynes was that in trying to make Britain warm to modern architecture, ultimately the poor build quality brought about by economic instability resulted in a backlash. Whereas modern architecture from the 1930s was well-built and in places such as the South of France or Brazil benefited from the bright, warm climate, in Britain, rain-proofing provided by traditional pitched roofs and architectural detailing was lost in a generation of modernist housing that became plagued by cold and damp. The financial instability of the 1970s combined with the desire to hit housing targets for construction resulted in deeply problematic housing. The New Towns were not alone in this catastrophe, which affected large volumes of public sector housing built in this period.

Netherfield, Milton Keynes (see also image on page 37).

Freedom of action

Broad social and economic changes taking place in Britain in the last quarter of the twentieth century impacted on the development of the New Towns. Although the New Towns were not as strongly affected as some other towns and cities, the trend of de-industrialisation in the 1970s and 1980s was nonetheless significant. In the New Towns this shift was compounded by a change in how the towns were run. Ebenezer Howard's method for town building had been based on local control of the town's assets, namely the freehold of all the buildings and the freedom to invest rental income on acquiring (or building)

more physical assets. A closed-loop of positive feedback was thereby created that amplified the available revenue over time, in turn meeting the ongoing interests of the town's residents and employers. It is for this reason that Howard is seen as one of the forefathers of the welfare state. Hospitals, schools, shops and factory sites could be built according to the whim of the Garden City Company, accountable only to its members. Howard's idea, formed in the pre-welfare state era, can be meaningfully compared to the left-wing political philosophy of anarcho-syndicalism. This is the democratic self-management of an organisation by its workers, or in the case of a Garden City, by its residents.

The fundamental logic of the Garden City concept and its New Towns offspring was an essential independence. This originally took hold because of Lord Reith's personal experience in running the British Broadcasting Corporation at the time of the Great Strike of 1926. Despite being publicly funded, Reith fiercely defended the operational and editorial independence of the BBC when the government attempted censorship of the strikers' views. For the New Town Development Corporation, necessary independence from government was a pre-eminent requirement of the Reith Committee's final reports.

> We assume that such a corporation will be invested with sufficient powers to enable it to carry out its task free from the administrative control and consequent interference which are necessarily associated with full and direct government responsibility. The appropriate Minister (the Minister of Town and Country Planning or the Secretary of State for Scotland) should have the power to give such directions as he may from time to time consider necessary in the public interest in any matter of major policy. Subject to that, the corporation must have freedom of action comparable with that of a commercial undertaking.
> (Reith, 1946)

A number of political and economic concepts are central to this situation. 'Autarchy' or self-control is what drove the profitability of the Garden Cities and New Towns. A second concept here is 'hypothecation', the dedication of a tax or income for a particular purpose. In the case of the Garden Cities and New Towns this was rental income on Company- or Corporation-owned land and buildings in the towns, reinvested into further town development or social amenities. Other examples include gasoline tax in the USA being used to pay for maintaining roads, London's Congestion Charge, introduced in 2003, where cars are charged to enter the city during peak times and the money raised is invested in improving the city's public transport. The BBC is of course also an example, where the mandatory UK Television Licence (rather than the government) funds the BBC's high-quality public service broadcasting.

Central government have always disliked this ring-fencing of budgets as it ties the hands of the state over what it can choose to invest in, reducing flexibility to respond to circumstances. The preference is to collect all taxes then centrally decide where to direct spending. However, the third relevant concept here is 'subsidiarity' – the principle that action should always be carried out at the smallest level of an organisation that is capable of carrying out the task. This inherently promotes decentralisation.

That the Garden Cities and New Towns were set using these principles is testimony to Howard's pragmatism in knowing what would be necessary for a project on the scale of town building to succeed. The family of joint venture construction firms created to build Welwyn Garden City are a notable example. The existence of the publicly funded yet independent development corporation model is a sign both of Reith's influence and also the way in which the New Towns Programme was rushed through in the months immediately after the war. Yet as the inherent profitability of Howard's model became apparent towards the end of the 1950s, the New Town Development Corporations were drawn inexorably closer to central government seeking to capture the benefits. The New Towns would become future gold mines for government, and the designation of the second generation of New Towns deepened the scale of future investment that might be recouped.

However, between the first official formulation of the New Towns Programme by the Reith Committee and its subsequent enacting under the New Towns Act of 1946, the long-term status of this independence remained ambiguous. Silkin, the minister ultimately responsible, stated publicly at the time,

It is the [Reith] Committee's view that the corporation should continue indefinitely, living side by side with the local authority . . . but I think that when its job is substantially done, the corporation must go, and the assets and liabilities be handed over to a local authority.

(Cullingworth, 1979: 316)

The Garden City Company was intended to continue indefinitely effectively as a localised welfare state. Reith assumed this should also be the case for the New Towns Development Corporations, as was the case for the BBC. However, the minister disagreed and expected a wind-up date, although how this should be determined remained unresolved for decades. The focus in the early years was on getting the programme started, not deciding how it might end. The Treasury loans that funded the development corporations were on the basis of a sixty-year term with interest payable at current rates. This meant that the first generation of New Towns was scheduled to repay their loans by no later than 2006 to 2010, and the third generation not later than between 2026 and 2030.

The New Towns Act ensured ultimate government mandate through ministerial power to dissolve the corporations and transfer their assets to a local authority or 'statutory undertakers' at any time. Although Silkin assumed assets would transfer directly to local authority control, the letter of the law left the door open for the New Town Development Corporation assets to be transferred to an alternative body, yet to be determined.

In the early 1950s, the Conservative Government was concerned that it represented a potentially bottomless drain on the Treasury. The designation of New Towns had proceeded at haste, before there was a clear understanding of the overall expenditure required, representing a potentially 'alarming commitment' for future expenditure (Cullingworth, 1979: 528). With the economic turbulence of the 1950s adding to the latent hostility towards the New Towns Programme from the Conservative heartlands, this issue became immensely political. The gloomy economic climate throughout the Macmillan years meant that there was little immediate prospect of the development corporations concluding their work and repaying their debts soon. However, a debate within government began as to whether local authorities should ultimately take wholesale control over the assets built up by the development corporations. By 1954, Macmillan was suggesting that the assets might better be held and managed by a single public corporation, who could then manage the disposal of the towns' assets with 'a shrewd discretion' (Cullingworth, 1979: 317).

The official line was that local authorities would not be capable of properly managing the unique and valuable assets of the New Towns: 'They will be authorities without sufficient experience or background to cope with problems of the size that will pass to them' (cited in Cullingworth, 1979: 317). An alternative view was that 'In the late 1950s, the Conservative government did not want New Town assets (which were beginning to show profits) passing to what were then predominantly Labour-controlled district local authorities in the New Town areas' (CLG, 2006: 51).

Since legislation was needed to create such a new government agency, it took several years for a suitable gap in the parliamentary timetable to open and see the proposals taken forward. The creation of a national holding corporation, called the Commission for the New Towns, was a major part of the New Towns Act 1959. This produced the only significant parliamentary debate to take place throughout the entire history of the New Towns. As Meryl Aldridge describes, the debate was fierce,

> It was considered quite unjustified that the Treasury should apparently want to reclaim not only the original advances, plus interest, but the profits too. It was suggested that the Treasury would not allow the Commission to use any of the surplus to provide amenities, or worse, that the Commission would become a disposals board, which was denied by the government. Attempts to limit the Treasury's claim on any surplus accumulation by the Commission were defeated, as were clauses to prevent the Commission from raising rents and to safeguard new town staff.
> (House of Commons Debates, vol. 608, cited in Aldridge, 1979: 86)

The Labour MP for Wellingborough said in parliament,

> Tory governments have persistently stinted the new towns . . . the primary purpose of the new body is to be a financial one, to enhance the value of the asset, while the comfort, welfare and convenience of the inhabitants, which used to be the primary object of the new towns, is now relegated to second place . . . merely something to which the Commission is to 'have regard'.
> (House of Commons Debates, vol. 596, col. 869, cited in Aldridge, 1979: 86)

The 1959 Act stated the Commission was to, 'have regard to the purpose for which the town was developed and to the convenience and welfare of the persons residing, working or carrying on business there'. The Commission was intended to act as 'good landlord' and not as 'a disposals body'. Its formal remit when it opened in 1961 was, '[1] to facilitate the economic and social well-being of citizens and businesses in the English New Towns and [2] To achieve the best price reasonably obtainable for the land and property when sold' (House of Commons, 2002a).

From the early 1960s onwards the Commission for the New Towns began to take over the assets of the first New Towns to be designated and reach their target populations. By 1966, the Commission had absorbed three development corporations, Crawley, Hemel Hempstead and the joint Welwyn and Hatfield. It came to own the freehold of all the housing and commercial property, including shops, offices and factories, as well as all the undeveloped land within what had been the development corporations' areas. It was able to acquire land and grant planning permission but unlike the development corporation had no powers of compulsory purchase (Aldridge, 1979: 87). The Commission effectively became an amalgamation of all the separate development corporations, with staff continuing to work in their old offices in the New Towns, only now under a different ultimate management. This was a somewhat peculiar phenomenon, as Meryl Aldridge describes,

> The Commission for the New Towns, during those first fifteen years, could be said to symbolise all the contradictions of the new towns policy. Claimed by many to be the most dramatic evidence of the switch from a social to a financial rationale for new town development, it was staffed by people with a long history of involvement in new towns and with an intense belief in the concept.
> (Aldridge, 1979: 90)

Gold mines of the future

Although Labour, returning to government under Harold Wilson in 1964, had promised to abolish the Commission, in reality there was little incentive to do so. Quietly, bringing the New Towns back under central control was in the interest of government. The Commission's 1966 annual report on progress of the four New Towns so far brought under their control showed a capital gain from the employment zones of 60 per cent, 'They are a clear indication that the Exchequer investment in new towns, far from imposing a burden on the taxpayer, has already proved a far-sighted and rewarding venture' (cited in *Town and Country Planning*, 1967a: 43).

On the back of the economic boom of the 1960s, the New Towns were starting to look like a good investment for government. The justification for centralisation, put forward by the Commission, was that the profits gained from the well-located New Towns, namely the London satellites, could offset the poorer returns from the New Towns built in areas of heavy industry such as Corby and Peterlee. Development also continued in the New Towns, with the Commission staff overseeing ongoing reinvestment. Meanwhile, the second generation of New Towns being designated provided further investment opportunities for the government. By the 1970s, with more of the first generation New Towns coming under Commission control, the New Towns Programme was a growing area of public sector property management.

Throughout the 1970s, a number of factors undermined enthusiasm within Whitehall for this arrangement, fuelling a growing concern that the additional New Towns did not represent such a sound investment. Falling population forecasts, growing doubt about the viability of some of the New Towns' locations, and widespread economic instability all contributed to this change of heart. For the practitioners building the New Towns there had long been a tradition of bamboozling the attempts of government to control things. As Keith Mason, Divisional Engineer of the Cumbernauld and Irvine Development Corporations, recalled,

The famous example was when the Secretary of the Cumbernauld Development Corporation got a phone call from the Scottish Office to say, 'Don't let that contract

for this lump of road.' His answer was, 'Too late, we've already started.' He put the phone down and said 'Get that job on the go!'

(Hill, 2007: 45)

For Milton Keynes, the development corporation staff ensured their vision became a reality through a similar attitude. Trevor Denton, one of the corporation architects, described the situation in 1971.

Nothing much had been achieved for about three years . . . The whole project hung in the balance. Unless something happened quickly, Milton Keynes wouldn't happen. So Fred [Roche, the general manager] moved first on the infrastructure. Roads started to go in, and sewers. He wanted to reach a stage where the place was so committed, it would be very difficult, having spent so many millions, to pull the plug.

(Hill, 2007: 37)

In their early stages of development, the New Towns sought to gain a critical mass quickly in order to get them off the ground. After the planning came the infrastructure, and then major construction of buildings could commence. Many towns faced long delays in getting to this stage as infrastructure works were often extremely complex. In Redditch, for instance, the demands of re-housing overspill population from Birmingham were delayed by over a year while a sewage treatment plant was built. Revised masterplans for Peterlee in the 1960s required re-engineering of existing services in order to accommodate the new changes.

The tail end of this process was the determination that the towns were largely complete, so the operations of the individual development corporations could draw to a close. In 1973, the development corporations for Crawley, Hemel Hempstead, Welwyn and Hatfield closed and the Commission for the New Towns, now holding their assets, was in a position to repay their Treasury loans plus interest (Aldridge, 1979: 38). On the termination of the development corporation, housing in the new towns was to become council housing of the relevant local authority (urban district council or county council) or housing association, while the commercial property and certain other strategic assets, known as ransom strips, plus the sub-soil rights, remained the property of the Commission.

After the development corporation assets for the first four towns had been absorbed, Stevenage, Harlow, Bracknell and Corby were expected to follow suit. However, in 1975 a sharp increase in interest rates, followed by unpredictable changes in their level, made the break-even dates for these towns extremely unpredictable. The changing economic climate meant the development corporations had to continually recalculate their budgets to account for the changing interest payments due. The first generation towns Stevenage, Bracknell, Harlow, Basildon and Corby, and the second generation towns Runcorn, Redditch and Washington, were then scheduled to close their corporations between 1980 and 1983. To help reduce costs, the government merged Runcorn's Development Corporation with that of nearby Warrington. Plans for Skelmersdale, just getting off the ground in the early 1970s, were cut back.

The relationships between the New Town Development Corporations, central government and the Commission for the New Towns became increasingly complex. The situation changed in 1979 with the incoming Conservative Government adopting a radical new attitude towards the New Towns. The tacit cross-party support that they had enjoyed came to an abrupt halt. Top of Margaret Thatcher's political agenda was the taking on of left-wing metropolitan councils, union-dominated industries and the 'quasi autonomous non-government organisations', the quangos, which included the New Town Development Corporations. The Thatcher Government was convinced of the need to end the supine approach to the unions taken in the mid-1970s, stop supporting uneconomic aspects of national industries and reduce the size of the state through a process of privatising public assets. This meant a changing role for the Commission for the New Towns.

In 1979, the timetable by which the New Town Development Corporations were to wind up their activities was accelerated and their assets sold on to a wide range of buyers. The last in England, the Milton Keynes Development Corporation, closed in 1992. In Scotland, with the Scottish Office holding ultimate responsibility, the process was slower and the Scottish Development Corporations closed between 1992 and 1996, their assets transferred to new single-tier local authorities. The

Commission for the New Towns eventually repaid the last of the Treasury loans, with interest and a substantial penalty for early repayment, in 1999 (Walker, 2007).

From 1992 in England, Wales and Northern Ireland, the towns were formally de-listed as a special area of government policy. In order to 'normalise' them, they were reclassified as equivalent to all other places in the UK within their relevant local authority. In turn, the particular local authority context varied. Some New Towns would be adopted by a district authority and would be one of a number of towns within the local government's remit. For example, Runcorn became part of Widnes and Halton Borough Council, Hemel Hempstead, part of Dacorum District Council and Skelmersdale run by West Lancashire District Council. In the case of Washington, the City of Sunderland became the host authority. Others would be two-tier authorities with a district council responsible for some aspects of the town, and the county council responsible for other aspects, especially education, health and highways. Two-tier authorities are subject to complex arrangements over responsibilities, particularly over highways. In some two-tier authorities arrangements exist such that in the autumn when the leaves fall they are regarded as litter and the responsibility of the district council environment department, but if it rains they then become a hazard on the highway and become the responsibility of the county council highways department. Numerous such arrangements exist and attempts at creating unitary authorities to eliminate such complex division of duty have been an ongoing area of government reform.

These different administrative circumstances could also result in different political contexts. Further to this, the local economic context in which the towns existed, and their regional connectivity such as good access to motorways, played a major role on their circumstances. With employment sectors in decline, such as aerospace in Stevenage and Redditch, chemicals in Runcorn or steel in Corby, many New Towns faced declining fortunes that echoed those in other towns and cities similarly dependent on single employers or sectors.

Furthermore, the arrangements by which the Commission for the New Town distributed the assets from the New Town Development Corporations varied too. Some towns such as Runcorn saw their housing stock transferred to independent housing associations, while others became part of the council housing run by the local authority housing department. The variety in circumstances faced by the New Towns in the 1990s prevented easy analysis of their subsequent performance of the New Towns or of any special treatment needed because of their unique designs.

Inevitably, the transition of the New Towns to normal town administration – as with any change in management regime – altered the unique circumstances under which the New Towns had thrived, leading to unanticipated long-term consequences. The problems that the New Towns faced because of flawed assumptions in their urban design principles, or poorly constructed housing, were exacerbated by a fragmentation of ownership. Their unique layout combined with the dramatic change in government attitude towards their management, created a state of affairs that is seen only in the New Towns. Only in Scotland, where the development corporation assets were passed directly to the local authorities, was fragmented ownership avoided. The coherent management throughout the development of the Scottish New Towns continued, with towns such as Livingston experiencing none of the problems of poor estate management that later blighted the English New Towns.

'A State within the State'

In England, the culture of privatisation in the early 1980s made the two fundamental objectives of the Commission for the New Towns (to enhance the value of the asset while having regard to the welfare of the inhabitants) incompatible. Operating until 1997, the Commission for the New Towns had primarily been a management agency rather than a development agency. From its creation until 1978 it owned the freehold of all the housing and commercial property, including shops, offices and factories, as well as all the undeveloped land inside the designated area.

The distinction between the social and financial remit, warned about during the parliamentary debate in 1959, remained problematic. The goals of financial returns and ongoing investment in social aspects of the towns could not be easily reconciled in the increasingly tough financial circumstances of the late 1970s and throughout the 1980s. The balance between

financial and social objectives was maintained in the early years of the Commission in the 1960s but after 1979 the volume of development corporation assets increased massively. The transference of the assets of the New Town Development Corporations as they were wound up and the desire to quickly liquidate these assets meant the social agenda of the New Towns rapidly faded.

A 2001 report by a House of Commons Select Committee, *The New Towns: Their Problems and Future*, gathered a wide body of evidence on the long-term issues. The change in mood following the Thatcher Government's decision on the Commission for the New Towns was described by Crawley Borough Council,

> In common with many, if not most, New Towns, this authority had enjoyed mixed relationships with the Commission for New Towns. They were often challenging to deal with and invariably seemed primarily interested in realising land value from their ownerships, with the consequence that the interests of the community were often insufficiently promoted.
>
> (House of Commons, 2002a)

The report from the City of Sunderland, who took on responsibility for Washington New Town, echoes this experience,

> The sudden closure of development corporations and handover of assets to the Commission for New Towns caused problems. The legislation under which the CNT was set up gave it a much narrower role than the development corporations. Through the CNT, the government became asset strippers selling of large amounts of land and assets.
>
> (House of Commons, 2002a)

The role of the Commission having shifted towards financial gain for the nation as a whole, via the Treasury, was clear from the chairman's introduction of the final Annual Report of the Commission for the New Towns. It reflected the wider political momentum of the 1979 to 1997 Conservative Government selling-off publicly owned assets in pursuit of the 'minimal state'. Under the sub-heading 'Excellent Levels of Disposals',

Chairman Dr John Bradfield perfectly captures the attitude of the time,

1996–97 proved to be a significant year in several ways. The Government resolved that from 1998, the Commission for the New Towns should not only continue with disengagement from the New Towns, but should also undertake the disengagement from the residual assets and liabilities of the Urban Development Corporations and The Housing Action Trusts. The disposals total is excellent given that the early years of disengagement, when the Commission for the New Towns was able to generate hundreds of millions of pounds from the disposal of major built assets such as shopping centres and office blocks have long since passed. In these later years, the main emphasis is on selling land for development . . . But as our examination of 50 years of history reminded us, the New Town Movement is above all about the creation of opportunities for people, whether they are individuals or families (including parents, school children, job seekers and the retired) or whether they are institutional investors, major manufacturers or start-up entrepreneurs. It is right then, that the Commission for the New Towns should continue to take as much care over the detail of the renumerative community related assets (CRA) packages, or 'Invest in Success' transfers, as it has previously taken, and continues to take over the sale of development land or the leasing of an office building. Only by doing so can we maintain the quality of life for the inhabitants that has been created over fifty years.'

(Commission for the New Towns, 1997)

The expectations of the Commission were not met. The publicly owned land assets acquired from the New Towns Programme and those left over from the privatisation of nationalised industries, managed by the Urban Regeneration Agency, were to remain in public hands. The 1997 election instead saw Tony Blair's New Labour party sweep to government with a massive landslide. In 1999, the Commission for the New Towns and the Urban Regeneration Agency were merged and rebranded as English Partnerships. Here, the objective was to secure economic and social regeneration through stakeholder engagement. Although the era of asset stripping was over, the main priority was on regenerating the inner cities. The regeneration of the New Towns remained a lower priority than the core cities in New Labour's urban renaissance.

With the Commission for the New Towns having sold the commercial assets it controlled in the New Towns to benefit the public purse, local authorities had been left with deeply dysfunctional towns. With the town centres often nothing more than shopping malls, large parts of the urban heart of the town was essentially gated, private space that would be closed to the public as soon as the shops were shut. For the housing, estates had been intended to be managed as a whole unit but with property owners mixed in with the renting tenants, estate management became complicated, and prospects of widespread demolition hampered by the needs to compensate owners unable or unwilling to sell up and move on. This was paralleled by uniquely complicated land ownership in the town, with the prime sites often sold to distant investors, and the Commission retaining ownership of strategically significant sites (House of Commons, 2002a). The land holdings in and around the New Towns were in many cases substantial. As Meryl Aldridge notes, 'the inexorable logic of the corporations' powers to buy at less than development value had led to . . . policies of rapid land assembly from the start' (Aldridge, 1979: 103).

In Newton Aycliffe, Corby and Telford the shopping malls that formed the town centres were all sold to remote private developers, disengaged from the local area and its needs. The local authorities, no longer able to control the towns, found it immensely challenging to shape the future development of the town centres or the housing estates. In many of the later New Towns this was made even more problematic by the fact the original development plans had been effectively cut short in the 1980s, and the towns never reached the target population they were designed for (see Table 10.1). As West Lancashire District Council, responsible for Skelmersdale, reported,

at the point of transfer of planning and development responsibilities from the CNT to the Local Authority, Skelmersdale in common with other new towns was not in its planned 'completed state'. Much remained to be done. To secure the development that will take the

Table 10.1 List of English Partnerships' undeveloped land-holdings in the English New Towns as of August 2001.

New Town (in order of size of landholdings)	Designated area (hectares)	Current population (2007 est.)	Remaining English Partnerships undeveloped land holdings, 2001 (hectares) – including community assets	2001, EP land with existing planning permission in place under Section 7.1 of the 1983 New Towns Act	Value as of 31 August 2001 (£)
Bracknell	1,337	50,100	9		£1,000
Newton Aycliffe	1,254	29,000	9		£486,000
Hatfield	947	27,900	14		£1,407,000
Corby	1,791	49,200	29		£622,000
Redditch	2,906	79,500	74		£10,114,000
Hemel Hempstead	2,391	81,000	84		£8,840,000
Basildon	3,165	100,000	118	1	£19,348,000
Skelmersdale	1,669	38,800	137		£4,067,000
Runcorn	2,930	61,200	183	75	£31,717,000
Washington	2,271	60,000	199	34	£4,137,000
Peterborough	6,453	161,800	404	43	£15,529,000
Northampton	8,080	202,800	495		£64,396,000
Warrington	7,535	195,200	726	295	£107,746,000
Central Lancashire (Preston City)	14,267	300,000	730	78	£76,535,000
Dawley / Telford	7,790	138,200	820	444	£91,258,000
Milton Keynes	8,900	184,500	1,352	574	£440,185,000
TOTALS	87,459	2,387,000	5,795	1,544	£914,988,000

Source: House of Commons (2002a).

New Town towards maturity and 'normalisation' requires resources that are beyond the District Council's means. If Skelmersdale is to continue to progress and to fulfil the sub-regional function originally envisaged for it, rather than slip into a slow decline because it has been starved of resources, it is important that regeneration initiatives are funded and commenced as soon as possible.

(House of Commons, 2002a)

The circumstances by which the New Towns' assets in land and buildings had been organised echoed the scenario presented in the 1959 debate. Rather than the assets being assumed to belong to the town, they were instead taken as booty for the State. Despite the original sixty-year loans that the Treasury made to the New Town Development Corporations having all been repaid with interest, the local authorities were not themselves allowed to sell any of their assets without giving a substantial percentage (sometimes as high as 72 per cent) of the proceeds to the Treasury. As West Lancashire District Council pointed out, the CNT/EP assets did not benefit the town when sold, and neither could the local authority raise revenue by selling its assets either,

[T]he proceeds are not reinvested locally, either to secure regeneration objectives or to help meet the sometimes exceptional costs of service provision, which are a legacy of the former New Towns design and layout. Furthermore, the former CNT assets now held by the Local Authority are subject to clawback on disposal.

(House of Commons, 2002a)

Many of the councils submitting evidence to the 2001 House of Commons Select Committee called for the government to simply transfer all of the remaining centrally controlled assets to local authority control. The Commission for the New Towns was created by the Conservatives to prevent the mass transfer of assets from the New Town Development Corporation to their adjoining local authorities, who as the towns had matured were invariably Labour-controlled councils. The CNT was instead to centralise the assets precisely because of the essential idea from Ebenezer Howard's day that land ownership and urban development should be subject to local control and 'autarchy'.

The intellectual environment of the late nineteenth century, when Howard had promoted the Garden City, had seen a wide range of perspectives on 'the social question'. The Land Nationalisation Campaign focused on hypothecation of rental income by the state to achieve social ends. Henry Spencer had promoted subsidiarity by declaring that it should be parish councils that should own their local land and invest proceeds from rent into community development. Then, there was Prince Peter Kropotkin, the Russian aristocrat who became a patron of anarchist movements. His focus on autarchy was essentially about the decentralisation of power. Yet, writing in *The State: Its Historic Role* in 1897, he grimly forecast the nature of state power, which a century later had indeed become the reality for Howard's legacies,

But the State, by its very nature, cannot tolerate a free federation: it represents that bogie of all jurists, 'a State within the State'. The State cannot recognize a freely-formed union operating within itself; it only recognizes subjects. The State and its sister the Church arrogate to themselves alone the right to serve as the link between men. Consequently, the State must, perforce, wipe out cities based on the direct union between citizens. It must abolish all unions within the city, as well as the city itself, and wipe out all direct union between the cities. For

the federal principle it must substitute the principle of submission and discipline. Such is the stuff of the State, for without this principle it ceases to be State.

The desire for central control of the New Towns by government was in total contradiction to their nature as Garden Cities based upon the idea of independence from government. The authority of the state and the liberalism and self-determination of the development corporation were in destructive conflict. Ebenezer Howard had warned his acolyte, Frederick Osborn, that state involvement was flawed and Osborn's response that without state involvement the Garden Cities would never be built. This took over fifty years to come to a head. The government's official history of the New Towns Programme by Professor J.B. Cullingworth, based on ministerial correspondence and the minutes of Cabinet meetings, shows how the fundamental paradox of the New Towns Programme as publicly funded but out of public control, created deep unease. Ultimately, this problem seemed to echo the view of Kropotkin,

Much of the anxiety about new towns expressed by the Chancellor of the Exchequer and the President of the Board of Trade stemmed from the fact that, once a commitment was made to a new town, issues of overall policy control were compromised. A new town could not be made subject to the same effective controls as could be applied to other building programmes. It had its own momentum (for which a specific development agency had been established); and it was not affected by local politico-financial constraints (as was an expanded town).

(Cullingworth, 1979: 530)

Control was not merely a matter of ensuring some sort of political obedience, but also stemmed from deep concern over competence. Repeatedly the files point to 'Treasury concern to elaborate an effective machinery of control over what they often saw as "the higher flights of fancy of planners"' (Cullingworth, 1979: 530). Did the development corporation staff really understand the potential expense or long-term implications of some of their more pioneering proposals, particularly regarding transport? The proposals in Runcorn for building a road network to be used only by buses was seen as, 'one of the occasions when the architect-planner has taken a short journey into Cloud Cuckoo Land' (Treasury File 2 EAS 420/01, cited in Cullingworth, 1979: 530). Cullingworth admits that there was even doubt about the true nature of the problem of the New Towns,

> Does the resistance lie in the fear that the new towns will become too autonomous in operation or that their accounting, already muddled by grants and subsidies, will become even less effective in assessing the costs and benefits of development. Perhaps it is merely the absence of a clear set of policy objectives.
>
> (Cullingworth, 1979: 530)

Urban planning as a 'wicked problem'

Regarding policy objectives, the New Towns Programme always had an explicit goal, dating from the Garden Cities Movement, of relieving the conditions of the urban poor in the inner cities and assisting the economically depressed rural areas through managed relocation into planned new settlements. Yet the second, implicit, goal was to assist the growth of British industry and promote a positive image of the country abroad to rebuild the economy after the war. The second objective in some ways undermined the first, since the companies relocating from the cities generally took skilled workers from the outer suburbs, and the problems of the urban poor in the inner cities remained a separate issue.

Measuring the overall costs versus benefits of the New Towns, establishing the facts and thus proof of whether there was a worthwhile return on investment by the government, was infernally complicated. As Cullingworth describes,

> The Treasury were faced with a real dilemma: initially anxious (or, to use the word which frequently appeared in their internal minutes, 'alarmed') about the long-term commitment which the new towns represented, they were increasingly concerned with ensuring their 'success'. Yet this did not fit easily into normal patterns of Treasury thinking; and in any case, they were unsure about how success could be measured; hence their concern with establishing objective criteria for performance . . .

The Treasury search for objective criteria proved in vain – neither the efforts of civil servants, nor those of academics proved able to provide what was intuitively hoped for. Moreover, studies of this nature inevitably took a long time; and (even when they reached a 'conclusion') the context changed before the final report emerged. All the effort to establish a 'scientific' approach ran into the sands, and the Treasury were forced back into their well-established role of attempting to subject departmental submissions to sharp questioning, objections and delay.

> (Cullingworth, 1979: 530)

The great tragedy of the New Towns is that the uncertainty over whether they were working or not resulted in actions that in some ways guaranteed their failure. The decision in 1979 to cut this Gordian Knot by bringing the programme to its conclusion as soon as possible, both undermined the fundamental logic of the New Towns Development Corporation and prevented their local authorities from taking over that role. Instead, the ownership of the various components of the New Towns was fragmented by the asset-stripping attitude of the Commission for the New Towns. The New Towns Programme, that had become a de facto land nationalisation policy alongside the nationalisation of industry in the war, was now subject to an effective privatisation on grounds that lacked clear long-term strategy, beyond the minimising of central government involvement.

Cullingworth, writing in 1979 before the implications of this policy shift became clear, gave a considered view of the challenge faced by government. Social and political objectives often cut across the remits of different government departments, but the New Towns did this in a particularly sharp way.

> New towns could not be abstracted from planning, industrial location, education, agriculture, health, housing, transport, and other fields which, being matters of national policy and resource allocation, were constantly in the forefront of the minds of departmental and Treasury ministers.
>
> (Cullingworth: 1979: 537)

The New Towns also impacted on the concerns of local government, so across the whole spectrum of government activity, the New Towns were a perennial concern. In the age of the Garden Cities, development could proceed in near total independence from central government which then provided relatively little. Prior to the twentieth century the private sector had contributed practically all urban development, from the routes of railway lines to volume house building, and the church and charities had been major providers of health and education services. Welwyn Garden City became a modern marvel in the 1920s simply by the extent of its tarmac roads – before such basic infrastructure became a national requirement overseen by local government.

With the government inverting this status quo to assume near total control in the wartime economy, Reith's conceiving of the New Towns as independent agents were seen as 'cuckoos in the nest' not only by the residents of the Home Counties but also by government. Public sector town building clearly cut across the remits of many different departments, and with quasi autonomous development corporations involved, the overall organisational structures required was challenging. As it turned out, arrangements were irregular and at times chaotic, a point that no party involved wished to draw attention to in public.

As the towns came to be built and populated, the inter-related social and economic circumstances were intensely complex. The rising role of the public sector in this area and the rationalist mindset of the technocrat meant a culture that assumed prediction and control were possible. However, in issues of urban growth, controlled experiments of true scientific enquiry are impossible. Ultimately, the principles of success can only be reviewed with hindsight since the timescales for success in town building of this scale must be measured in generations. At the time of building, government was faced with a profound difficulty. They were attempting to understand and control something that it was logically impossible for them to do so.

This was something that went against the grain of any of the ideas within the professions involved. Le Corbusier, who was awarded the RIBA Gold Medal in 1953, and regarded as the most influential of all architect-planners, regularly referred to divine order as the essential inspiration for harmonious urban design (Liscombe, 2003). For a Swiss born into a family of clock makers, Le Corbusier's view of the world was that of an essentially mechanistic universe that should, if designed properly,

work like clockwork. This view was the legacy of Newton, Laplace and the various other scientist-philosophers of the European Enlightenment. The belief in control and predictability remained central until the 1960s, after which, across a whole range of academic study from meteorology to psychology, it became clear that the real world was in some cases too complex to be predictable.

In urban theory, this idea emerged from the work of Professor Melvin Webber, who had earlier advised Milton Keynes against a public monorail system and towards a car-based future. Along with his colleague Horst Rittel, Webber published a paper, 'Dilemmas in a General Theory of Planning', in 1974, which outlined what they called 'wicked problems'. These were ones that could not be solved by application of conventional scientific method as they involved the inter-relationships of huge numbers of variables in circular and interdependent fashions. They were 'messy' and non-linear, unlike the 'tame', linear problems familiar from games such as chess. Urban planning, they argued, was riddled with these sorts of intractable problems. Attempts to solve the problems would lead to further unintended side effects, themselves wicked problems. Understanding the issues would not lead to definitive black and white answers, but to shades of grey, where apparent contradictions prevailed, and answers were little more than 'perhaps better' or 'perhaps worse', not 'absolutely right' or 'absolutely wrong'.

These circular effects are now at the heart of understanding sustainability, and the formal study of these issues is emerging from the new scientific paradigm of systems theory. The story of the New Towns Programme is thus one of the attempts of a rationalist mindset to understand a social phenomenon that essentially could not be understood using their methods of analysis. With government certain of its role as supreme authority, this situation led inexorably to the conflict Kropotkin had forecast. The scale of the New Towns Programme, and the conflict seeded by Reith's insistence that independence was essential, was incompatible with the mindset of command-and-control demanded by Whitehall.

New Towns would only succeed if people had faith that they would succeed. If doubt as to their worth set in, it produced a feedback effect that destabilised their chances of success. In the early years, when they were growing they were dynamic, new industrial centres, offering social mobility to people living in poor conditions. Yet the inability to be sure that this was going to last, and that the money invested was going to produce a return, prompted the government to pull the plug in 1979. Shutting the development corporations down as soon as possible was seen as the safest bet. As with the later privatisation of rail, the shift in organisational structures produced huge unanticipated side-effects. For the New Towns as a whole, and for some specific sites in some of the New Towns, the result was profound social decay.

These problems were on a lesser scale than similar social and economic decay resulting from the closure of major nationalised employers across Britain's industrial heartlands. Yet, the problems that emerged in the New Towns had a similar source. Since they had ostensibly become skilled working-class towns, predominantly with jobs focused on manufacturing, distribution or clerical work, the New Towns were always a left-wing cause.

Ebenezer Howard's original intention of an independent entity to control a whole town was anathema to the sensibilities of the late 1970s and the new right-wing Thatcher Government.

New Towns in the age of sustainable communities

The future renewal of the New Towns may unlock their potential as low-carbon, sustainable communities. Image shows a cargo-cycle on Milton Keynes' red-way network.

The question of the long-term success of the New Towns is fundamentally one of the notion of sustainability. Since the 1990s, sustainable development, defined by The United Nations Brundtland Report, has sought to ensure that decisions in the present do not undermine the quality of life of those living in the future. Social and economic sustainability relate to the continued existence of fundamentals such as decent schools or employment needed to underpin the success of a place. The British planning system was created in the 1930s precisely because a boom of poorly planned urban development had failed to provide the basic amenities to ensure places that functioned properly. As described in Chapter 2, residents of the vast council housing estates created in the interwar period sometimes had to pay so much money to commute to work that they could not afford to eat. Even the middle class commuter suburbs forced people into spending over two hours a day sat on a train.

The New Towns gave this vision of the planned community the opportunity to prove itself. Seeking balanced communities, echoed the later goal of the sustainable community. In its original version, the Garden City idea, that prompted the New Towns, had the goal of self-sufficiency in food and electricity foreshadowing later concerns over environmental sustainability. So how might the New Towns be said to have been socially, economically and environmentally sustainable communities? And to what extent can any failure in this be addressed in future? In terms of towns and cities, unsustainability in social and economic terms was clear from problems of urban decline. Places that were getting worse, not better, were not able to sustain themselves. Buildings that were in need of refurbishment, or at risk of demolition, highlighted the difficulties in achieving sustainable places.

The Sustainable Communities Plan was the name given to the UK Government's national planning strategy of 2003. The definition of a sustainable community was, in its simplest formulation, 'Places where people will want to live and work, now and in the future' (CLG, 2003). The plan was backed by some £22 billion of public investment to address sites where new development could be encouraged that would contribute to such future communities. This essentially saw a return to the ideals of the post-war planners to banish urban deprivation through a rational approach to development aimed at achieving a higher quality of building and place making. Of primary concern was the dire state of the inner cities, to be galvanised through a programme of urban renaissance. In the wake of privatisation and de-industrialisation in the 1980s and 1990s, many industrial towns and mining towns had their main source of income eliminated. These communities had become effectively socially and economically unsustainable. Second, a lack of housing supply in the south created other problems of social sustainability. A lack of available housing supply meant that key workers, such as firemen or nurses, could not live near to their places of work, and had to commute extremely long distances to provide essential services.

The eighteen years of the Conservative Government from 1979 to 1997 had transformed Britain in many ways, shedding old heavy industry and nurturing the growth of a knowledge economy instead. The closure of mines, steel works and car factories resulted in population migration and the onset of urban decay, arguably the greatest since the Second World War.

Some New Towns were directly affected by the process of deindustrialisation in the 1980s and 1990s, such as Corby, the town originally built by private enterprise around a new steel works in the 1920s. In the early 1990s the end of the Cold War meant that in Stevenage, Hatfield and Redditch, defence contracts being halted, led to layoffs in the large numbers of local private firms supplying components to major military and aerospace programmes. With globalisation opening-up foreign competition, the light engineering firms that many New Towns hosted also started to suffer.

By 2002, the House of Commons Select Committee responsible for scrutinising the government's housing and planning policy, drew attention to the state of the New Towns. Evidence from a range of groups including the local authorities responsible for the towns revealed problems related to the way they had been designed and managed.

Infrastructure, housing and other buildings, were all growing old at the same rate, suddenly leading many councils with repair and refurbishment bills far higher than their annual budgets could handle. The change in the way the towns were managed, from control by dedicated development corporations to a combination of local authority, central government agency and private sector could also confuse attempts to address these issues.

Problems in the physical condition would lead to a declining image, and as people would choose to live or work elsewhere these problems could become amplified. Yet at the level of national statistics pockets of poverty could be masked by the relative success of the wider local authority boundaries in which some New Towns now found themselves. Being located in the south east, in close proximity to London, with good transport links meant a popular location for businesses to set up and lower than average unemployment and higher than average cost of living. Yet individual wards could often show worse than average on common social indicators such as teenage pregnancy or school exam pass rates. In Crawley for instance, despite having had an exceptional record on employment because of the quantity of work provided by neighbouring Gatwick Airport, in terms of education parts of the town featured in the bottom 10 per cent of the country's most deprived wards (evidence submitted by Crawley Council, cited in House of Commons, 2002a).

The consequence of this was that declining estates declined further. Low educational attainment fed back into higher unemployment, greater welfare dependency, greater incidence of crime and anti-social behaviour, and – in the most extreme cases – housing abandonment or widescale demolition. How did the New Towns get to have such major problems, when their creation so ardently sought high-quality communities? When did they go from being places that were growing, to ones that were shrinking? How did the ambition for what would now be a sustainable community fade away in reality?

That the New Towns changed from a heyday when they attracted the best new industries in the UK, to one where they became marked by decline, must be contrasted with the state of the country as a whole. Job losses in the manufacturing sector or mining affected towns and cities across the country on far greater scales than existed in the New Towns. Yet, the problems that the New Towns faced were compounded by the fact that they were young places, and that their local governance and management was altered. The government's response to the Select Committee report pointed out that firstly, the New Towns were subject to regeneration programmes. Many were in growth areas, and the national regeneration agency, English Partnerships (formed by a merger of the Commission for the New Towns and the Urban Regeneration Agency) was actively involved in working in strategic partnership with the local authorities, the Regional Development Agencies, the private sector and others to improve the conditions of the New Towns, revitalise their town centres and attract new housing and employment. Secondly, the problems of the inner cities or former industrial towns were of a far greater scale and thus were more needing of direct government support. Nonetheless, the existence of deprivation within the New Towns speaks of the troubles of urban policy, especially given the ambition of the creators of the New Towns Programme was to eliminate the appalling conditions present in cities in the early twentieth century. A single example, submitted by a resident to the 2002 Select Committee, is a reminder of the social outcome of poor building and poor management. Mrs P.E. Denne, chair of the residents association of the Five Links Estate in Basildon, recalls the phases of change, and the vicious spiral of social decline,

With my family, we came to live on the estate in August 1973 . . . we got a mutual exchange to move from Dagenham. This was a place everyone wanted to come to, in its design it was modern, pedestrian walkways only so no traffic was allowed, laid out in courtyard fashion, which were all landscaped, and family friendly, children could play outside their front doors, parents knew where they were. It made for an excellent community feeling. There were gardeners, regular cleaning teams, including drains . . . For the first ten years things were great, then the word was we were to change landlords. It did not make much of a change, then gradually the upkeep started to deteriorate. Through lack of money the cleaning facilities started to disappear, maintenance of the estate became minimal, the whole area started to slowly look like a slum, broken walls, un-repaired foot paths, broken slabs in courtyards. . . . Trees that had been planted all around the estate, even in the courtyards, through lack of coppicing, just grew out of order. This started to cause damage to properties, walls, damage to foot paths and safety roads, because of root growth, subsidence became inevitable, once again lack of maintenance.

After about 15 years of neglect, and being fed up not being listened to, residents decided to get together to

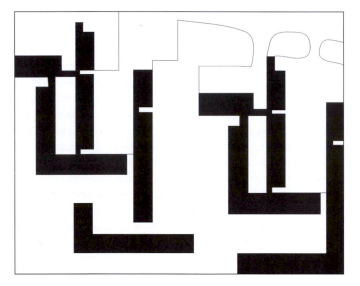

The Courts, Telford.

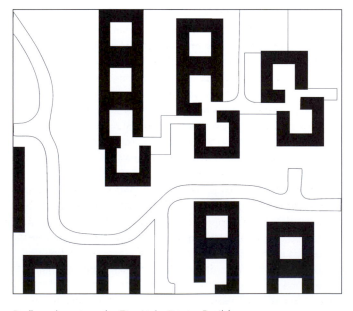

Radburn layout on the Five Links Estate, Basildon.

Car-free housing layouts in the Firbeck estate in Skelmersdale.
Courtesy of West Lancashire District Council.

form a group to try and get the local council to wake up to their responsibilities, towards the residents complaints. This was in May 1997.

(evidence submitted by Five Links Estate residents association, Basildon cited in House of Commons, 2002a)

The poor physical conditions soon attracted criminal activity. Houses were easy to break into as windows and doors were easy to force open. Pedestrian-only routes reduced natural surveillance. Stolen cars and fly-tipping would be dumped on the estate. Overall, this represented a failure of estate management. Social housing estates descending into this state of disrepair and disrepute had long been common, largely as a result of a lack of on-site presence from estate management, unlike some of the nineteenth-century housing estates (Power, 1987). Although problems on estates were not uncommon, in the New Towns the situation resulted in a rapid change from being managed by the housing department of the development corporation to becoming a new responsibility of a local authority's housing department or of a housing association. Both such organisations would be responsible for a large number of estates across a wider region than the development corporations, and would have none of the long-standing knowledge and experience of the estates and their occupants. (ODPM, 2002: 6).

Run for decades by responsive local staff engaged in achieving the best for the towns, in the wake of their 'normalisation' some New Towns and specifically certain neighbourhoods in certain towns became deeply troubled. Yet, as the official response to the House of Commons Select Committee 2002 investigation into the New Towns pointed out,

The Government accepts that some of the New Towns have problems relating to their non-traditional housing design and infrastructure. There are, however, many other urban areas that are not New Towns but were built at the same time and to the same specifications. This is not a problem specific to the New Towns.

(ODPM, 2002: 12)

Indeed, the change in ownership exacerbated problems that were there, but these problems were also found elsewhere

and on larger scales. The New Towns may have suffered severe deprivation in some areas but these areas were smaller in size than similar issues in post-war housing elsewhere such as the inner cities, and were generally not coupled with scale of economic collapse that marked Britain's old industrial and mining towns. The 'worst first' approach to regeneration, administered through the Neighbourhood Renewal Fund, focused on the local authorities ranked the worst in the country. For the New Towns, the overall performance of the local authority in which they resided could mask the levels of deprivation in some neighbourhoods. Only when viewed at the scale of local wards – which, naturally, in the New Towns followed the boundaries of the neighbourhood units – was it clear that the majority of the New Towns included wards in the bottom 20 per cent of most socially deprived wards in the country (Gardiner, 2004).

Adaptability: responding to future changes

Responding to the poor condition resulting from poor build quality in some of the New Town estates, major refurbishment programmes were set up in the 1980s and 1990s. In Harlow, the 'three hills' estates – Fernhill, Honeyhill and Clarkhill, built as part of the 1960s extension – were the most progressive in their design, demonstrating car-free housing areas in a complex of modernist buildings. Yet some parts of the estate suffered acute problems of damp and decay in the buildings. Flat roofs were taken out and replaced with pitched roofs to prevent leaking, and car parking was provided in garages rather than parking bays to reduce vehicle crime. Yet by 2000, it was deemed that these refurbishments had failed and plans were put forward for demolition and rebuilding. In some cases the residents objected, claiming that an aesthetic prejudice against modernist architecture was being applied. The neighbouring Bishopsfield estate, also featuring modernist architecture and car-free arrangements, gathered a spirited local and national campaign to defend against its demolition (*Building Design*, 2008).

The investment in infrastructure, roads, water and sewage systems, gas pipes, electric cables, telephone wires, which the development corporations had to struggle so hard for in the early days, illustrate how wasteful poor-quality construction,

Woodside, Telford – a Radburn estate whose regeneration programme has involved public realm improvements to the car-port areas to make them into more people-friendly 'home-zones'. Images courtesy of Transforming Telford.

long-term neglect and subsequent demolition could be in the long run. The first housing estate in the UK built to the Radburn principles, Laindon in Basildon, was demolished in the 1990s and rebuilt to a tight but suburban arrangement of houses on culs-de-sac with garages at the front and gardens at the back. James Stirling's Southgate estate in Runcorn and parts of Milton

Keynes also faced demolition. An inevitable factor was the relative value of the land and potential increases in value from replacing housing of a low spec built in low-density arrangements, with a greater number of units of a higher spec.

However, part of the peculiar circumstances of the New Towns' neighbourhoods meant that in some instances demolition has not been an option. The case of the Woodside neighbourhood in Telford provides a strong example of this challenge. With around 80 per cent of the properties privately owned as a result of the right-to-buy policy, demolition was restricted to a cluster of problematic deck-access flats known as The Courts. The remaining 2,000 homes were also in themselves good quality. The problems were the surrounding environment and its Radburn layout, which had altered the traditional relationship between buildings and streets. Instead of the street combining pedestrian and vehicle movement, Radburn layouts separated these two functions, in order to create extensive car-free areas. The local road network led to car parking areas at the rear of the properties, while the fronts of the houses faced onto pedestrian-only walkways that connected via nearby green spaces to the neighbourhood centres. Unlike in the original Radburn, New Jersey, a desirable leafy suburb a few miles from downtown Manhattan, in British Radburn estates few people used the pedestrian footways. Instead, people invariably relied on their cars for daily needs, so always entered their houses by the service entrance at the rear. In the case of Woodside and other Radburn estates, extremely complex, expensive and time-consuming processes were needed to work out how the overall area could be improved, without resorting to total demolition and remodelling.

When a process of regeneration began in Telford in 2003, the Woodside Estate achieved the worst score on the government's Indices of Multiple Deprivation (IMD) for the town and was in the worst 5 per cent nationally. The initial design approach applied to regenerate the estate proposed to invert the logic of the Radburn layout through a 'turnaround solution'. This suggested inverting the internal layouts of the houses back again, so that the vehicle-facing entrance became the formal front of the house and the vehicle areas remodelled to more closely resemble a normal street. At the other side of the house, the underused pedestrian routes would be sealed-off to become back gardens.

However, this design proved unworkable as, first, residents did not like the disruption of having rooms such as kitchens moved from one part of the house to another, or the possible inconvenience of carrying everything to their now landlocked gardens through their house. Second, the utilities companies ruled-out converting the underused pedestrian walkways into closed back gardens, as this was where the services had been laid. Uninterrupted access was needed for future repairs to water, sewers, gas pipes or electricity wires, which would be impossible if they had gardens laid over them. Whereas in the traditional street services ran under the road or pavement, in the Radburn estates the apparently less disruptive laying of services along pedestrian walkways and adjoining green verges prevented any alteration of the unsuccessful layout (Schofield, 2008).

The solution eventually adopted was devised by a firm of Dutch architects who, through a community-led design process, modified the service areas according to the idea of the Home Zone. This turns car-dominated areas into more people-friendly places by changing the design of the streetscape (see www.homezones.org). Asking residents what they wanted provided vital feedback on maintaining the positive aspects of the existing buildings. In terms of establishing the success of these alterations, Woodside housing manager, Will Schofield, said,

It is difficult to get scientific measures, but we have been carrying out resident satisfaction surveys over a long time looking at the differentials between different areas. Satisfaction levels are rising faster in the parts of the estate that have had the works done than those which have not. Property values are also rising faster in the areas that have been done, than those that have not.

(Schofield, 2008)

At the larger scale of the area or neighbourhood-level development further examples of a fundamental lack of adaptability can be seen in the road structure. In Washington, the large-scale road network, arranged in a grid predating that of Milton Keynes, resulted in neighbourhood units – called villages – being cut off from one another. As the local authority described it, 'The road network acts like a collar therefore new development and change is unable to straddle more than one village' (House of Commons, 2002a). Separating the cars into their own dedicated network meant high mobility, which was good, but long-term severance, which was bad. The dedicated pedestrian-only movement routes also created problems. The extensive use of cycle ways and pedestrian paths separate from roads creates problems of safety and way-finding. As the authorities in Washington described,

> Whilst all the villages are interlinked with footpaths, these are often poorly lit and fail to create an attractive environment conducive to encouraging more people to walk. The separation of roads from pedestrians means that the town is difficult and confusing to navigate.
>
> (House of Commons, 2002a)

Furthermore, these car-free routes are expensive to keep in good condition. As the local authority for Runcorn reported, 'Maintenance costs can be disproportionately high due to the difficulties of machine access away from the road' (House of Commons, 2002a). The legacy of the celebrated decision to separate road, pavement and cycle path thus reveals the huge natural efficiencies that existed in traditional street patterns by having these three modes of transport all sitting adjacent to each other. The innovation of the Radburn design, transferred into a practice of car-free neighbourhood design and total segregation of different modes of movement, had a huge impact on the nature of place created in the New Towns.

The situation encountered in the New Towns of poor physical condition has counted against their becoming sustainable communities. Their poor build quality is amplified by the weakened economic status of the towns themselves. For a time they ceased to be places that people wanted to live and work. Writing in *The Guardian*, journalist Jason Cowley, who grew up in Harlow in the 1970s, described how his town changed from a booming to a declining place.

> When I lived in Harlow, in the 1970s . . . it seemed to offer everything an energetic young boy could want in those days: department stores, an Olympic-size swimming pool, a hi-tech sports centre, a dry-ski slope, a skating rink and a golf course set in a landscaped park through which a river meandered. It even had its own water gardens, at the gateway to which was a Henry Moore sculpture of a family – which, my father told me, symbolised all the new families that had started in the 1960s when Harlow was known as 'pram town' . . . It had a leftwing council, a progressive, liberal intelligentsia, which congregated around the excellent local playhouse, eight comprehensive schools and a well-funded network of children's playschemes and recreational sports facilities (Glenn Hoddle emerged from the Harlow leagues). It was a well-organised town . . . Just outside the town centre was a football stadium, the home of Harlow Town, who, for a brief period in 1979, became the most celebrated non-league club in the country by beating Leicester City, among others, on their way to the fourth round of the FA Cup. Harlow eventually lost 4–3 away to Elton John and Graham Taylor's Watford in a thrilling game that was shown on *Match of the Day*. I was in the crowd that afternoon when, for large parts of the game, my home team dominated. In retrospect, that match was the high point of my time in Harlow. Not long afterwards, my parents moved away, already alarmed by what they saw as the precipitous onset of decline.
>
> (Cowley, 2002)

The New Towns enjoyed a spirit of optimism, community and growth when they were being built, and when they were run by their local development corporations. The end of the development corporation changed the fundamental functioning of the towns, and arguably they have struggled to find their feet in the wake of this, alongside other challenges such as national economic change and issues with their designs. Yet, just as things changed for the worse, in time as the British economy shifts again, their economic prospects are likely to improve. In time, the quality of the built environment, and the quality of the towns as a whole, will improve.

Sustainability as a changing understanding of the natural world

The challenge of sustainability is fundamentally to ensure the upward direction of social progress. This is impossible in the face of unstable economic conditions and the persistent growth of environmental pollution and resource depletion. The concerns of sustainability are therefore the primary concerns of the planning system – a point that the TCPA have been hammering home throughout the last few years to great effect (see www.tcpa.org.uk). Fundamentally, the TCPA have always been at the forefront of new directions in planning, with public interest being the primary objective: homes for all, sustainable development and community empowerment. These objectives of planning are still valid, even if the precise methods for achieving these objectives are continually refined.

The New Towns serve as a vital body of knowledge about how particular design principles or decisions over strategic planning have turned out in the long run. The examples of inflexible layouts caused partly by their physical design, partly by their ownership, or segregated pedestrian and cycle routes made troublesome by high cost of maintenance and fear of crime. Each of these is the result of wider social and political factors that were impossible to anticipate when the designs were first conceived. The difficulty in predicting the future evolution affected the designers but also the civil servants in charge of the finance. As discussed in Chapter 10, in the 1960s, the Treasury, desperate to establish whether the New Towns Programme was providing good value for money, determined that it was logically impossible to separate the complex variables at work or draw meaningful comparison between different economic conditions or other parallel programmes such as the 1950s Expanded Towns Programme (Cullingworth, 1979: 537).

Research into the New Towns represented what Melvin Webber was later to call 'a wicked problem', one that was essentially too complex to be capable of simple answers. But this is not to say that there cannot be useful empirical knowledge learnt. Rather than being predictive, like the science of ballistics or mechanical engineering, the study of towns should be perhaps more like the science of biology. This produces significant scientific knowledge but in a different form. Towns are, after all, natural phenomenon just as human society is. Until the late 1960s, the mindset of those involved in the design of the New Towns belonged to an age of mechanical reason, after which the subsequent ecological mindset started to gain ground.

The urban development underway at the cusp of this change was Milton Keynes. One of the architects, Christopher Woodward, described their approach saying, 'We regarded existing new towns are inadequate, sentimental, insufficiently rigorous, not theoretically based, and patronising' (Hill, 2007: 23). Another Milton Keynes Development Corporation architect, Stuart Mosscrop, said of the grid pattern of the town, 'The straight line is the only distinctive mark that man can make on the face of the Earth. Nature can make any other kind of shape but can't make a perfectly straight line' (Hill, 2007: 15). The urban designers and architects applied their vision of the modern age in the built fabric of towns such as Milton Keynes. The flat landscape of Bradwell Common was to have the geometrically pure concept of the grid imposed upon it by the architecture, planning and civil engineering of Central Milton Keynes. This attitude sought to impress upon nature a rigid, scientifically justified mark, as proof that humankind had conquered the natural world. This view was the essence of the mechanical concept of nature that understood humanity's role upon the earth as controlling nature for the benefit of human needs. This view had grown throughout the nineteenth century with the industrial revolution and had been furthered by every new technological marvel, from the steam train to the spaceship.

In the design of Central Milton Keynes this belief manifested itself in the street pattern of the city. The continuous line of Midsummer Boulevard reaches from the train station to the shopping mall centre, through it and on to Campbell Park beyond in a single uninterrupted line. The aesthetic experience of walking along this straight line is one of a persistent and extreme vanishing point. The interior of the Central Milton Keynes shopping centre is similar to being in an airport, which were subject to major growth at the same time.

Yet just as the philosophical ideas underpinning modernist architecture were being implemented in the plan for Milton Keynes, science itself was becoming more sophisticated in its view of the world. The ecology movement was starting to demonstrate the impact that industrialised human action was having on the natural world, and the Apollo missions to the Moon showed that the whole Earth was just a tiny marble in a sea of infinite darkness.

Appreciation of the link between people and nature was then revolutionised in the 1970s by the work of environmental psychologists such as Stephen Kaplan, Rachel Kaplan and Daniel Berlyne. Their work proved from extensive research that

Milton Keynes' unique public realm produces an aesthetic experience different from traditional British towns. The grid system produces strong vanishing points, especially for pedestrians, except where the footpaths dip under the roads. The Centre, Britain's first 1 million square foot shopping mall, bares a similarity to the British airport concourses designed around the same time.

Central Milton Keynes.

certain environments were naturally more appealing to people. This rang with the logic of evolutionary biology. Our aesthetic experience had a rational basis. Detailed, interesting views that offered basic qualities of shelter and exploration were naturally appealing. Their work also proved that exposure to nature automatically relieved mental fatigue that built up from repetitive views or contained spaces.

There was a fundamental preference, common to all people regardless of cultural background, towards certain types of view. What people innately found attractive and comforting were scenes akin to an open valley with trees in it. A vista should allow one to see danger approaching, offer somewhere to shelter – from attack or from the rain – and, crucially, an element that appeared hidden that encouraged exploration. In an urban context, a bend in the road or entrances of buildings provided naturally compelling views (Kaplan et al., 1998). According to the Kaplans, urban layouts with roads that form clear sections of 100 metres or so make naturally more successful communities than long terraces. Such street patterns are often found in historic European towns and cities – either because they have grown gradually, and thus show incremental and organic change, or because the designer had an instinctive appreciation

for these universal aesthetic principles. The curve of Regent Street in London's West End is a clear example. Similarly, buildings with views of trees or open space are inherently more appealing and more calming to be in. In light of this fact, the aesthetic experience of Milton Keynes' repetitive clean lines and vanishing points, from a pedestrian point of view at least, is alienating. In the car, of course, it is a different experience, and the car-based residents are rightly proud of their unique city with its tree-lined boulevards.

An aesthetic analysis of Central Milton Keynes is far from clear-cut, but does suggest positive or negative qualities of design. Grid cities exist across the world and throughout history, and the qualities of their spaces have numerous factors to consider, from sense of enclosure to level of activity on the street. Such an assessment of the New Towns on the grounds of environmental psychology would find various complex questions. The maturity of the New Towns is reflected in that of their trees and hedgerows. In many cases the New Towns preserved their mature trees. Milton Keynes even built its main shopping centre around an existing oak tree. On the surrounding streets, the trees in Milton Keynes will take ninety years to mature. This means that by the middle of the century – assuming they survive the onset of global warming – it will be possible to see clearly across Midsummer Boulevard. The extensive presence of trees and landscaped green banks, throughout the New Towns, according to Kaplan and Kaplan means inherently calming and attractive locations. Yet how is this effect countered by the pedestrian experience of traffic or a repetitious street experience, with unattractive underpasses? Clearly, the presence of trees and plants is preferable to a barren and hard public realm, but questions remain as to whether such greenery in the New Towns might be revitalised. Might it better provide habitat for promoting biodiversity, and should town planners treat their urban green infrastructure in light of climate change (see BRANCH, 2007)?

In terms of the overall pattern of streets, the grand geometric boulevards of nineteenth-century Napoleonic Paris served a specific purpose of allowing the military to control the city. The statement of control over chaos was not merely a philosophical one, but a pragmatic one. The barricading of tight and complex medieval streets had been a crucial element of success in the French Revolution. The bold new avenues meant cavalry could move rapidly through the city and create firing lines across which people could not move. These principles were soon established in city building across continental Europe from the Baltic to the Black Sea.

The vision of order in the urban layout of towns, built on the geometric rationalism and impression of control over untidy nature, or the mob, did however also epitomise the mindset of the industrial age. The 1970s mark the start of a new way of thinking about humanity, technology and the natural world. The ecology movement grew until by the 1990s its stark warnings of the impact of the industrial mindset were finally taken seriously by the political establishment, and by the 2000s became a mainstream concern. Today, the contribution to climate by pollution from power stations, factories and vehicles – especially cars – has meant an urgent need to address the environmental sustainability of our towns and cities. The fundamental principles of urban industrial society are challenged by these new agendas. Future development is expected to meet new standards and new design principles. Existing settlements must be refurbished in such a way that their negative environmental impact is reduced, and that they can adapt to the now inevitable changes in the climate.

The New Towns offer a great example in this respect. First, their story reminds us that this zeal for radically altering the nature of urbanism leads to unforeseen side-effects. Second, demands change as society changes, and as such the attributes of a place may turn from a disadvantage to an advantage again. Third, the New Towns are places that are in many ways ideally equipped to pioneer the move to sustainability.

The New Towns were built to be socially sustainable communities, in sharp contrast to the bleak estates or suburban sprawl of the 1920s, where local facilities or sense of identity may be absent. They have been economically sustainable wherever the mix of employment has meant a sufficient variety of work in event of the collapse of any particular employer or sector. In terms of environmental sustainability, all the New Towns have extensive habitat such as woodlands, comprehensive cycle paths that other towns could never dream of, and a range of sites that are already pioneering a range of environmental aspects, from industry to housing. The new paradigm of sustainable development, more holistic, organic, accepting of limitations, not naively asserting control over nature begins at the point the designs of the New Towns end. Yet even though the grand gestures of the New Towns plans may have epitomised the mechanical view of humanity asserting control over nature, the future belonged to the new wave. Throughout the 1970s, the TCPA was involved in campaigns such as Greentown, Milton Keynes, and the Lightmoor Community in Telford. These were prototypes for low-impact developments, but Greentown was rejected, and Lightmoor was extremely small scale (Hardy, 1991b).

The clamour today is that all towns must be sustainable. Rather than Parker-Morris room sizes and industrial system building, the new standards are for 'eco-homes'. Essentially, the regulations such as the Code for Sustainable Homes are encouraging super-insulated buildings, oriented to achieve maximum solar gain and with technological features such as heat-recovery ventilation systems, grey-water recycling systems and roof-mounted solar panels. Heating, electricity and water systems are also being re-considered at a neighbourhood level, with 'energy from waste' plants capturing low carbon bio-gas from rubbish dumps and sewage works, in place of high carbon fossil gas. These ambitions are driven by careful consideration of policy objectives, yet there is a risk that they will eventually deliver precisely the same unforeseen consequences as housing standards in the past. Just as in the past, these might take decades to come to light. Achieving three goals of high-quality housing, in large volumes and with rapid delivery, is generally never met. Either there is high-quality build, delivered quickly, but in small quantities, or large volume of homes, delivered quickly but of lower quality, or large volumes of high quality, but delivered slowly. This problem is by and large intractable.

The lessons of the New Town design concepts

In the New Towns, where mass-production techniques were encouraged to speed the delivery of housing targets, these produced buildings with low potential for future modification. In places that included parts of Harlow, Basildon, Runcorn and Telford, whole neighbourhoods have been marked as impossible to refurbish. By contrast, the high volumes of late Victorian housing, or interwar suburban semi-detached houses, often built by small teams of builders, were of variable quality, but the building design was inherently adaptable. Extensions could be added to the back or the side, lofts could be converted, details augmented or removed, and each would have its own drive, giving space for one or more cars outside the front door. The New Towns development corporations largely ignored this housing type, opting instead for lines of terraces surrounded by open space. Suburban semi-detached housing was predominantly built by private developers, but this represented a small proportion of the total.

At the level of the street, the way that repetitive terraces were built prevented individual buildings being replaced. In the town centres, the large 'monumentalist' block structures also lacked the quality of traditional street patterns where small building plots with diverse ownership could be individually replaced over time. This fine-grain pattern can respond to the changing needs of a place over time. Clear examples of this can be seen in the post-war reconstruction of Köln in Germany compared to Coventry in England. As with the New Towns, Coventry centre was built as a modernist superstructure, where coarse-grain buildings containing office and retail surrounded

pedestrian precincts. These need to be refurbished as a whole, and the essential properties of the buildings are difficult to alter. In Köln, the city centre had also been destroyed in the war and only one in ten of the original buildings remained. Unlike Coventry, the city was rebuilt to the old medieval street pattern, reproducing the plot sizes and building heights that had been there before. The result is that whereas Coventry feels partly like a product of the 1950s and 1960s, Köln largely feels like a historic city even though practically all the buildings in the centre are post-war. Its streets, now largely pedestrianised, have an attractive lack of regularity, many hidden spaces and buildings that can be removed and replaced over time, creating a richly textured urban environment. Each building can be removed and replaced if desired. Poor-quality buildings might be replaced with a higher spec one, offices can become apartments or vice versa, depending on what the building owners decide to do.

The coarse grain centres throughout the New Towns were favoured by department stores and retail chains, but made specialist independent retail less likely. The designers of Milton Keynes were aware of this and getting the shopping centre they hoped for proved to be a challenge. As Allen Duff, Commercial Director of MKDC from 1978 to 1983, recalled,

> We took advice from a lot of people, and one of the most vociferous was Terrance Conran [Britain's leading furniture magnate] . . . He argued that specialist retail made shopping centres different. You don't go to another town to go to Woolworths because you've got one of your own. But you might go for a really good book or music shop. We took this advice very seriously, agreed with it completely, but found that the quality specialist shops were usually family-run businesses. [They'd] been in a particular location for a long time, owned the freehold on their property [and were] successful because of their good will and personal attention.
>
> (Hill, 2007: 31)

To try to get small retail in, certain tenants were offered zero rent up to £100,000 turnover per annum and 10 per cent thereafter. An arcade was dedicated to smaller shop units. As MK's Centre took off however, it became impossible to

In the post-war era Köln was rebuilt to its traditional street pattern, building heights and plot sizes, keeping the character of the streets, their sense of enclosure and intricate public spaces, with buildings essentially 80 per cent new build.

A further benefit of this urban form is that over time single buildings are easily capable of being removed and replaced to reflect changing needs and producing an engaging, fine-grain street. Images above show Clerkenwell in London.

Modern, up-market, self-build houses in Amsterdam's Eastern Docklands show extremely creative responses within a coherent pattern of traditional building heights and plot size outlined by a neighbourhood design code.

enforce this mix. Tenants were offered huge sums of money to move out by national retailers desperate to take their place (Hill, 2007: 51).

Research conducted in 2005 by the think tank the New Economics Foundation noted that, throughout Britain, town centres were becoming indistinguishable because major retailers were becoming dominant. Individualistic places defined by specialist retailers were becoming rare. They dubbed this the rise of 'clone towns' (NEF, 2005). In new urban development

today, creating a high-quality town centres with interesting specialist retailers would benefit from fine-grained streets where affordable commercial plots are available for sale, preferably with small mortgages. This should complement the recognised need for affordable mortgages for key public workers such as the police and fire service.

At the wider scale than the individual building or street, the neighbourhood unit and zoning were major design principles of the New Towns. This rejection of the historic urban form from

In Britain's New Towns – and elsewhere – single large structures containing a set number of housing units or retail units of a set size could prove extremely difficult to adapt to different uses in the future. The 'form-follows-function' argument meant a built-in lack of flexibility to changing needs of society over time. Photo: Stevenage town centre.

the 1940s onwards was intended to solve perceived problems in cities blighted by traffic, factory smoke and poorly maintained housing. Housing arranged into neighbourhood units of around 5 to 10,000 homes, with shops in a local neighbourhood centre, and separated by major roads, produced physical severance. Today, as the English Partnerships Urban Design Compendium notes,

> The neighbourhood unit can provide a useful organising device – but only when it is overlaid on an integrated movement framework and conceived as a piece of town or city whose activities and forms overlap. This is to move away from large-scale projects envisaged or described as neighbourhoods, but designed as disconnected enclaves. It is also to move away from estates and layouts – terms which in themselves serve to emphasise single use and segregation.
>
> (EP, 2000: 41)

The design principles in the New Towns were put into practice in the 1940s, 1950s and 1960s, with an appearance of scientific rationality, but no strong understanding of how they would work in reality. Such an understanding was never going to be easy to determine, as the effects would take time to become apparent, and unforeseen consequences were an inevitable consequence of social and technological change. The clear example of this is the impact of the car on the validity of the design principles. This point was argued extensively over the years, with the modernist architects and the highways engineers carrying far more influence than public transport lobbyists or Garden City idealists. Only in the last twenty years has the trend reversed and the focus shifted towards the necessity for sustainable transport.

The failure to understand movement patterns can be seen clearly in the case of the first New Town, Stevenage. Movement plays a fundamental role on the nature of place so changes in movement patterns mean changes in the way a place functions. Nick Matthews, editor of the TCPA journal and a resident of Stevenage, describes this change,

> The large scale road infrastructure ensured rapid mobility, yet this increased mobility meant the neighbourhood centres only had residual usage. In general, the neighbourhood units were successful, but in the

1960s, increased mobility diffused sense of identity at the neighbourhood level.

(Matthews, 2008)

Ironically, bike shops are an example of successful retail in a neighbourhood shopping centre, yet this zero-carbon mode of transport is not ideally catered for. In many New Towns, the cycle network goes to the town centre, but not through it. The lack of movement through the centre is the long-term result of the design principle that traffic should move to and not through centres. These have led to long-term concerns for the future development of the town centre. As Matthews describes,

The problem with the town centre is there is no flow. It is in the centre of a ring of dual carriageways so there is no opportunity for organic growth. It is in the hands of a single, institutional management. It is very difficult to make it feel like a place you want to visit.

(Matthews, 2008)

As discussed in Chapter 9, road systems that encouraged rapid movement by car meant people could as easily drive away from the centres of the New Towns as into them. In Stevenage, ironically, the centre of historic Stevenage Village was a more common draw for some residents than the New Town centre.

The old town centre is the strongest of the neighbourhood centres because it has a large supermarket (Waitrose). It has lots of pubs because of its old coaching history, and a plethora of takeaways. For a long time it was the centre of the town's nightlife, until the Leisure Centre opened on part of the old industrial estate.

(Matthews, 2008)

This trend is seen elsewhere too. For Crawley, the historic high street that had built up along the old London to Brighton coaching route, sits to the side of the New Town shopping precinct opened in the 1960s. In the 1980s, a major new shopping centre, The County Mall, again shifted the centre of economic activity to a new site. Ultimately a car-based leisure park in the 1990s, with a multiplex, bowling alley and franchise restaurant chain, shifted evening entertainment away from the centre (see photos on page 86).

A further significant aspect of changing movement patterns relates to speed. In terms of retail provision, Stevenage centre struggled to pull people in from a larger area, partly because of the ease with which people nearby could get to London. The Garden City rationale of locating satellite towns a certain distance away from their parent cities was eroded by changes in the speed of rail services. Where Stevenage was once effectively self-sufficient by virtue of it being around an hour from central London by rail, since the late 1970s the same journey could be done in half the time.

Increases in rail speed affected all the London satellite towns, including as far away as Peterborough. Not only was day tripping to the retail or cultural amenities of the capital extremely easy, but also these New Towns became attractive locations from which to commute to London. If one worked relatively close to the relevant mainline station in London, it could be a quicker door-to-door commute from a satellite New Town than commuting from another part of London. The ambition for social balance and a lack of outward commuting was undermined by increased mobility, as was the economic success of the town centres.

How the New Towns were affected varied, depending on the regional context. Bracknell for instance suffered from its proximity to the shopping facilities of Reading. Despite being in a highly populated area of the country, Bracknell, like Stevenage, could not attract people in from other nearby towns. The town centres had been designed to meet the needs of their surrounding neighbourhood units, but these people did not necessarily see the need to use the town centres when better shopping was available elsewhere, and outsiders thought the same.

On the other extreme, Peterborough is a major local centre with excellent transport links to the rest of the country as a whole, but located in the sparsely populated East Midlands region it could not draw many people in to support its retail or leisure sectors. By comparison, small cities such as Oxford and Reading in the Thames Valley are surrounded by a large number of towns with modest populations in the tens of thousands, and are within easy striking distance of each other, and large towns such as Swindon. As such, a large population

The Stevenage Leisure Centre on part of the former industrial estate immediately to the west of the train station and the town centre, represents a major new centre of activity for the town. As with Crawley (described on page 86) this new development represents growth but also draws economic life away from the former places of activity in the town.

in the surrounding area support the shopping and nightlife of both Oxford and Reading.

The prize for the best plan for regional connectivity belongs to Milton Keynes. Located far enough from London and of a sufficient scale, it instantly became a regional centre in its own right. It is also located midway between the vast centres of London and Birmingham, connected by motorway and mainline rail, and also lies midway between the top tier university towns of Oxford and Cambridge. The government's Sustainable Communities Plan identifies this as the east–west science arc, with Milton Keynes being a major point for growth at its centre. The strategic value of its location is that Milton Keynes has ready access to the markets of Britain's largest two cities, and provides space for the commercial development of innovations generated by the adjacent university towns. Its role today is a new investment focus for British technological innovation.

The Point in Milton Keynes opened in 1985 and was Britain's first multi-screen cinema.

This role continues that the tradition of all post-war New Towns in providing business premises and workforces for emerging British industries.

The heritage value of the New Towns

Questions of how the New Towns should be regenerated extend from their housing through their road layouts to the nature of their centres. How can such interventions be done in a way that respects the existing place, as the recent government guidance requests? The New Towns have always had something of a 'science-fiction' aesthetic – parts of Kubrick's *A Clockwork Orange* were filmed in Harlow, and the futurist pyramid of Milton Keynes' Bletchley leisure centre became part of an alien world in *Doctor Who*. These progressive designs produced places that are unique, even if their reputations have become tarnished. This provides something of a challenge for their ongoing refurbishment. Should they attempt to preserve the ethos of the 1950s and 1960s, or is that a lost cause? Incremental changes have seen the originally bold architecture and never completed super structure of Cumbernauld town centre, crowded out by 1990s big box retail stores. In Harlow, the public park area of Gibberd's Water Gardens was converted into an additional shopping mall and multi-storey car park. These changes may have secured employment and commercial gain in the short term, but have created changes that challenge the prospects for building in keeping with the original intentions.

The first generation New Towns were products of the 1950s. Their designers and early residents felt like pioneers, not only because they were moving to new lands but because they sought to build a new way of life using new techniques. Whereas house building in the early twentieth century had used horse and cart to bring building materials to site, by the 1950s new machines were massively extending human capabilities. As such, engineers were designing features such as extensive landscaping and vast pedestrian underpasses with greater ease than before.

These early New Towns also belonged to an era defined by a paternalistic view that the authorities did what was best. Reith, for instance, forbade the inclusion of dog racing tracks in the New Towns, even if there had been demand. The New Towns were founded on the idea that life consisted of a steady job and weekends of idle bliss tending to one's garden. By the later New Towns, the liberal and progressive mood of the swinging sixties meant different values, reflected in the personal mobility made possible by the car. The civic amenities of the town were its sports centre and swimming pool, its library and arts centre. Many clearly demonstrate principles that are resolutely of their time, and should be respected as such.

Against the backdrop of changing political attitude, acute areas of deprivation and depressed town centres that demand regeneration, the New Towns nonetheless have an architectural character and a place in history that should not be lightly dismissed. With their reputation sullied by negative press, especially in the wake of major unemployment affecting Corby, Runcorn, Skelmersdale or Hatfield, the significance of the New Towns has been lost. The New Towns can in some ways be seen as identical to their contemporary buildings in the Expanded Towns or in the inner cities, yet these lacked the coherence and

scale of the New Towns. Leading the campaign for this period of architecture as part of British heritage is The Twentieth Century Society. Campaign director, Jon Wright, described the challenges,

> Generally in the New Towns there is a lack of understanding about what was trying to be achieved. Until the late 1970s, the buildings, public art and street patterns of the Victorian era were considered poor quality, out of touch with modern needs and best demolished. Today the same is occurring in the New Towns. Large architectural statements of the era that are now listed such as the Byker Wall in Newcastle or Park Hill estate in Sheffield, are widely known, but the New Towns are neglected. They are not places that people other than their residents or people working there ever visit.
>
> (Wright, 2008)

The unique character of the New Towns is shaped by their origins in the Garden City Movement and what it aimed to achieve. This Edwardian vision that sought to combine the best features of both urban and rural environments, the town and the country, mean that the New Towns green space and balance of housing to jobs are extremely significant. However, many New Towns have been afflicted by the poor consequences of their strategic location, uncertainty over their intended size, poor build quality, or later alterations or additions. A fundamental shift in Britain's economy away from manufacturing was inconceivable in the early days of the New Towns. The prospect of future economic decline of the New Towns was never considered by their original masterplanners.

Interestingly, as a product of their time, the New Towns heritage points to some of the key – and perhaps not widely known – figures of the twentieth century. Telford of course was renamed as such, from its original name of Dawley, to pay tribute to Thomas Telford, the civil engineer whose construction projects helped develop the industrial revolution in nearby Ironbridge. A less well known figure in New Town heritage – other than to local residents that is – is Caroline Haslett DBE, from Crawley; an Edwardian physicist who campaigned for the benefits of domestic electricity supply to be understood. The Electrical Association for Women she co-founded produced the first 'all-electric' home in 1935; a pioneering idea when few homes had electric light, let alone appliances. Housework was toil, she argued, and so electrical machines should be invented to liberate us. Twenty years later the National Grid was built to bring electrification into British homes.

Electrification led to electronics and computing (originating in the work of Alan Turing, at Bletchley Park, which coincidentally is now part of Milton Keynes). These new industries were as significant in the 1960s, 1970s and 1980s as the rise of the car in the 1950s and 1960s, or the radio and telephone in the 1920s and 1930s. Various post-war New Towns, such as Stevenage, Glenrothes and Cumbernauld, provided brand new facilities for new emerging market sectors and so were at the forefront of building computers – or tabulating machines – as they were originally known. The New Towns have thus been the centres for innovation in Britain. They have thus been vital in developing new sectors for British industry and have played a critical role in shaping the whole of the modern world. Besides their scientists and engineers, the New Towns also have their fair share of world famous actors, musicians and sports stars.

The economic sustainability of any town is based by and large on the strategic value of its location, and the range and type of employers that prosper there. In their heyday, prior to the economic downturns and asset stripping of the Thatcher and Major years, the New Towns performed impressively. Between 1960 and 1978, overall national manufacturing output fell by 11.5 per cent but in the New Towns increased by 25 per cent. By 1989, this had extended to new, high-tech industries, 50 per cent of the urban centres for new technology jobs were in the New Towns (CLG, 2006: 63). Furthermore, the goal of creating well-balanced towns where all residents could work locally was achieved. The towns were remarkably self-contained (CLG, 2006: 61). However, the technological change that brought them success, and the rising consumer culture that brought domestic appliances and the private car, ultimately upset the goal of a balanced community. Clearly, a return to the vision of low commuting via local employment, and spaces designed to attract new businesses, perfectly fits the contemporary goal of the sustainable community.

In the first decades of the twenty-first century this also means the New Towns are starting to contribute to the challenge of environmental sustainability. Their engineering and manufac-

turing bases will become the centres for the development of low-carbon products and services. Already there are powerful moves in this direction. The Corby steelworks site now hosts the Eurohub rail-based freight centre that links the heart of England to the whole of continental Europe via the Channel Tunnel. The Nissan plant in Washington was among the first to be powered by wind energy, and the nearby Smith Electric Vehicle company has been a leader in the delivery of zero-emission service vehicles. Peterborough has re-branded itself an 'eco-city' to focus on its cluster of environmental companies and new eco-housing. Glenrothes is home to the Fife Energy Park, pioneering the construction of major sustainable energy infrastructure, such as off-shore wind turbines.

The constant waves of technological change and social change can be seen in Hatfield. The former aerodrome site, now the Hatfield Business Park, is host to numerous firms including mobile phone company T-Mobile and the online grocery store Ocado. The vast computerised distribution facility for Ocado is a creation of the Internet age. It can distribute goods to 60 per cent of the country with a lower total carbon footprint than any conventional supermarket (even when the customer walks to the store) given that its total distribution pattern is so much more efficient in comparison. In a carbon-constrained world this approach may become dominant.

A final example of how the New Towns have been advancing the agenda of environmental sustainability is in recent housing provision utilising the eco-homes standards. Due to the public sector land-ownership transferring from the Commission for the New Towns to English Partnerships (becoming the Homes and Communities Agency in 2008), and English Partnerships requiring all housing on their land to be built to the government's Code for Sustainable Homes standard ahead of it becoming a mandatory requirement, the New Towns have hosted some of the first and largest developments built to this new standard. These include the exemplar sustainable urban extension at Upton in Northampton, and major sites in Telford, Corby, Peterborough and Milton Keynes. These have all aimed to apply new environmental standards ahead of these being required for all new house building. In Bracknell, English Partnerships and the local strategic partnership have been adapting the former RAF training college, located close to the centre of town, into a site of several thousand new eco-homes (see table on page 143 for the volume of English Partnerships land in the New Towns and its values as of 2001).

So what are the lessons from the post-war New Towns that future town builders should take on board? Towns are around for a long time, so they must be made to accommodate change. First, they must be large enough to be self-supporting and expand over time. Second, they need a built form that is adaptable to change. A broad range of employers should be attracted, but since their needs might not yet be known, commercial sites should be adaptable to alternative uses over time. Housing must be physically capable of being altered over time. Mortgage lenders have to be on board, as their failure to be brought into the New Towns was a major barrier to the development of a balanced demographic that included the home-owning middle classes. Small-scale developers, building small numbers of units (as happened in the late Victorian housing boom) or self-build to design codes, will create a varied and adaptable townscape. To encourage interesting, specialist retail, affordable commercial plots need to be made available for purchase. A fine grain, traditional street pattern, as seen in the post-war reconstruction of Köln, is preferable to the coarse-grain superstructures seen from Welwyn Garden City to Central Milton Keynes, or the effectively short-term metal sheds of big box retail

At the level of strategic planning, new towns in the future should be located in the right place. The long-term fortunes of the New Towns show that new settlements must be built on strong existing movement routes. Towns must also be intended to be of a sufficient overall size. Towns should be big enough to be self-supporting, but also – to avoid the fate of Skelmersdale or Newton Aycliffe – it is important that the agreed targets are not revised (either up or down) midway through their construction.

Ebenezer Howard thought that once towns had reached the right size they should stop. Yet, towns are never really finished. Change goes on continually over the decades. The ebb and flow of urban inflow that fuels high density, versus the decentralisation to suburban expansion or the building of brand new settlements, is like a decades-long in and out breath of our towns and cities. The moment of these turning points are the political decisions, taken by small groups of people in a certain position at a certain time. Howard created the Garden Cities as campaign and real construction programme. Osborn took it

on to Silkin, Reith and Abercrombie who formally created the policy of urban decentralisation. Gibberd and Stein helped build the first New Towns. Macmillan decided to form the Commission for the New Towns to take over when the construction was complete. Shore decided to end the decentralisation policy. Thatcher decided to wind up the development corporations as soon as possible. Today, small numbers of dedicated people will set future paths for urban development. Just as in the past, ideas should not be adopted dogmatically just because they appear to be the latest thing. Ideas should be tested by reasoned debate, and with an understanding of what happened in the past.

Howard saw the Garden City as an invention, but really it was a hypothesis. It was an idea about how we could build that needed to be tested in reality to prove whether it was valid. This experiment was an immensely complicated one. It would take generations to run, and be subject to so many influences, it would be hard to get to the bottom of it. The scale of knowledge to be gained from the New Towns Programme remains vast. This account has merely scratched the surface. Each town has a wealth of insight to be gained from its experiences, both positive and negative. The different national context of the Scottish, Welsh or Northern Irish New Towns has been neglected in this account. Yet certainly, some insights are clear.

Howard's model for self-financing urban development introduced in the Garden Cities, and taken forward by Reith into the New Town Development Corporation model, was immensely successful. It was blown off course by the unstable economic conditions of the 1970s. Yet, today, the Letchworth Heritage Trust, and the Milton Keynes Parks Trust – the only two independently surviving elements – remain immensely successful. The Milton Keynes Roof Tax that funded infrastructure for new developments has also been a successful revisiting of this idea. These show the benefits of being allowed to control one's own affairs. Indeed, Community Land Trusts are now widely recognised as a vital tool for establishing sustainable communities. Understanding the needs of a place – whether a whole town, or a modest housing estate – is best done by people on the ground with a personal stake in getting it right.

The story of the New Towns is really one of scale. Political power, technological power, public will and the desire to create a break with the past and promote the new, all came together to allow very different ideas to be put into place on a very large scale. The greatest risk for new development in the twenty-first century may be that thinking big will be disastrous. Mistakes would thus be replicated on massive scales. An incremental, fine grained, individualist approach to buildings is needed to be able to adapt to change. The technological change of the industrial revolution wrought social change, and ultimately environmental change. Predicting the long-term changes that will face society is difficult, but what is certain is that there will be change.

Conclusion

The lessons of the New Towns

CHAPTER 1

Bishopsfield, Harlow. Courtesy of the Museum of Harlow.

This book has attempted to tell the story of the New Towns; where they came from, how they were put together and how they have fared over time. Establishing the wide historical context and underlying philosophical and practical issues, hopefully has provided a useful introduction to a subject long-neglected by urban theorists and current practitioners. For policy makers, the call for systematic research was expressed by the 2002 House of Commons Select Committee. The government answered this call in a major literature review commissioned from Oxford-Brookes University that looked at the possible transferable lessons for the 2003 Sustainable Communities Plan. The report, begins by stating,

> One key finding from this extensive literature review has been that there is, in fact, very little research-based material relating to the New Towns programme as a whole, which, arguably, is both objective and useful. There are some notable exceptions; but the team were surprised by this lack of quality in the literature. This is undoubtedly due to the fact that the NTs programme has never been reviewed systematically.
>
> (ODPM, 2006: 5)

As shown by the government's official history of the New Towns Programme (Cullingworth, 1979), the internal attempt by the Treasury to systematically study the New Towns realised fundamental problems of reviewing a programme of some thirty towns, each with their own geographical and demographic context, subject to an ever-changing wider political and economic context. By addressing the New Towns as a narrative, rather than as a given set of data, the intention of this book has been to tell the story of the New Towns rather than establish any fundamental scientific truths about the nature of town building. Nonetheless, the experience of the New Towns reveals some significant facts that may be of importance for practitioners, policy-makers and researchers whose work would benefit from understanding how towns really work. It is vital that we gain a better understanding of how towns evolve over the long term. What are the essential elements that make a town a successful place?

The New Towns represent a scale of construction that was hugely impressive. It dominated the lives of a generation of practitioners, and has influenced the lives of millions who at some point in their lives have been residents. In attempting a broad-brush approach to cover the scale of the New Towns Programme and the long chain of events that led to its creation, this book has inevitably only scratched the surface of many aspects. There is a vast ocean of potential knowledge yet to be tapped. The lessons can be positive or negative – both have value – and there are general points about the way we regard towns in policy and practice.

The first general point is about time. Towns take a long time to plan and build, and once built they age slowly. Their lifecycles are far slower than the individual buildings they are composed of. The process of town building also lasts longer than the duration over which any particular government is likely to be in power. Cross-party support for the New Towns Programme right up until 1979 was vital for their success up to that time. The 2006 Transferable Lessons report noted that cross-party support for the major planning policies of Growth Areas or the Eco Towns Initiative had not been established (ODPM, 2006). The story of the New Towns Programme also shows that parties can change their mind about a policy once in power and more keenly aware of the reasons behind it, as the Conservatives did regarding the failure of the Expanded Towns Programme and subsequent resurrection of the New Towns Programme in 1960, and Labour did regarding the role of the Commission for the New Towns in 1964.

The need to co-ordinate the funding and delivery of infrastructure remains a major issue today, but having privatised utilities is a major difference. Consultation to get all key agencies on board and the raising of private finance are all central aspects of modern planning. Local people are also widely consulted and able to contribute to designs via community planning workshops. Ensuring the co-ordinated input of various government departments with separate programmes for health, education or transport services can remain problematic. As such, the lessons of the New Towns are salient. Provision of medical services was problematic throughout the New Towns Programme. In Redditch, development suffered major delays until additional sewage works could be provided. When the Ministry of Transport decided to change the route of the new M11 motorway to lie to the east instead of the west of Harlow, it undermined the fundamental logic of how the town was laid out. The resulting traffic congestion caused by commercial vehicles needing to traverse the town remained a highly difficult and contentious issue to address.

Movement is clearly a vital component for successful places. Many New Towns benefited directly from their location relative to the brand new motorway network. Built around the same time as the New Towns, new industries immediately benefited from faster access to other parts of the country. On the other hand, the commercial life of the town centres has been undermined by the ease with which people could drive to other centres for their shopping and entertainment. The town centre regeneration plans for Bracknell are one of a number of attempts to reinvent the retail offer of the town in relation to its neighbours.

Bracknell's challenge, shared with many other New Town centres, is also how they can improve movement routes. For cyclists in particular, existing routes go to the centre but do not go through it. A clear lesson for future development is that walking and cycling routes should run alongside roads to increase accessibility, ensure safety and cost-effective maintenance, and not be segregated from main roads.

In terms of masterplanning, the layout of the New Towns highlighted the problems that could come from the rapid application of a new design idea with little understanding of how it might turn out in reality. At the macro-scale, neighbourhood units severed by dual carriageways prevented coherent urban growth. In terms of block structure, large-scale commercial buildings could not respond to changing needs and became expensive to refurbish. In terms of housing, low cost terraces were the majority. In some places, the use of a wide range of mass production panel systems became a major problem. The suburban semi-detached of the 1930s (inspired by the architecture of Howard's Letchworth Garden City) was however an extremely popular housing type as it was endlessly adaptable and expandable, with large gardens and space to park a car outside the door. The New Towns largely denied this housing type, instead seeking a break from the past, and the delivery of the largest number of units for a given cost.

Howard, Osborn, Reith and Abercrombie outlined concepts for town planning and urban design, drawing on their experience of the Garden Cities, and exchanging ideas with the likes of Perry and Stein in America. But in attempting to do away with the complexity of the urban form of the historic city, which forced housing to be squeezed into narrow plots, and car traffic to snarl up in roads designed in an age when far fewer people travelled at much slower speeds, they produced a new urban form that had a different set of problems. In some senses, the historic urban form has a complex structure but the individual buildings are relatively simple. Each can be individually replaced to create a rich-texture fine grain, able to adapt to changing needs over centuries. In the modern estates of the New Towns (plus, to a lesser extent the Expanded Towns or inner cities) the urban form has been simplified; it has been differentiated into dedicated areas for housing, retail, leisure and work, spread apart and separated by green corridors and large road systems. Yet the individual buildings within this simplified arrangement are relatively complex. Major new structures such as swimming pools or shopping malls have aged in unexpected ways. Using new techniques and materials – particularly concrete, glass and steel – has presented new challenges for building refurbishment, which lack the benefit of the centuries of experience in historic building materials. In housing too, although seemingly simple, they were often built as effectively large structures subdivided into separate dwellings. Victorian terraces by contrast are composed of dwellings built by large numbers of small firms to essentially the same pattern book or design code, forming a coherent whole but with significant independence.

In the New Towns, streets or neighbourhoods were built simultaneously using a mass-production model where possible to maximise output. The requirement to innovate in construction techniques was an inherent part of this. The result is that refurbishment may have to happen at a street-wide level; individual modification or expansion of dwellings was difficult. Finally, the provision of services within grassed verges or pedestrian walkways has made alterations to the position of buildings within the street a more expensive undertaking. The fundamental ability of the built form to change was never considered by the designers. There is a long-term value in well-built, simple buildings, which are easy to upgrade or replace.

A general point about the way in which the new design principles were applied is that they illustrate the mindset of the age. The mechanical model of architecture and urbanism (originating with Howard's conception of the Garden City as a mechanism, and furthered by Corbusier's idea of the house as a machine for living in) assumed a mass-production method where one-size fits all. The design principles seen in the New Towns were taken to be easily replicable, and as such the same issues are seen across virtually all of the New Towns. In each case, the concept of this new approach to urbanism dominated over the local context. From the late 1960s onwards, a paradigm shift toward a new mindset began. The biological model of towns or buildings instead sees each building as a unique construction in a unique context. In the same way that a doctor regards each patient as unique, this new approach recognises that towns and buildings are subjected to great and complex forces that influence urban life. In order to act in the best interests of the patient, one must first understand them as an individual, and then proceed on the basis of science, judgement and compassion.

In terms of planning guidance in the UK, all new developments are supposed to respond to the local context in terms of topography and regional character, and benefit, rather than undermine, existing communities. How new developments – whether urban extensions, inner city or town centre sites, village extensions or new towns – progress the more biological approach may be seen in the treatment of block structure, plot sizes and movement routes; a richly varied townscape may be created by enabling smaller housing developers, or self-builders, to contribute to a greater degree.

The break between the mid-twentieth century mindset of the New Town designers and more contemporary ideas is not a clean one. Despite the attempts by government bodies such as CABE or English Partnerships to promote good practice that adopts the new, more contextual, responsive and long-term approach to design, there are many buildings and neighbourhoods built in recent years that continue repeating the beliefs of the previous era. Others meanwhile take a different view, seeking to learn from traditional urbanism rather than deliberately denying it. Some commentators may abhor this as an artificial pastiche, whilst others may criticise the inherent futurism of new architecture or urbanism as arrogant hubris, lacking in rational, empirical justification. Nevertheless, both sides are engaged in progressive thinking, and both will be central in forging a sustainable future. A vital lesson is that new approaches to urbanism and architecture should never be adopted dogmatically but must always be challenged.

For the New Towns there is also much that is to be acknowledged. The ambitions held at the dawn of the New Towns Programme are the same as those held today, but the degree to which these ambitions were achieved and the challenges that were overcome are of great relevance for future urban development. The financial model of closed-loop reinvestment was the most successful aspect of the New Towns and was a direct legacy of the Garden Cities Movement. The emergence of Community Land Trusts (www.clt.org.uk) or other forms of locally controlled financial vehicle, from community centres to wind farms, are rediscovering the benefits of locally controlled finance. Localism is an idea that has gained cross-party support in recent years, and the creation of successful new places in Continental Europe and Scandinavia is directly linked to the ability of local government there to control a wider range of investment in infrastructure and services than has been possible in the UK.

In contrast to the housing-led development of recent years, the New Towns' employment-led approach initially created strong communities with virtually no unemployment and little outward commuting. This may seem an unambiguously successful policy, but it had an inescapable long-term effect on the sort of places the New Towns became. With the early populations shaped by the staffing needs of the firms that chose to relocate there, the long-term impact undermined the desire to create balanced communities.

The town's employment shaped the population in direct ways. The middle classes, who aspired towards home ownership, never moved to the early New Towns. Economic depression in the wake of the Second World War meant mortgage lenders weren't capable of engaging with the New Towns Programme. As such, all the housing was built for rental only. Even after twenty years, private developers sometimes contributed as little as 5% of the total housing, meaning many New Towns consisted almost entirely of public housing. The long-term demographic impact of this policy in some of the New Towns has remained hard to address, and links the nature of the housing stock to the nature of place.

For major new developments in the future, the provision of public housing, affordable key-worker housing or joint ownership schemes, must address the potential long-term implications of a town's population. The issues of the right-to-buy, labour mobility, local employment, training opportunities, are all related to the way in which a town can adapt to change.

The employment-led approach of the New Towns also meant some towns were dominated by a single large employer (such as British Steel in Corby, British Leyland in Livingston or ICI in Runcorn) or by a single industrial sector, such as defence or aerospace. The most successful New Towns were those that attracted a wide range of employers, such as Glenrothes and Milton Keynes.

Employment mix rapidly influences the type of place a town becomes. The nature of a place is inescapably coupled to the nature of its population and where they work. People living in a town can thus strongly identify themselves with it and seek to defend their town's reputation, as those living in the New Towns do today. Those who moved to the New Towns in their early stages of growth even felt personally involved in the creation of a new community. The development corporations became successful at contributing to this as establishing a strong image and identity for the towns helped promote them to business.

The current regeneration of the New Towns also depends on the image they have. Just as the development corporations knew that early success was largely a matter of winning a battle of perception, today, people's psychology towards the New Towns is essential. Believing in the New Towns' future is fundamental in helping create it. The negative image that some have been labelled with in recent years, as a reflection of some of their real physical and social challenges, does not address the fact that times change. Compared to many other places the New Towns are still young, and it is absurd to write them off, as careless commentators or practitioners may do from time to time.

Addressing the long-term economic and social sustainability of the New Towns remains a challenge, but they represent such an investment in urban fabric that they must be renewed to become sustainable communities. The cost of building an equivalent scale of urban infrastructure today is prohibitively expensive. The New Towns represent an existing investment that must be maintained.

Their story is intertwined with the wider social changes of the twentieth century. Their ambition of a well-balanced town assumed a stable vision for society and failed to appreciate social and technological change, meaning that some now face regeneration challenges. The environmental ideals of the Garden City can still be seen in the provision of open green space and they were intended as cycle-friendly places, though they have high levels of car-use. Between the Edwardian ideal of the walk-to-work community and the 1960s reality of mass car-ownership, the design principles of the New Towns went from being ahead of the times to behind the times very quickly.

As all places must, the New Towns need to reinvent themselves in the twenty-first century, and perhaps can do so by considering their roots. Their origin was in giving people better living conditions. As such they should not be regarded as a 'social experiment', but as a comprehensive programme to sort out deeply flawed places, of which Britain had a great many in the 1930s; pit towns with Dickensian living conditions, plot-land homes with no sewers, water or roads, deeply overcrowded inner city slums, sprawling housing estates built with insufficient facilities and workplaces sited in the middle of nowhere.

For industry, the tailor-made factories of the New Towns gave businesses the physical space to expand at a vital time for the British economy. They promoted the UK overseas as open-for-business and forward-looking in the wake of a long period of economic stagnation and war. This led to inward investment and the development of new British industries such as electronics, in which the country remains a world-leader. In the future, the New Towns will be among the first parts of the country to develop the new products and services of the green industrial revolution. Today, learning the lessons of the New Towns means appreciating the role that they have played in the past, and the role they can play in the future, as towns where people want to live and work.

Bibliography

Abercrombie, P. (1944) *Greater London Regional Plan, Standing Conference on London Regional Planning*, Ministry of Town and Country Planning.

Abercrombie, P. and Forshaw, J.H. (1943) *County of London Plan*, London County Council.

Aldridge, Meryl (1979) *The British New Towns: A Programme without a Policy*, Routledge & Kegan Paul Ltd, Henley-on-Thames.

APA (2004) American Planning Association, *Individuals Who Influenced Planning Before 1978*, www.planning.org/25anniversary/influentials. htm (last accessed 30 September 2008).

BBC (2007) *Redeveloping Essex's Fallen Utopia*, David Sillito, http://news.bbc.co.uk/1/hi/uk/6264579.stm.

BBC (2007a) Liz Leyh interviewed on The Reunion, broadcast Sunday 22 April 2007 11:15-12:00, Radio 4 FM. http://www.bbc.co.uk/radio4/ thereunion/pip/z2ika/

Beevers, Robert et al. (1991) *Garden Cities and New Towns: Five Lectures*, Hertfordshire County Council.

Bishop, Jeff (1986) *Milton Keynes: The Best of Both Worlds: Public and Professional Views of a New City*, Bristol School for Advanced Urban Studies, Occasional Paper 24, 1986.

Booth, Phillip (2006) *Towards a Liberal Utopia?* Continuum International.

Boyd Whyte, Iain (ed.) (2003) *Modernism and the Spirit of the City*, Routledge, Abingdon.*Building Design* (2007a) 'Unhappy customers', 30 May.

BRANCH (2007) *Planning for biodiversity as climate changes, Natural England*, www.branchproject.org.uk.

Building Design (2007a) 'Unhappy customers', 30 May. www.bdonline. co.uk/story.asp?storyCode=3084063 (last accessed 23 October 2008).

Building Design (2007b) 'Defending suburbia, interview with Milton Keynes chief architect Derek Walker', 6 August. http://www. bdonline.co.uk/story.asp?sectioncode=577&storycode=3092887 (last accessed 23 October 2008).

Building Design (2007c) 'Never say Nether again', 31 July. http://www. bdonline.co.uk/story.asp?sectioncode=427&storycode=3092493 (last accessed 23 October 2008).

Building Design (2007d) 'Debate: Should Milton Keynes go high density', 7 August, www.bdonline.co.uk/story.asp?storycode=3093026 (last accessed 23 October 2008).

Building Design (2008) 'Demolition threat to Harlow's Bishopfield estate', 2 May, www.bdonline.co.uk/ story.asp?storyCode=3112748 (last accessed 23 October 2008).

Bullock, Nicholas (2002) *Building the Post-war World: Modern Architecture and Reconstruction in Britain*. Routledge, London.

Buchanan, Colin (1963) *Traffic in Towns*, Ministry of Transport, London.

Carr, Bob (1995) 'Greater London Industrial Archaeology Society', newsletter, August.

Carruthers, Judith (ed.) (1996) *Brave New World: Early Memories of Stevenage New Town*, Stevenage Museum, Stevenage Borough Council, Herts.

Clare, John (2008) *History of Newton Aycliffe*, http://greataycliffe. sedgefield.gov.uk/ccm/greataycliffe/history/town-history.en (last accessed 23 October 2008).

CLG (2003) *The Sustainable Communities Plan*, definition, www. communities.gov.uk/archived/general-content/communities/whatis (last accessed 22 October 2008).

CLG (2006) *Transferable Lessons from the New Towns*, www. communities.gov.uk/documents/housing/pdf/151717.pdf.

Clapson, M. (1998) *Invincible Green Suburbs, Brave New Towns*, Manchester University Press, Manchester.

Clarke, C.J. (2006) 'Basildon: mood of a nation', *British Journal of Photography*, no 7564.

Clarke, C.J. (2008) interview with the author, 21 July.

Commission for the New Towns (1997) *Annual Report 1996–97*.

Cowley, Jason (2002) 'Downtown', *Guardian*, 1 August, www.guardian. co.uk/society/2002/aug/01/urbandesign.architecture (last accessed 22 October 2008).

Cullingworth, J.B. (1979) *Environmental Planning 1939-69 Vol. 3: New Towns Policy*, Stationery Office Books, London.

Darling, Elizabeth (2006) *Reforming Britain: Narratives of Modernity Before Reconstruction*, Routledge, Abingdon.

DETR (1999) *Towards and Urban Renaissance*, Department of the Environment, Transport and the Regions, London.

DETR and CABE (2000) *By Design, Urban Design in the planning system: towards better practice*, Department for Environment, Transport and the Regions and the Commission for Architecture and the Built Environment, London.

Devine, David (2008) curator at the Museum of Harlow, interview with the author, 26 February.

Downie, Leonard (1972a) 'The Disappointing New Towns of Great Britain', *Washington Post*, 1 November. Supported by the Alicia Patterson foundation and available online at www.aliciapatterson. org/APF001971/Downie/Downie.html (last accessed 7 October 2008).

Downie, Leonard (1972b) 'The Urban Order of the North', *Washington Post*, June. Supported by the Alicia Patterson foundation and available online at www.aliciapatterson.org/APF001971/Downie/ Downie10/Downie10.html (last accessed 7 October 2008).

Edwards, M. (2001) 'City design: what went wrong in Milton Keynes?' *Journal of Urban Design*, vol. 6, no. 1, 87–96.

Elwall, Robert (1999) *Building a Better Tomorrow: Architecture in Britain in the 1950s*, John Wiley & Sons, Chichester.

EP (2000) The Urban Design Compendium, English Partnerships, London.

Franklin, John (1999) 'Two decades of the Redway cycle paths in Milton Keynes', *Traffic Engineering and Control*, July/August.

Gallagher, Dominic (2001) *From Here to Modernity*, Open University, Milton Keynes, www.open2.net/modernity/3_10.htm (last accessed 11 June 2008).

Gardiner, Joey (2004) *The New Towns: Special Report, Regeneration and Renewal*, 29 October.

Gatti, R.F. (2008) *Radburn: The Town for the Motor Age*, www.radburn. org/geninfo/history.html (last accessed 17 March 2008).

Gibberd, F. et al. (1980) *Harlow: The Story of a New Town*, Publications for Companies, Stevenage, Herts.

Girardet, Herbert (2004) *Cities People Planet*, John Wiley & Sons, Chichester.

Guardian (2007) 'Brave New World by Jonathan Glancey', *Guardian*, Saturday 11 February.

Hall, Peter (2008) 'Nightmare estates had idyllic origins', *Regeneration and Renewal Magazine*, 11 January.

Hall, Peter and Ward, Colin (2000) *Sociable Cities: the Legacy of Ebenezer Howard*, 2nd edition, John Wiley & Sons, Chichester.

Hardy, Dennis (1991a) *From Garden Cities to New Towns*, Routledge, Abingdon.

Hardy, Dennis (1991b) *From New Towns to Green Politics*, Routledge, Abingdon.

Harlow (2005) *Homes for Harlow: Harlow's Housing Strategy 2004–2007*, Harlow Council, www.harlow.gov.uk/docs/housingstrat2004-05b.doc (last accessed on 28 October 2008).

Harwood, Elain (2000) 'Post-War landscape and public housing', *Garden History*, vol. 28, no. 1, 102–116.

Hayes, Dennis and Hudson, Alan (2001a) *Basildon, Mood of a Nation*, Demos, London.

Hayes, Dennis and Hudson, Alan (2001b) *Basildon Man: Beyond the shellsuits*, 5 April, www.spiked-online.com/Articles/000000005552. htm (last accessed 10 October 2008).

Hennesey, Peter (1992) *Never Again: Britain 1945–51*, Jonathan Cape, London.

Hill, Marion (ed.) (2007) *The Story of the Original CMK*, Living Archive, Milton Keynes.

House of Commons (2002a) *The New Towns: Their Problems and Future*, DETR Select Committee, www.parliament.the-stationery-office.co.uk/pa/cm200102/cmselect/cmtlgr/603/60304.htm (last accessed 1 October 2008).

House of Commons (2002b) *The New Towns: Their Problems and Future*, DETR Select Committee, Memorandum by City of Sunderland (NT 21) www.publications.parliament.uk/pa/cm200102/ cmselect/cmtlgr/603/603m25.htm (last accessed 1 October 2008).

Howard, Ebeneezer (2003) *To-morrow: A Peaceful Path to Real Reform* (with commentary by Peter Hall, Dennis Hardy and Colin Ward), Routledge, Abingdon.

Jacobs, Jane (1961) *The Death and Life of Great American Cities*, Random House and Vintage Books, New York.

Jefferies, Julie (2005) *Focus on People and Migration*, Office of National Statistics, London.

Kaplan, Rachel, Kaplan, Stephen and Ryan, Richard (1998) *With People In Mind*, Island Press, Washington DC.

Kynaston, David (2007) *Austerity Britain, 1945–51*, Bloomsbury, London.

Liscombe, Rhodri Windsor (2003) '"Cities more fair to become the dwelling place of Thy children": transcendent Modernity in British reconstruction', in Boyd Whyte, Iain (ed.) *Modernism and the Spirit of the City*, Routledge, Abingdon.

Matthews, Nick (2008) interview with the author, 2 September.

MKDC (1980) Central Milton Keynes advertising campaign (uploaded onto youtube.com).

Mornement, Adam (2005) *No Longer Notorious: The Revival of Castle Vale, 1993–2005*, HAT Media, UK, www.cvhat.org.uk/media.html (last accessed 30 September 2008).

NEF (2005) *Clone Town Britain, New Economics Foundation*, London, www.neweconomics.org/gen/news_clonetownbritainresults.aspx (last accessed 23 October 2008).

NLP (2008) *Development of Options for the West Midlands RSS in Response to the NHPAU Report, Nathaniel Lichfield and Partners*, www.nlpplanning.com/wmrsshousingoptions/ (last accessed 6 February 2009).

Northern Echo (2004) *Aycliffe Angels*, www.aycliffeangels.org.uk (last accessed 25 September 2008).

ODPM (2002) Government's Response to the Transport, Local Government and the Regions Committee Report: 'The New Towns: Their Problems and Future'.

ODPM (2003) *Sustainable Communities Plan*, Office of the Deputy Prime Minister, London.

ODPM (2006) *Transferable Lessons from the New Towns*, Department of Planning Oxford Brookes University, July 2006, Department for Communities and Local Government: London. www.communities.gov.uk/publications/housing/transferablelessons (executive summary) and www.communities.gov.uk/publications/ housing/ transferable lessons2 (full report) (last accessed 10 February 2009).

Onslow, J. et al. (1990) *Garden Cities and New Towns*, Hertfordshire Publications.

Osborn, Frederick. J. and Whittick, Arnold (1977) *New Towns: Their Origins, Achievements and Progress*, 3rd edition, Routledge, Abingdon.

Owens, Bill (1999) Suburbia, Fotofolio, New York. First published 1973.

Parker, Selwyn (2008) *The Great Crash: How the Stock Market Crash of 1929 Plunged the World into Depression*, Piatkus, London.

Peterborough (2004) *Sustainable Travel Town study*, www.peterborough.gov.uk/page-586.

Phippen, Peter (2008) PRP architects, interview with the author, 1 September 2008.

Plymouth (2005) *Plymouth Rapid Urban Characterisation Study 2005*, www.plymouth.gov.uk/urban_characterisation (last accessed 1 October 2008).

PRP (2007) *Place and Home: The Search for Better Housing*, Black Dog Publishing, London.

Power, Anne (1987) *Property Before People*, Allen & Unwin, London.

Purpose (1955) *Purpose* magazine, issue 1, Stevenage Development Corporation.

Ravetz, Alison (2001) *Council Housing and Culture: The History of a Social Experiment*, Routledge, Abingdon.

Reith (1946) 'Interim report of the New Towns Committee (Lord Reith)', Final Report, Cmnd 6794, HMSO, London.

Rowthorn and Wayne (1988) *Northern Ireland: The Political Economy of Conflict*, Polity Press, Cambridge.

Risky Buildings (2008) www.riskybuildings.org.uk/docs/23pasmore/index.html (last accessed 19 March 2008).

Schofield, Will (2008) housing manager, Transforming Telford, interview with the author, 15 March.

Stevenage (2005a) Interview with Ray Gorbing, conducted 16 January 1987 by Eric Grierson for the Stevenage Oral Project, Stevenage Museum, Herts.

Stevenage (2005b) Interview with Mary Tabor, conducted 6 December 1985 by Elizabeth Davis for the Stevenage Oral Project, Stevenage Museum, Herts.

Stevenage (2005c) Interview with Michael Cotter, Stevenage Oral Project, Stevenage Museum, Herts, www.stevenage.gov.uk/leisureandculture/museum/stevenagevoices (last accessed 3 October 2008).

Stevenage (2007a) Interview with Leonard Vincent OBE, conducted 20 November 1986 by Eric Grierson for the Stevenage Oral Project, Stevenage Museum, Herts.

Stevenage (2007b) Interview with Jack Franklin, Stevenage Oral Project, Stevenage Museum, Herts, www.stevenage.gov.uk/leisureandculture/museum/stevenagevoices (last accessed 3 October 2008).

TCPA (2007) *Best Practice in New Settlements and Urban Extensions*, TCPA, London, www.tcpa.org.uk/downloads/20070606-NSUE.pdf (last accessed 23 October 2008).

Telegraph (2002) 'Cumbernauld, radiant city or carbuncle?' 31 August.

TEST (1991) *Changed Travel – Better World? A Study of Travel Patterns in Milton Keynes and Almere*, TEST, London.

Town and Country Planning Journal (1967a) January, The New Towns special issue.

Town and Country Planning Journal (1967b) February, The Expanded Towns.

Turner, M. et al. (1987) Little Palaces: The suburban house in North London, 1919-1939.

Walker, John (2007) Former Chief Executive, Commission for the New Towns, speaking at TCPA Eco-towns conference, Regent's College Conference Centre, London, 14 December.

Ward, Colin (1993) *New Town, Home Town: The Lessons of Experience*, Calouste Gulbenkian Foundation, London.

Webber, M. (1963) 'Order in diversity: community without propinquity', in, London, W. (ed.) *Cities and Space*, Johns Hopkins Press, Baltimore, pp. 25–54.

Webber, M. (1974) 'Permissive planning', Working paper 18, Centre for Environmental Studies, London.

Welch, Adrian (2007) Glasgow Architecture website, www.glasgow architecture.co.uk/cumbernauld_centre.htm (last accessed 7 October 2008).

Whittick, Arnold (1987) *FJO: Practical Idealist; A Biography of Sir Frederic Osborn*, Town & Country Planning Association, London.

Williams, R.J. (2004) *Anxious City*, Routledge, Abingdon.

Wright, Jon (2008) Campaign Director, Twentieth Century Society, interview with the author, 8 August.

Index